The Dialectics of Art

The Dialectics of Art

John Molyneux

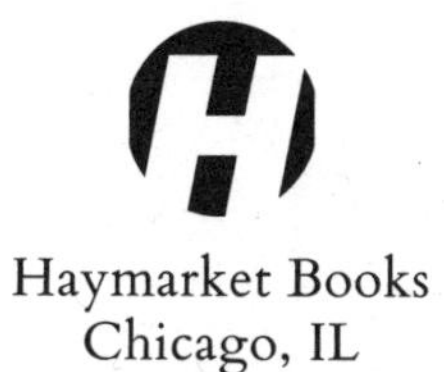

Haymarket Books
Chicago, IL

Published in 2020 by
Haymarket Books
P.O. Box 180165
Chicago, IL 60618
773-583-7884
www.haymarketbooks.org
info@haymarketbooks.org

ISBN: 978-164259-131-6

Distributed to the trade in the US through Consortium Book Sales and Distribution (www.cbsd.com) and internationally through Ingram Publisher Services International (www.ingramcontent.com).

This book was published with the generous support of Lannan Foundation and Wallace Action Fund.

Special discounts are available for bulk purchases by organizations and institu-tions. Please email orders@haymarketbooks.org for more information.

Cover photograph of a detail of Michelangelo's *David* by mkistryn. Cover design by Rachel Cohen.

Printed in Canada.

Library of Congress Cataloging-in-Publication data is available.

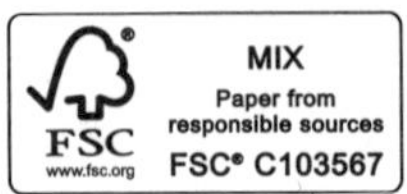

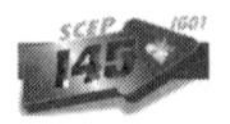

This book is dedicated with gratitude to Mary Smith and to my former students at the University of Portsmouth, in dialogue with whom many of its ideas were worked out and developed.

Contents

	PREFACE	ix
	Introduction	1
1.	What Is Art?	6
2.	How We Judge Art	43
3.	Michelangelo and Human Emancipation	77
4.	Rembrandt and Revolution	96
5.	A Revolution in Paint: One Hundred Years of Picasso's *Demoiselles*	122
6.	State of the Art: A Review of the *Sensation* Exhibition at the Royal Academy of Arts, September–December 1997	136
7.	The Emin Phenomenon or the Phenomenal Emin	153
8.	The Liberty of Appearing: The Photographs of Yasser Alwan	171
9.	Shorter Reviews	181
	Jackson Pollock	181
	Andy Warhol	185
	Francis Bacon	189
	Peter Paul Rubens	191
10.	How Art Develops	194
11.	The Dialectics of Modernism	213
	CONCLUSION	236
	NOTES	239
	INDEX	258

Preface

This book is the product of a lifelong engagement with art and a brief meeting with activist-historian Paul Le Blanc in Dublin in 2018.

Paul Le Blanc and I share an interest in Lenin. He has written several acclaimed books on Lenin and Leninism, and I had published *Lenin for Today* in 2017. When Paul visited Dublin in summer 2018, we got together to compare notes. In the course of our conversation, I asked if his publisher, Haymarket Books, might be interested in publishing or republishing any of my work. He put me in touch with Anthony Arnove, and I put forward some proposals, one of which was for *The Dialectics of Art*. So I should start by expressing major thanks to Paul and to everyone at Haymarket.

As for my engagement with art, it began with my childhood drawings, which my mother put up on the kitchen wall until it was covered from top to bottom. It was the 1950s, and we lived on the ground floor of a large house in Belsize Park in London, the upstairs rooms of which my mother let to boarders. The tenants were a very heterogeneous, multicultural bunch, including Irish, Africans, Indian communists and a young artist, Sheila Fell, who, with her boyfriend Clifford, rented two rooms on the top floor, one of which served as a studio. Sheila was from Aspatria, in Cumberland, and painted marvellous landscapes of the Cumberland countryside and mountains. I remember, aged about eleven, seeing one painting of a mountain in the studio room which made a deep impression on me which has stayed with me all my life.

Sheila also painted a portrait of me when I was about seven, which remains in the possession of my son. Art world people used to come to the house to visit her, including L. S. Lowry, who became her patron, and the leading art critic of the day, David Sylvester. Oddly, I recall that it was when it was explained to me who David Sylvester was that the idea first came into my head I might like to be an art critic.

My engagement with art broadened and deepened at secondary school. This was a fairly traditional grammar school, Westminster City, just off Victoria Street in central London. In the sixth form, which I entered at fifteen, we were allowed to give up games and do art instead. The school was located midway between the National Gallery in Trafalgar Square and the Tate Gallery (now Tate Britain) at Millbank, on the Thames. Both were in walking distance, and after initial school trips the art master allowed me to go, on my own or with a friend, to these galleries on Wednesday afternoons. As a result I spent more or less one afternoon a week in these great galleries, and so many of the paintings I saw there – Piero's *The Baptism of Christ*, Holbein's *The Ambassadors*, the wonderful Rembrandts, Rubens's *Het Steen*, the van Goghs, Matisse's *Snail*, the Francis Bacons – stayed with me permanently. Many feature as examples in this book. In 1964 my relationship to art changed again when I went to a Robert Rauschenberg exhibition in the Whitechapel Gallery in the East End. Going into the Whitechapel, I had little understanding of what I was about to see, and not much more when I did see it. But when I stepped out of the gallery into the streets of the East End, I experienced something of a revelation. The art I had seen inside – works like *Charlene* and *Rebus* – reflected and represented what was in front of my eyes on the street. Art, I suddenly realised, was not just about great masters from the past or 'eternal beauty' and suchlike; art was relevant *today*, to the life I was living *now*. This changed and intensified my view not only of visual art but also of the literature I was studying for A level English – Shakespeare, Keats, Fielding, T. S. Eliot and the like. Then, in my second year in the sixth form, I entered an essay competition for a travel scholarship; by writing about the Renaissance, I won a trip to Florence and Rome. The trip took place in August 1965, affording me the privilege of seeing Brunelleschi's Duomo, Giotto's Campanile, Michelangelo's *David* and *Slaves*, Botticelli's *Primavera* in the Uffizi Gallery, works by Titian in the Pitti Palace, the Sistine Chapel and so on.

I never lost my interest in art – I went back to Florence and Rome in 1971 and regularly visited art galleries – but from 1968, when I got caught up in revolutionary politics, it took a back seat to political activism and Marxist theory, as well as the complications of my personal life, which were considerable. It was in terms of Marxist theory that I developed as a writer, publishing books such as *Marxism and the Party* (1978) and *What Is the Real Marxist Tradition?* (1983). Then in 1992, after many vicissitudes, I took a job as history and theory lecturer in the School of Art and Design at the University of Portsmouth. Over the years my work became more and more focussed on the Fine Art course, and eventually my office was located in the middle of the Fine Art studio. I found this work very rewarding. I greatly enjoyed lecturing on the Art and Society courses (which were my own creation) and supervising dissertations, many of which were very interesting projects. And I got on very well with my students, especially the art students: quite a number remain my friends to this day. In the process, my knowledge of art increased and my ideas became clearer. After five years or so, I felt ready to start writing about art. My first published piece was a review of the Young British Artists (YBAs) *Sensation* show in 1998, which is reproduced in this book.

Another important element in my engagement with art was organising and curating the *Left in Vision* art shows at the annual Marxism Conference at the University of London Union in Bloomsbury; these shows were held for four successive years from 2007 to 2010, when I retired and moved to Dublin. They were open to artists broadly on the left, and all kinds of art was welcome – of course, much of it was overtly political, but it did not have to be. I had no funding for these shows and relied entirely on the limited resources provided by the School of Art and Design, as well as huge amounts of effort and goodwill on the part of a number of my students and a number of socialist activists and artists. Obviously the standard of the work varied – it could not be otherwise – but I think that overall the shows got stronger year on year and that in the process we featured some really outstanding work, including pieces by May Ayres, Roxanne Chappell, Dave Garner, Leon Kuhn, Red Saunders, Yasser Alwan and others. During this period I continued to write about art, as well as Marxism and current politics, especially for the journal *International Socialism*, along with shorter reviews for the *Socialist Review* magazine and the *Socialist Worker* newspaper, as well as the odd piece for *Art Monthly* and other publications.

In terms of intellectual influences on my art writing, John Berger was clearly an important figure. This has often been remarked on by people commenting on my work, including one critic who called him my 'mentor'. In the literal sense of actually being taught by him, this is not true – we never met – but even metaphorically it is a certain overstatement. I saw the brilliant, pathbreaking *Ways of Seeing* on TV in 1972 and read the book, followed by his *Permanent Red* and *The Success and Failure of Picasso*, along with many of his other books and essays over the years. What I took from him especially, along with his hugely important analysis of the relationship between oil painting and capitalism and his always-acute sense of history and historical context, was his conviction that it was possible to respond humanly and directly to the experience of a work of art. Many academics, including some on the left, reject this or are not interested in it (they would see it as 'humanism'), being concerned only with documentary research and what can be proved by the same. But I believe that if a direct response is ruled out, art loses a lot of its human value. Berger demonstrated how 'official' and 'mainstream' art history and commentary has an extraordinary ability not to see what is in front its eyes – such as Frans Hals's feelings about the *Regents* and *Regentesses of the Old Men's Almshouse* – and that was very useful to me. And, of course, I admired Berger the person, with his lifelong commitment to both art and human liberation.

At the same time, I quite often differed sharply with Berger's specific judgments, especially of artists in the post–Second World War period. Francis Bacon and Jackson Pollock, whom I consider major figures, are obvious examples, though I shared his love of Rembrandt and Jack Yeats.

Another important influence was Leon Trotsky. Trotsky's main influence on me was in terms of revolutionary theory, and I wrote an analysis of his theory of revolution back in 1983, but his *Literature and Revolution* and his essays in *Leon Trotsky on Literature and Art* made a huge impression. I very much agreed with his vehement defence of artistic freedom, including under the dictatorship of the proletariat, and his insistence that art should be judged according to the 'law of art'. However, I don't think Trotsky, who had rather a lot of other things on his plate, ever really explained what the 'law of art' was. Anyway, it got me thinking, and some of the results can be seen in this book.

But by far the most significant theoretical influences on my ideas about art have been Marx and Engels themselves. Marx's theory of alienation and alienated labour, first expounded in the *Economic and Philosophic Manuscripts of 1844* (which I read in 1968) and then developed through the *Grundrisse* and on into *Capital*, has been a continual point of return and provides the foundation for my answer to the 'What is art?' question. Equally important is the Marxist theory of history, historical materialism. I am a convinced historical materialist and approach the history of art through that lens, just as I would the French Revolution or, indeed, contemporary politics. In relation to art, it is crucial that the historical materialism we are talking about is not any kind of crude or mechanical economic determinism. (This is even more important for revolution, by the way, but that is another story.) In relation to art, it is necessary to remember that art both arises out of (and is always conditioned by) a definite historical and social context – a concrete moment in the long history of class struggle – *and* represents a specific, active human response to that context. Here I should mention Engels's late letters on historical materialism and his highly suggestive comments on the Renaissance and the Reformation in his introduction to *Dialectics of Nature*, which underpinned my analyses of Michelangelo and Rembrandt. Finally, my attempt to define art in the capitalist epoch was shaped, indirectly, by the way Marx went about unravelling the meaning and value of commodities at the beginning of *Capital*. For Marx, the value of a commodity is determined not by its inherent properties as an object but by the quantity of socially necessary labour involved in its production. In an analogous move, I locate that which makes an object a work of art not in the object but in the nature of the labour that produces it. 'The Fetishism of commodities', wrote Marx, 'has its origin in the peculiar social character of the labour that produces them.' I say something similar about art, whose existence in capitalist society *as something separate and distinct from other human artefacts* is, indeed, a form of fetishism.

The structure of this book needs a word of explanation. It is like a sandwich, the filling of which consists of a selection of my writing on specific artists and exhibitions over the years. These studies have all been published already and are reproduced here as they first appeared, save a few small adjustments for style. I decided not to correct or retrospectively alter such errors of judgment as they may have contained. In one or two cases, I have added a note to acknowledge subsequent developments, such as Tracey Emin becoming a Tory, or what happened to the Egyptian working class. The bread of the sandwich is provided by two chapters at the beginning – 'What Is Art?' and 'How We Judge Art' – and two at the end – 'How Art Develops' and 'The Dialectics of Modernism' – all of which were written specifically for this book.

One consequence of this structure is that the part of the book that is likely to be the most difficult, most contested and, in some ways, least appealing – the attempt to crack the fearful and perhaps tedious 'What is art?' question – comes first. A case could have been made for putting it last, maybe as an appendix, but on balance I thought it was logically necessary as it is clearly foundational for the enterprise as a whole. I cannot resist noting again here the parallel with *Capital*, in which the first chapter is famously the hardest. (Though in making these comparisons, I should stress that I am not for one moment comparing myself to Marx or this little book to the mighty *Capital*).

Another consequence, which I actually hope for, is that the studies of specific artists and the observations on the trajectories and current situation of modern art are an application, fairly consistently, of the methodology and approach set out in chapters 1, 2 and 10. What makes this possible, at least in a broad sense, is that my basic ideas on art were formulated before any of the pieces in the book were published and, although they have developed, they have in essentials remained the same.

This is not a work that fits into an academic or art world niche. I am not a specialist in the Renaissance or the early twentieth century or any other period, and my tastes and concerns range from Rembrandt to Rauschenberg, Titian to Tracey Emin; nor am I in any sense a player on the art scene. These are deficiencies that bring with them serious disadvantages, but perhaps they also carry certain advantages. In any case, I hope so.

Finally, I should say that the rapidly changing art world and its innumerable productions globally, combined with the even more rapidly changing material world of economics, politics and nature, means that my reflections at the end of the book on the present situation of art and its immediate prospects may already be out of date by the time they are published. But of one thing I'm pretty confident: such is the nature, at once chronic and acute, of the environmental crisis the world has entered that it is bound to generate a powerful artistic response.

John Molyneux
Dublin, July 2019

AUTHOR'S NOTE: This book is packed with references to specific works of art, particularly as examples illustrating historical and theoretical arguments. Ideally I would have liked similarly to pack the text with images of those works. Unfortunately this was not possible without inflation of the price of the book beyond what either I or the publishers consider acceptable. I would remind readers, therefore, that virtually every work referred to in this book is easily accessible online on any computer or smart phone.

Introduction

This is a Marxist book about art. It is not a Marxist history of art, but a series of reflections on art and art history from a Marxist standpoint. It is written in the belief that visual art matters. I don't just mean it matters to the minority who passionately care about fine art; I mean it matters, objectively, to society as a whole and for its development.

This needs some explanation and clarification. It is not that paintings or sculptures have been or will be prime movers in the immense social changes that will be necessary if humanity is to have a decent future. That role has been and will be played by mass popular struggle as it was in the French Revolution and the Russian Revolution. Nobody reading the history of those momentous events, or of any of the major revolutions and struggles of the last two centuries, could seriously claim that they were caused or driven by works of visual art. Art was there and played its part – think of Jacques-Louis David's *Oath of the Horatii* (1784) and *The Death of Marat* (1793) in France, and Kazimir Malevich, Alexander Rodchenko and El Lissitzky in Russia – but it is not really its direct political role that makes art important. Rather, what matters most is the ability of art to articulate the social consciousness of an age in a way that aids the development of the human personality and our collective awareness of our natural and social environment.

This is not an exclusively Marxist view. For instance, the American conservative commentator David Brooks writes in a 2016 *New York Times* op-ed: 'A person who has appreciated the *Pietà* has a greater capacity for empathy, a more refined sense of the different forms of sadness and a wider awareness of the repertoire of emotions.'[1] However, this does not make it anti-Marxist, any more than the fact that many conservatives and bourgeois think Shakespeare was a great writer means that Marxists should deny this. What distinguishes the Marxist view is that it is particularly, though not exclusively, concerned with the development of the personality of the working class and the oppressed. In *Literature and Revolution*, Leon Trotsky wrote: 'What the worker will take from Shakespeare, Goethe, Pushkin or Dostoievsky will be a more complex idea of human personality, of its passions and feelings, a deeper and profounder understanding of its psychic forces and the role of the subconscious, etc. In the final analysis the worker will become richer.'[2] All good art does this to a greater or lesser extent, but visual art does it by means of visual imagery, which in one way is quite a specialised and easily neglected activity, but in another way is all-pervasive. Some examples:

Picasso's *Guernica* (1937) did not stop the Spanish Civil War, nor did it prevent the victory of General Franco and his fascists; indeed, it probably had negligible impact on the course or outcome of the war. However, what it did do was fix in the minds of many millions of people, for generations to come, an image of the horror of modern warfare. And it provided us all with an array of specific visual images (the mother with a dead child in her arms, the screaming horse, etc.) which can be utilised in a variety of situations and have become part of our symbolic armoury.

Piero della Francesca's *The Baptism of Christ* (ca. 1450) and Matthias Grünewald's *Crucifixion* (1512–16) are paintings of considerable historical importance in that they embody rival visions of Christ at a crucial turning point: a Catholic vision of Christ as serene and majestic, and a Protestant vision of a Christ with whom it is possible to establish an intensely personal connection. Yet they both retain a contemporary significance, even though that historical moment (of the Renaissance and the Reformation) has long departed and the role of Christianity and religion in our collective consciousness has receded: the values of quiet and stillness so extraordinarily captured in the *Baptism* and of deep empathy with extreme suffering which drives the *Crucifixion* both remain relevant, inspirational even, amid the pressure, stress, cruelty and indifference of modern capitalism. Much the same applies to the deep human tenderness expressed in Rembrandt's *The Jewish Bride* (ca. 1665) (and many of his other works) in the face of our contemporary alienation. In a different way, in the early twentieth century the De Stijl artists (above all Piet Mondrian) and the Russian Constructivists profoundly influenced the whole aesthetic of the modern capitalist world as it is designed and built.

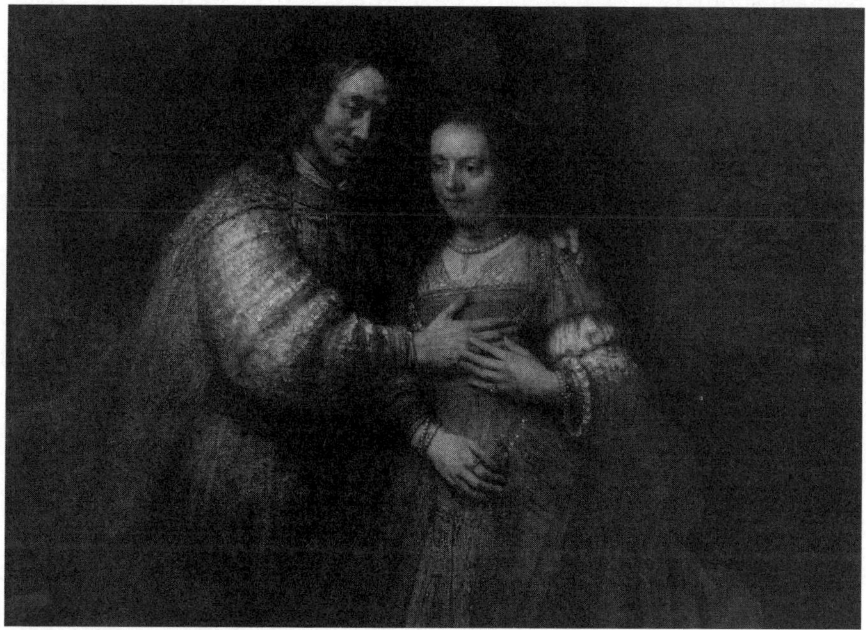

Rembrandt van Rijn, *The Jewish Bride* (ca 1665)

What enables art to exercise this influence, out of all proportion to its quantity in relation to the immense accumulation of visual images with which we are bombarded on a daily basis? It is not just the great skill of its foremost practitioners (undoubted as that is), but a qualitative difference between art and other forms of image production – namely, that it is made by free creative labour in a world dominated by the opposite. I explain and defend this view in depth in chapter 1, but here I will just say this: the general tendency of capitalism is to destroy all creativity in labour, not only in manual labour on production lines and in factories, but also in mental labour, in white-collar work. This is despite the fact that there is major discourse about the importance of 'creativity' and 'the creative industries' in contemporary capitalism. This is 'artwashing', akin to so-called greenwashing by companies and governments that continue to pollute the earth and pump greenhouse gases into the atmosphere.

In *The Communist Manifesto*, Marx wrote: 'Owing to the extensive use of machinery and to division of labour, the work of the proletarians has lost all individual character, all charm for the workman. He becomes an appendage of the machine.' But as the political economist Harry Braverman showed in his 1974 *Labour and Monopoly Capital* and many other studies have confirmed (and increasing strike activity in these areas also testifies), many formerly 'professional' jobs are being more and more 'proletarianised', more and more deprived of any autonomy. And 'the machine' is not just the physical machine, but the bureaucratic machine of the modern state and modern corporation with its increasing panopticon-like surveillance and control. However, this alienation meets with resistance, and the resistance takes various forms: trade union struggles to widen the scope of worker control and freedom in the workplace; generalised political activism; and the attempt to engage in creative labour – the making of art.

This makes art, independent of its explicit political or ideological content, a human value for socialists: 'a model of freedom', as John Berger called it, something to be defended, explored and celebrated. It is for this reason, I would contend, that so many of the greatest Marxist revolutionaries – Marx, Engels, Plekhanov, Lenin, Trotsky, Luxemburg, Gramsci, Lukács, Serge – not only wrote about art but also were drawn to it and had an affinity with it in some form or another.[3]

Of course, art also remains, like other forms of mental and physical production (and art is both), dominated by the ruling classes – under capitalism by the big bourgeoisie – but it also develops, in the capitalist epoch, in recurring tension with those rulers and their economic system: think of Rembrandt, Goya, Géricault, Turner, Courbet, Manet, impressionism, Seurat, van Gogh, Rousseau, Picasso, Léger, Kollwitz, Dadaism, suprematism, surrealism, Grosz, Heartfield, Rivera, Kahlo, CoBrA, Tàpies, early Warhol, Andre, Beuys, Basquiat, Mary Kelly,

Rosler, Kruger, Smithson, Art and Language, and so many others, all the way down to Whiteread, Emin, Ai Weiwei, Hirschhorn, Jeremy Deller, Banksy and 'the social turn' of the twenty-first century.

Insofar as this diverse book, which brings together work from different times and on different artists, has a unifying theme, it is the exploration of this always-dialectical tension.

CHAPTER 1

What Is Art?

What is art? Three simple words – a very tricky question.[1]

For example, the best-selling art book of all time, *The Story of Art* by E. H. Gombrich, begins with the statement: 'There is really no such thing as Art. There are only artists.'[2] This, or something like it, is a popular view, particularly among artists; indeed, I often heard Tracey Emin, faced with the challenge that her work *My Bed* was not really art, reply that 'art is what artists do' or perhaps that 'art is what artists say it is', and that therefore, since she, an artist, had declared *My Bed* to be a work of art, it must be so. There is much more to be said about this view, and various attempts have been made to justify or elaborate it. But as it stands, it contains a very obvious logical problem: If art is what artists do (or say it is), what makes someone an artist? You would think, would you not, that an artist was someone who made art? But then Gombrich's or Emin's answer turns out to be both circular and empty. And this kind of problem keeps recurring whenever we try to answer the 'What is art?' question.

In fact, in order even to attempt a serious answer to 'What is art?', we have to answer a raft of prior questions, such as: By 'art', do we mean visual art, whatever that may be (painting, sculpture, etching, drawing, installations, video art, film, performance art), or do we mean art in the more general sense (novels, plays, poetry, music, opera, pottery, dance, photography, film)? Or do we mean the word 'art' (the art of cookery, the art of motorcycle maintenance, the 'noble art' of boxing, or Art, short for Arthur)? Do we mean art everywhere and for all time, throughout human history, from before the Lascaux cave paintings to Ai Weiwei today? Or do we mean art over a specific period of time in a specific society? By 'What is art?', do we mean, 'What is the *definition* of art?' Are we trying to define a word, or a thing – or a set of things? What would it mean to define art? What do we mean by a definition? What makes us think art can be defined? Is it desirable that it should be? These questions fold into each other like opposing mirrors, seemingly ad infinitum (or maybe ad nauseam). So, given that the question is so tricky, why bother with it at all?

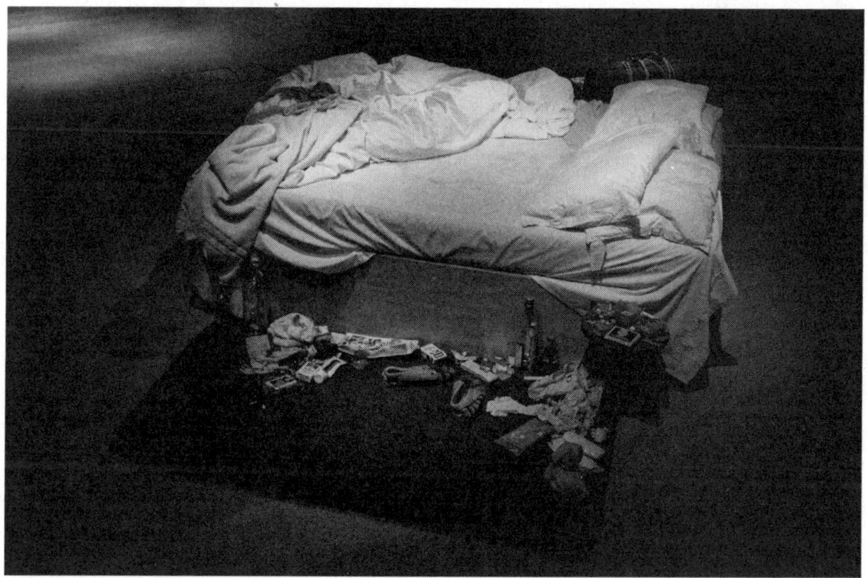

Tracey Emin, *My Bed* (1999)

Well, to deal with the last question first, it might seem a good idea, in a book about art, to know what we are dealing with. Moreover, the question is out there; a quite disproportionate amount of media coverage of modern visual art proceeds, and has proceeded for quite a long time, under the rubric 'But is it art?'. It was hearing this challenge repeatedly put to work of Christo, Hirst, Whiteread, Emin and others (as it has previously been put to that of Picasso, Brâncuși, Pollock, Warhol, Andre, etc.) and realising that the people who put it had no criteria by which to judge it other than whether it resembles what they were used to thinking of as art (paintings by Vermeer or Constable or Monet or whoever), that first led me to try to investigate it. Then – and this is the most important reason for addressing it here – I found, in the process of the investigation, that it pointed to a number of significant conclusions (truths, I believe), not only about art itself but also about the nature of human life and labour in class-divided societies – capitalist societies especially. Furthermore, I found that these conclusions have political implications.

The question 'What is art?' as I am posing it here is a call for a *definition*. A definition, according to my copy of the *Concise Oxford English Dictionary*, can be either a statement 'of the precise nature of a thing' or a statement of 'the meaning of a word'.[3] This is very unhelpful; how can one state the precise nature of anything, let alone a category like 'art' that necessarily involves millions of different 'things'? Moreover, the word 'art', as I noted above, has many different meanings. More useful, perhaps, is the same work's first entry for 'define' – 'mark out limits of' – and for 'definite' – 'having exact limits; determinate, distinct'. Anyway, what I am seeking to do is to *define art*, in the sense of establishing criteria for distinguishing works of art from other things which are not works of art. This is so as to be able to answer questions such as 'Is Carl Andre's *Equivalent VIII*[4] or Kazimir Malevich's *Black Square on White* a work of art?' or 'Is the rhyme in my birthday card a work of art?' or a song by One Direction or a solo by Louis Armstrong and so on, without the answer depending on whether I happen to like or approve of the particular work.[5]

For various reasons, definitions are always a problem. Dictionary definitions, like those cited above, are generally of little use when trying to establish the meaning of complex and disputed concepts, things or events. A dictionary definition of feudalism might be useful if you have never come across the term, but it won't help much in deciding whether or not Russia in 1914 or Britain in 1642 was feudal, any more than a dictionary definition of socialism (which dictionary, whose definition?) will settle whether Russia in 1936 was socialist. Moreover, *all* definitions, even the most apparently precise, have a tendency to fray at the edges. This is because definitions aim to distinguish between things (or concepts) – a very necessary task for human beings generally – but in reality 'things' are processes, processes of coming into being and passing out of being, and therefore not, in the end, separate and distinct entities. And the same is true of the concepts we develop in order to try, as we must, to pin things down. 'The concept', says Leon Trotsky in his *Philosophical Notebooks*, 'is not a closed circle, but a loop, one end of which moves into the past, the other – into the future. If you pull at its end you can undo the loop, but you can also knot it.'[6] So the definition of art that I propose is bound to be, in a sense, imperfect, and there are bound to be problematic transitional cases between art and nonart. This, as we shall see, is an important qualification. But the fact that day merges into night through twilight does not mean we should dispense with the concepts of day and night.

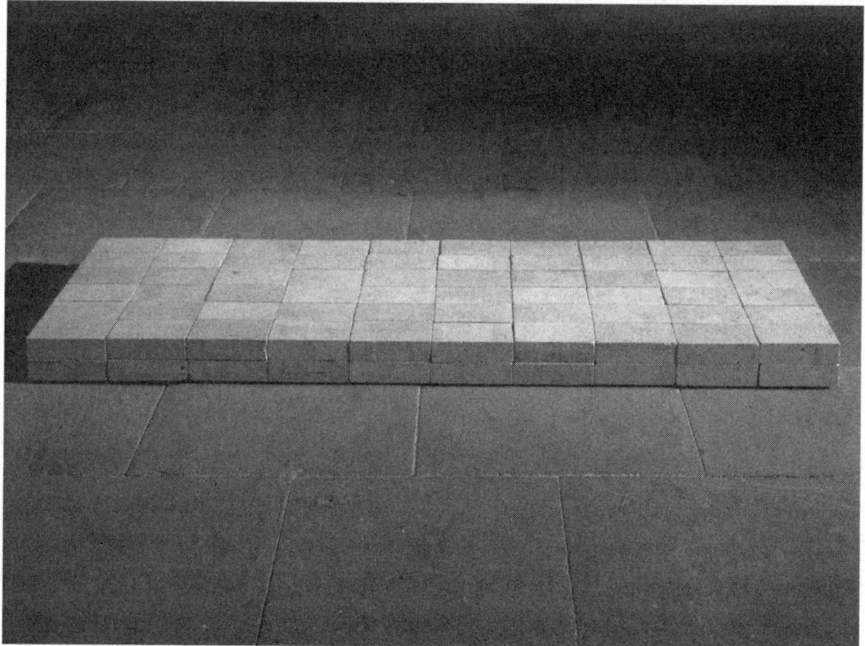

Carl Andre, *Equivalent VIII* (1966)

Then there is the fact that in order to establish a 'definition' of something, in the sense that I intend – namely, a statement of its limits or defining criteria – you first have to have a rough idea of what it is you are trying to define. What I am attempting to define here is not just 'visual art', but art in the general sense listed above (painting, music, literature, cinema, pottery, etc.) as it is commonly spoken of; but not all uses of the word 'art'. So if it turns out that boxing does not meet my criteria (and it doesn't), the fact that it is sometimes referred to as 'the noble art of self-defence' is not a problem for my argument. But if it turns out that T. S. Eliot's *The Waste Land* or a composition by John Coltrane or a novel by James Joyce doesn't meet my criteria, that would be a serious problem.

Secondarily, my aim is to define art for what I will call the *capitalist* or *bourgeois era*: that is, roughly from the beginning of the Renaissance (in Europe) through to the global present. It is clear that something we would now call art has existed since at least the Upper Paleolithic period (e.g., cave paintings dating back over thirty-five thousand years) and that every human society or culture of which we have evidence was engaged in activities (painting walls, making music, dancing, storytelling, etc.) we would now be likely to call art. But it is also clear that the modern use of the word 'art' to denote a specific sphere of activities and objects, comprising painting, music, literature and so on, distinct from other nonartistic activities and objects, did not apply to many or most of those periods or cultures. Now, it may well be that much of what I have to say will apply to some extent to art-type activities of the distant past and from many cultures – to the cave paintings of Lascaux and Chauvet, to Homer, to Haiku poetry and Benin bronzes – but I am deliberately limiting my attempt to provide a definition to the capitalist era, and if it can be shown that it doesn't work for Aztec sculpture or the architecture of ancient Zimbabwe, then so be it.

This is partly because I don't wish to bite off more than I can chew, or to claim a universality or timelessness for my views that is likely to prove unsustainable. But there is a more important point involved here: the concept of art, as it is widely used today and as I want to define it, did not exist before the bourgeois era. The word existed, but its meaning, and thus its use, was fundamentally different. The word 'art' comes from the Latin *ars/artis*, which in turn is a translation from the Greek *techne*, which simply meant skill. The modern use of art, as in 'the art of cookery', which I have referred to above, is a residue of this old meaning.

As Władysław Tatarkiewicz writes in a very useful article on the history of the concept of art:

> ['*Techne*'] in Greece – '*ars*' in Rome and in the Middle Ages, even as late as the beginnings of the modern era, in the age of the Renaissance – meant skill, namely the skill required to make an object, a house, a statue, a ship, a bedstead, a pot, an article of clothing, and moreover also the skill required to command an army, to measure a field, to sway an audience....
>
> Art, understood as it was in antiquity and in the Middle Ages, thus had a considerably broader scope than it does today.... Consequently not only painting or tailoring could be regarded as art, but so also could grammar and logic – precisely as sets of rules, as kinds of expertise. Thus at one time art possessed a broader scope: broader by the handicrafts and by at least part of the sciences.[7]

There was also a distinction made between the *liberal* (liberated) and the *vulgar* or *mechanical* arts. The former involved only mental labour, whereas the latter required also physical effort. The liberal arts were considered to be greatly superior to the common or mechanical arts, and painting and sculpture were considered lowly activities among the mechanical arts.

During the Middle Ages the liberal arts were considered to be grammar, rhetoric, logic, arithmetic, geometry, astronomy and music – seven in number. For the sake of symmetry, attempts were made to reduce the numerous mechanical arts to seven categories, and in the process painting and sculpture (considered of little importance) often fell off the lists altogether. Poetry was 'regarded as a kind of philosophy or prophecy and not as art'[8] and failed to make any of the lists.

It was during the Renaissance that the modern concept of art began to emerge. The Marxist art historian Arnold Hauser identifies Michelangelo as a key figure in this process and argues that '[t]he fundamentally new element in the Renaissance conception of art is the discovery of the concept of genius, and the idea that the work of art is the creation of an autocratic personality, that this personality transcends tradition, theory and rules.'[9]

And it was during the second half of the eighteenth century and the nineteenth century that this modern concept was consolidated and became hegemonic. Tatarkiewicz sums up the process as follows:

> The history of the concept [of art] in Europe has thus lasted for 25 centuries and falls *grosso modo* into two periods, each of which entertained a different concept of art. The first period – that of the ancient concept – was very long, stretching from the 5th century BCE to the 16th ad. Over these long centuries art was construed as production in accordance with rules. . . . The years 1500–1750 were years of transition: the erstwhile concept, though it had lost its earlier position, nevertheless still persisted, while the new one was already being prepared. At length, around 1750, the old concept yielded place to the modern one.[10]

It is this 'modern' concept that I am concerned with trying to analyse, and while Tatarkiewicz does not mention this, a Marxist cannot fail to note that his periodisation corresponds, more or less exactly, to the emergence and development of capitalism. It is worth noting here that the first public art galleries and museums emerged in the eighteenth century and that the world's largest and historically most important art museum, the Louvre, was established in 1793 as a direct result of the French Revolution.

Moreover, I believe that my analysis of the nature of art will help to explain why 'art' in its modern sense and usage emerged as a distinct category and sphere in the capitalist era.

I said earlier that it is necessary to establish whether one is defining a word, a thing or a set of things. Since Wittgenstein, we have known that the meaning of words is determined in and by their use, and that the same word (i.e., a sound or set of letters) can have different meanings when used in different ways and different contexts. I can *play* a tune, *play* football and go to a *play*. I can sit in a *chair*, or *chair* a meeting, or hold the *chair* of philosophy in a university. But it does not follow from this, as some post-structuralists have claimed, that there is no necessary link or connection between words or concepts and the 'real' or material world. Rather, I believe, with Marx, that that connection is established in human practice. 'All social life is essentially practical,' he writes in his

Theses on Feuerbach. 'All mysteries which lead theory to mysticism find their rational solution in human practice and in the comprehension of this practice.'[11] And I believe that the word 'art', in the way in which it has been used for several centuries to distinguish certain activities and objects from nonart activities and objects, does correspond to or represent (broadly) a real distinction which exists 'out there' in social practice. My aim in attempting to answer the 'What is art?' question is to try to identify the basis of that distinction.

This book will focus mainly on visual art, but I think the example of writing and literature helps clarify the distinction I'm talking about. The society we live in is full of writing: there are handwritten notes and letters, typed letters, emails, tweets and Facebook posts; there are business letters, bills and invoices, technical instructions on products, signs and notices at airports and train stations, adverts, newspaper articles, scientific papers and so on, endlessly. Out of this immense amount of writing, a tiny fraction of it gets to be considered, by anyone, to be art. On what basis? You could answer that it is mainly poetry, short stories and novels that receive such consideration, but, setting aside the difficulty of defining poetry, short stories and novels, this is not an adequate answer, because it leaves out (some) essays, (some) drama, (some) film scripts, (some) radio scripts, (some) written music and so on. Nor can the answer be given in terms of the persons – "art writing is writing produced by artistic writers" – since all 'art' writers (Yeats, Eliot, Neruda, Dostoyevsky, Roy, Pinter, whoever) did lots of writing which neither they nor anyone else ever suggested was art.

One further preparatory point: I know from considerable experience that when I try to define the concept of art, many people think I mean good or great art. They think if I am arguing that Damien Hirst's *Mother and Child Divided* (his cut-up cows) is definitely a work of art, then this can be answered by saying they don't like it or don't think it is any good. This misunderstands my point. There has always been any amount of mediocre or downright poor art (or poetry, or music, etc.) – the art galleries, libraries and music shops are full of it – but it is still art. In the same way, there is Cristiano Ronaldo or Lionel Messi, and then there are the lads kicking a ball around in my local park, but they are all playing football, just as there is Garry Kasparov or Magnus Carlsen, along with myself and others worse than me, all of whom play chess. It is the category I'm concerned with here, not the quality. The question of what makes art good or great I shall deal with in the next chapter. At the same time I recognise that, in this culture, the categories 'art' and 'artist' are not completely neutral like 'cat' or 'fish' or 'furniture'; rather, they carry a certain positive status (even if they are not very good art or artists). This is something else I believe my definition and analysis will help to explain.

Art and Labour

Writing just over one hundred years ago, the then influential art critic Clive Bell argued as follows:

> [E]ither all works of visual art have some common quality, or when we speak of 'works of art' we gibber. Everyone speaks of 'art', making a mental classification by which he distinguishes the class 'works of art' from all other classes. What is the justification of this classification? What is the quality common and peculiar to all members of this class? . . . There must be some one quality without which a work of art cannot exist; possessing which, in the least degree, no work is altogether worthless. What is this quality? What quality is shared by all objects that provoke our aesthetic emotions? What quality is common to Sta. Sophia and the windows at Chartres, Mexican sculpture, a Persian bowl, Chinese carpets, Giotto's frescoes at Padua, and the masterpieces of Poussin, Piero della Francesca, and Cezanne? Only one answer seems possible – significant form.

The moment Bell starts to explain what he means by his answer, significant form, I find myself in radical disagreement with him. For Bell significant form is a combination of 'lines and colours' that 'stir our aesthetic emotions'. The aesthetic emotion, he claims, is a distinct emotion independent of and different from all other emotions, and independent of all knowledge and experience of the world, 'which all sensitive people agree' is 'provoked by works of art'. If (like me) you don't agree, that simply proves that you are insensitive, like 'a deaf man at a concert'. This is as circular and empty as the notion that art is what artists say it is, with the difference that here art turns out to be what Clive Bell and 'sensitive' people who agree with him say it is – with the addition of a heavy dose of barely concealed upper-class arrogance. But setting his answer and its accompanying elaboration aside, what of Bell's premise that 'either all works of visual art have some common quality, or when we speak of "works of art" we gibber'?

The logic of this claim has been strongly contested on the basis of an argument developed by Wittgenstein in his *Philosophical Investigations*. Wittgenstein maintained that for some terms, which he called 'family resemblance terms', no such common denominator existed:

> Consider for example the proceedings that we call 'games'. I mean board-games, card-games, ball games, Olympic games and so on. What is common to them all? – Don't say: 'There *must* be something common, or they would not be called "games"' – but look and see whether there is anything common to all – for if you look at them you will not see something that is common to all, but similarities, relationships, and a whole series of them at that. To repeat: don't think but look!

The implication of this passage, says Nigel Warburton, is 'that "game" cannot be defined, at least not in terms of necessary and sufficient conditions',[12] and Morris Weitz and other philosophers have maintained that the same applies to 'art'; there is no factor or characteristic common to all works of art. Art should, by its nature, be seen as a concept that is 'open', not 'closed', capable of continued modification and extension through human creativity: 'Aestheticians may lay down similarity conditions but never necessary and sufficient ones for the correct application of the concept. With "art" its conditions of application can never be exhaustively enumerated since new cases can always be envisaged or created by artists.'[13] There are major attractions to this idea that it is wrong to even try to define art, not least the way this position allows for future developments as yet unseen and unforeseen; but there are also major problems. The first is that if we say, à la Wittgenstein on games, that art is characterised by a web of family resemblances, we still have to say what those family resemblances are; so in a sense we still have the problem of definition. The second is the danger, as pointed out by Stephen Davies, that 'everything resembles, or can be made to resemble, every other thing, so the invocation of resemblances cannot explain the unity and integrity of any concept.'[14] The third is that if we go back to Wittgenstein, we find that he argues, 'don't say there *must* be something common', but not that there *cannot* be anything common. That's why urges us to 'look and see.' So let's look again.

Once we do look, it is evident that *all* works of art – symphonies and poems and dances and songs and films, as well as paintings and sculptures – have in common the fact that they are all produced by human labour, mental and physical. Moreover, this not at all a trivial or banal point, because nature produces numerous things, scenes and so on, which human beings find beautiful, 'sublime' or moving in some way, but these are not (more or less ever) considered works of art. Paul Cézanne's numerous *Mont Sainte-Victoire* paintings are art of a high order; Mont Sainte-Victoire itself is not. Percy Shelley's 'To a Skylark' is art; not so either the skylark or its beautiful song. (This is despite the fact that Shelley calls the skylark's song 'unpremeditated art', professing, 'Better than all treasures / That in books are found, / Thy skill to poet were'.) Bell, like many other aestheticians, misses or ignores this point because he seeks his 'common factor' in the art objects rather than in how they are produced. Now, it's clear that being a product of human labour cannot itself be sufficient to define art, as this applies to a multitude of objects – art and nonart alike. Nevertheless, it raises the possibility that a defining characteristic of art may be the nature of the labour that produces it.

For a Marxist this is immediately intriguing because labour is such a central concept in Marxism (in Marx's philosophy, theory of history, sociology and economics) and because Marx has so much to say about it. For Marx, labour, together with nature, was the source of all wealth. It was also the source of all value, surplus value and profit; indeed, the labour theory of value is Marx's core economic doctrine. But more than that, Marx writes that 'the entire so-called history of the world is nothing but the begetting of man through human labour'.[15] This idea, that labour is the means by which humans create their world and themselves, was elaborated on by Engels in his remarkable essay 'The Part Played by Labour in the Transition from Ape to Man'. And one could, with some justice, describe the Marxist theory of history (usually known as historical materialism) as the 'labour theory of history', since it regards social labour as the means through which humans differentiated themselves from animals,[16] and the development of the forces of production (i.e., the productivity of labour) as the fundamental driving force in human history. Human labour is thus an immensely creative force, one that Marx describes, in a famous passage from *Capital*, as follows:

> We shall, therefore, in the first place, have to consider the labour-process independently of the particular form it assumes under given social conditions.
>
> Labour is, in the first place, a process in which both man and Nature participate, and in which man of his own accord starts, regulates, and controls the material re-actions between himself and Nature. He opposes himself to Nature as one of her own forces, setting in motion arms and legs, head and hands, the natural forces of his body, in order to appropriate Nature's productions in a form adapted to his own wants. By thus acting on the external world and changing it, he at the same time changes his own nature. He develops his slumbering powers and compels them to act in obedience to his sway. We are not now dealing with those primitive instinctive forms of labour that remind us of the mere animal. An immeasurable interval of time separates the state of things in which a man brings his labour-power to market for sale as a commodity, from that state in which human labour was still in its first instinctive stage. We pre-suppose labour in a form that stamps it as exclusively human. A spider conducts operations that resemble those of a weaver, and a bee puts to shame many an architect in the construction of her cells. But what distinguishes the worst architect from the best of bees is this, that the architect raises his structure in imagination before he erects it in reality. At the end of every labour-process, we get a result that already existed in the imagination of the labourer at its commencement. He not only effects a change of form in the material on which he works,

> but he also realises a purpose of his own that gives the law to his modus operandi, and to which he must subordinate his will. And this subordination is no mere momentary act. Besides the exertion of the bodily organs, the process demands that, during the whole operation, the workman's will be steadily in consonance with his purpose.[17]

But here we immediately face a paradox. In capitalist society, the labour of the overwhelming majority of people – especially, but not only, working-class people – might be thought in many respects to more closely resemble that of a bee than that of an architect. By contrast, creativity, which Marx ascribes to all labour, appears to be the province of a small minority, primarily artists.[18] Marx calls this kind of uncreative work 'alienated labour'.

The first point Marx makes about alienated labour is that it results in the worker's alienation from the product of their labour: '[T]he object which labour produces – labour's product – confronts it as something alien. . . . The worker is related to the product of his labour as to an alien object.'[19] But then he goes on to ask: 'How would the worker come to face the product of his activity as a stranger, were it not that in the very act of production he was estranging himself from himself? The product is after all but the summary of the activity of production.'[20] This shifts Marx's focus to what he calls 'the essential relationship of labour . . . the relationship of the *worker* to production', and he provides an extended description of this relationship.

What, then, constitutes the alienation of labour?

> First, the fact that labor is *external* to the worker, i.e., it does not belong to his intrinsic nature; that in his work, therefore, he does not affirm himself but denies himself, does not feel content but unhappy, does not develop freely his physical and mental energy but mortifies his body and ruins his mind. The worker therefore only feels himself outside his work, and in his work feels outside himself. He feels at home when he is not working, and when he is working he does not feel at home. His labor is therefore not voluntary, but coerced; it is *forced labor*. It is therefore not the satisfaction of a need; it is merely a *means* to satisfy needs external to it. Its alien

> character emerges clearly in the fact that as soon as no physical or other compulsion exists, labor is shunned like the plague. External labor, labor in which man alienates himself, is a labor of self-sacrifice, of mortification. Lastly, the external character of labor for the worker appears in the fact that it is not his own, but someone else's, that it does not belong to him, that in it he belongs, not to himself, but to another. Just as in religion the spontaneous activity of the human imagination, of the human brain and the human heart, operates on the individual independently of him – that is, operates as an alien, divine or diabolical activity – so is the worker's activity not his spontaneous activity. It belongs to another; it is the loss of his self.[21]

This description, and it is really analysis as well as description, applies not only to the labour of nineteenth-century factory workers but also, in my view, to the labour of the majority of people on the planet today:[22] to the teeming millions in the factories in Guangdong, to the fighting textile workers of al-Mahalla in Egypt, to the metal workers of São Paulo, but also transport workers everywhere, to call-centre workers in India, fast-food workers in the United States or Britain, clerical and other white-collar workers in Europe and so on. But it does not apply to the labour of artists, that is, to the labour responsible for the production of works of art.

This can be illustrated by many examples. Thus Marx says of alienated labour that it is shunned as soon as there is no physical or other compulsion. This is not true of 'creative' labour: Michelangelo, Titian, Renoir, Monet, Matisse, Picasso and many other artists went on working right up to their deaths and long after any economic compulsion had disappeared. Leo Tolstoy was never under any economic or other external pressure to write, yet he undertook the immense labour of *War and Peace*. Was W. B. Yeats 'forced' to write 'Easter, 1916,' or Giuseppe di Lampedusa to write *The Leopard*? Chuck Berry was still performing into his eighties and announced a new album at ninety. Bob Dylan, with an estimated fortune of $180 million, is touring still. Of course, artists of all kinds want and need to earn a living, but in case after case it is clear that neither economic compulsion nor economic acquisitiveness is the motivation for artistic labour.

Marx says that in alienated labour 'man does not affirm, but denies himself'. This is manifestly not the case with artistic labour, in many instances explicitly so: think of Rembrandt's self-portraits, of Whitman's 'Song of Myself,' of the art of Tracey Emin, of the monologue at the end of Joyce's *Ulysses* or Cézanne's statement, 'My nervous system is enfeebled, only work in oils can sustain me.'

These examples can be multiplied indefinitely, but there is something more fundamental at play than the artist's subjective motivations or attitude. Even where the artist is substantially motivated by personal gain, as seems to have been the case with Salvador Dalí, for example,[23] there is still a distinction between alienated wage labour and artistic labour. In artistic labour it is the artist who controls the process of production (and in most cases also owns his or her immediate means of production). This is not only true empirically – painters control the making of their paintings, poets the writing of their poetry, composers the composing of their music and so on – but *it must be so*, or 'artists' would disappear as a social category. Art would simply be manufactured in mass production like shoes, cars or mobile phones.

Viewing this historically, as we should, we can say that 'art' as a social category (in the sense we are talking about and are attempting to define) emerges to cover a variety of distinct and diverse activities – painting, sculpture, poetry, novel writing, composing music, playwriting and so on – in tension with and opposition to the growth of waged, alienated labour with the rise of capitalism. As the bulk of production, especially the manufacture of goods, becomes subsumed under wage labour and the rule of capital, so humanity, or rather some humans and overwhelmingly humans from a relatively privileged class position, carve out a sphere of production – art – not performed by alienated labour.

To avoid misunderstanding, let me stress emphatically that this does not mean artworks are not commodities; on the contrary, artworks have been systematically commodified since at least the seventeenth century (think of Dutch art and Rembrandt). It means that the labour that produced them was controlled by the producer/artist.

This, then, is the first element in the definition of art I wish to propose: art is work produced by unalienated human labour.

Form and Content

However, to say that art is unalienated human labour clearly cannot be the end of the story, because there is a great deal of unalienated labour that is not and does not produce art. Some examples:

(a) A person's work on an allotment and the vegetables they grow for their own consumption

(b) The 'work' of playing sport for pleasure or walking in the countryside

(c) Voluntary political activity – organising, campaigning and suchlike

(d) The work of producing scientific or social theory

What distinguishes art from the first three of these activities is that it embodies meaning. Of course, everything, even an ordinary bunch of carrots, embodies 'meaning' to some extent, but artworks, in contrast to vegetables, games in the park and country walks, are charged with meaning to a qualitatively different degree: they make statements to and about the world; they possess and express an intellectual and/or emotional content. I am well aware that the way modern visual art has developed, bunches of carrots, games in the park and walks in the countryside could easily be presented as artworks (and indeed have been, e.g., in the work of Richard Long) just as a urinal and a hatstand were selected and presented by Marcel Duchamp, or Campbell's Soup cans and Brillo boxes by Andy Warhol. My argument is that it is not the physical nature of the object itself which decides whether or not it is art – any object has the capacity to be made a work of art – but the nature of the labour involved. It is the *labour* of Long, Duchamp and Warhol that is charged with meaning and produces work that embodies that meaning, that is to say, has content.

However, the same is clearly true of political campaign work and works of scientific and social theory: they are the products of labour under the control of the producer, and they are packed with meaning. Yet they are not regarded as art. Why not?

The answer lies in the nature of the relationship between form and content that prevails in these categories, as opposed to the relationship that obtains in art. In a work of scientific or social theory, the content is not only much more important than the form, but it is also to a large extent detachable from it. In a work of art, the content/meaning is totally bound up with the form and is inseparable from it.

This claim is best explained and clarified by means of examples. But first I should state that by 'content' I mean not the 'subject matter' but the sum total of a work's emotional/intellectual/psychological meanings. There are thousands of paintings of the Crucifixion – they have the same 'subject' – but the content of Matthias Grünewald's *Crucifixion* is very different from that of Giotto's or Dalí's. Michelangelo made three *Pietàs* (statues of the body of Christ in the arms of the Virgin Mary), but each has a very different content. And by 'form' I do not mean genre or formal structure, as in a poem that is a sonnet or in rhyming couplets, or in a watercolour painting, or in music, a blues piece or a concerto. I mean the concrete form of a particular work: in the case of a poem, every single word in that exact order; in the case a painting, every single brushstroke as laid on the canvas, and in a song, every single note and every word as sung in that performance.

Now let us compare a great work of social theory – Vladimir Lenin's *The State and Revolution* – with a well-known, relatively simple but very powerful poem, 'A Red, Red Rose' by Robert Burns. In *The State and Revolution*, the importance of its content – Lenin's version of the Marxist theory of the state – far outweighs the importance of the particular form it is given in this text, and we can be confident that Lenin would have agreed with this judgment; he was a very effective and powerful writer but no great stylist (compared to, say, Marx or Trotsky). I do not read Russian, so I have only read *The State and Revolution* in translation. I do not believe I have missed much of its meaning because of this. What counts above all in this work are the ideas it contains. It is not that the specific words do not matter – if you change 'smash the state machine' to 'take over the state machine', the essence of Lenin's argument is lost. But the sound and rhythm of the words don't matter much.

Things stand quite differently with the Burns poem. It contains little in the way of ideas, nothing that would count as 'theory'; it is simply a declaration of love, but it is an exquisitely beautiful declaration, and here the exact word, every exact word, matters. 'My love is like a red rose' does not convey the same feeling as 'O my Luve is like a red, red rose'. The repetition of 'red' alters and intensifies the emotional impact of the poem. The same is true of the eighth and ninth lines: 'Till a' the seas gang dry. / Till a' the seas gang dry my dear'. 'A' the seas' is subtly different, more romantic, than 'all the seas', and again the repetition reinforces the point.

Now let us take the example of Strange Fruit. The words of this poem/song were written by Abel Meeropol, and they are a strong indictment of lynching in their own right.

> Southern trees bear strange fruit
> Blood on the leaves and blood at the root
> Black bodies swinging in the southern breeze
> Strange fruit hanging from the poplar trees.
>
> Pastoral scene of the gallant south
> The bulging eyes and the twisted mouth
> Scent of magnolias, sweet and fresh
> Then the sudden smell of burning flesh.
>
> Here is fruit for the crows to pluck
> For the rain to gather, for the wind to suck
> For the sun to rot, for the trees to drop
> Here is a strange and bitter crop.

But the performance of it by Billie Holiday brings about a qualitative transformation in the power of this artwork. Holiday's unique phrasing and the expressiveness of her voice produce an intensity of both anger and sorrow that makes her version of the song an extraordinary masterpiece. The difference in form of the Holiday song from the Meeropol poem generates a different content.

Obviously I have chosen examples which illustrate my argument, but I want to suggest that this fusion of form and content is a general characteristic of what we call art. In a poem it is the specific combination of words in a specific order, with all their associations and their sound (rhythm, rhyme, alliteration, assonance, onomatopoeia) that make up the poem's content. When John Keats writes of autumn as the 'season of mists and mellow fruitfulness', the very sound of the words contributes to the meaning or content of the poem. The same is true of the particular brushstrokes and the thickness of the paint in Vincent van Gogh's *Sunflowers* or the particular colours and strength of line in an abstract painting by Piet Mondrian.

Moreover, I think this unity of form and content in art, across the board, is recognised in practice by both artists (in producing the work) and by critics (in assessing it).

It should be said that this unity or fusion is not absolute, nor always perfectly realised. Rather, it constitutes a goal towards which art and artist are constantly striving and by which the work can be judged. Consequently, a work can be criticised for failing to achieve the required fusion. Thus T. S. Eliot regarded *Hamlet* as a failure as a play because, in his view, there lay at its heart some 'intractable material', some 'disgust', for which Shakespeare was unable to find an adequate 'objective correlative'.[24] And sometimes Picasso's *Guernica* has been criticised on the grounds that it's preindustrial imagery was inadequate to convey the horror of modern warfare. (I cite these criticisms as examples of the kind of argument that can be made, not to agree with them – which I do not.)

To conclude, art is work produced by unalienated human labour and characterised by a fusion or unity of form and content. Furthermore, there is a connection between these two elements in the definition in that, generally speaking, it requires unalienated labour to achieve such a fusion of form and content.

Support from the Marxist Tradition

To the best of my knowledge, the precise definition of art presented here has not been advanced previously,[25] but there are numerous statements from within the Marxist tradition that either point in this direction or lend it support. We can begin with Marx himself.

Marx never wrote systematically on the question of art, but the notion of an antagonism between capitalist production and art, between artistic/

creative labour and alienated labour, is a theme in Marx that appears on a number of occasions, starting as early as 1842 when, discussing the freedom of the press, he wrote: 'A writer must of course earn a living to exist and be able to write, but he must in no sense exist and write so as to earn a living. . . . In no sense does the writer regard his works as a means. They are ends in themselves. . . . The first freedom of the press consists in its not being a business.'[26] In 1842 Marx was not yet a Marxist and had not yet developed his theory of alienation; consequently, the formulations here are somewhat idealistic. Nevertheless, he insists on a contrast between writing simply for a wage, for money, as a mere means to earn a living, and writing as an end in itself.

Much later, in his *Theories of Surplus Value*, Marx writes:

> Milton, for example, who wrote *Paradise Lost*, was an unproductive worker. In contrast to this, the writer who delivers hackwork for his publisher is a productive worker. Milton produced *Paradise Lost* in the way that a silkworm produces silk, as the expression of *his own* nature. Later on he sold the product for £5 and to that extent became a dealer in a commodity. But the Leipzig literary proletarian who produces books, e.g. compendia on political economy, at the instructions of his publisher is roughly speaking a productive worker, in so far as his production is subsumed under capital and only takes place for the purpose of the latter's valorisation.[27]

Marx is focussed here on the question of productive and unproductive labour (from the standpoint of capital), which is not our concern; but he makes two distinctions which do relate to my definition of art. The first is between the nature of Milton's labour in writing *Paradise Lost* and the fact that he sold the product. Marx compares this labour to the way 'a silkworm produces silk' as 'an activity of his nature'. Of course, this is a rather inaccurate way of describing the writing of poetry; however, he clearly means by this that it was labour in which Milton affirmed and expressed himself (i.e., unalienated labour), and he insists that the character of this labour is not changed by the subsequent fact that the product is sold as a commodity. The second distinction is between Milton (the artist) and the 'literary proletarian' who 'delivers hackwork' on the orders of a publisher. In practice these distinctions may not be simple or absolute, with intermediate cases where the pressures of the market react back on the writer or artist without totally controlling their work, as is the case with normal wage labour. Nevertheless, they point to features that are typical of the situation of the artist under capitalism. Turner, Matisse, Bacon or Emin makes work and passes it to a dealer to sell; Mann or Joyce writes a novel and looks for a publisher to produce and sell it; Bergman, Fellini or Loach gets funding for a film and hopes to get a deal for its distribution; but in each case the artist retains control and, initially, ownership of what they produce.

In the *Grundrisse* Marx critiques Adam Smith's wholly negative view of labour as nothing but a sacrifice of leisure or free time. Smith is right, he says, that, 'in its historic forms as slave-labour, serf-labour, and wage-labour, labour always appears as repulsive, always as *external forced labour*; and not-labour, by contrast, as "freedom, and happiness"'. But Marx argues that 'the individual, "in his normal state of health, strength, activity, skill, facility", also needs a normal portion of work, and of the suspension of tranquillity' and writes of 'real freedom, whose action is precisely labour.' And when he looks for an example of really 'free' work, he cites the composition of music – an artistic activity. 'Really free working, e.g. composing, is at the same time precisely the most damned seriousness, the most intense exertion.'[28]

Again in *Theories of Surplus Value*, dealing once more with productive and unproductive labour, Marx writes:

> Because Storch does not conceive material production itself *historically* – because he conceives it as production of material goods in general, not as a definite historically developed and specific form of this production – he deprives himself of the basis on which alone can be understood partly the ideological component parts of the ruling class, partly the free spiritual production of this particular social formation. He cannot get beyond meaningless general phrases. Consequently, the relation is not so simple as he presupposes. For instance, capitalist production is hostile to certain branches of spiritual production, for example, art and poetry. If this is left out of account, it opens the way to the illusion of the French in the eighteenth century which has been so beautifully satirised by Lessing. Because we are further ahead than the ancients in

> mechanics, etc., why shouldn't we be able to make an epic too? And the *Henriade* in place of the *Iliad*![29]

Here, as is very often the case with Marx, he throws out numerous extremely interesting and suggestive asides in the course of discussing something else, which for that reason remain unexplored. Thus we have the distinction between material and spiritual production – one which is not as straightforward as it might seem. Is Michelangelo's *David* spiritual or material production, or both? It is certainly a material object, as is Chartres Cathedral or even, when we think about it, a novel or a film or a record. But most interesting is the claim that 'capitalist production is hostile to certain branches of spiritual production, for example, art and poetry'. The truth or otherwise of this claim depends, partly, on what we think it means.[30]

It could be taken to mean that the capitalist class (the bourgeoisie), taken as a whole, are hostile to art. There may be an element of truth in this, in that many, probably most, capitalists are vulgar boors and philistines interested only in making money.[31] But as a generalisation about the capitalist class *as a class*, it would appear to be false in that its more intelligent representatives clearly take the question of cultural hegemony seriously and ensure that some of their number both sponsor and control the commanding heights of the arts: think of the Rockefellers with the Museum of Modern Art (MoMA) in New York (or the Whitneys, Guggenheims and Gettys) or Pompidou in France, or the role of Kenneth Clark, Herbert Read and Lord Gowrie in Britain. Moreover, there is no sign, either in the capitalist era as a whole or in late capitalism, of the disappearance or (quantitative) decline of art. There may well be more paintings, sculptures, novels, poems, songs, musical works, photographs and films made today than ever in the history of the world. If, however, we interpret Marx's statement to mean that there is an inherent contradiction between capitalist methods of production and the production of art, and that art cannot and will not be produced by the normal methods of capitalist production (i.e., by means of wage labour in which the employer determines more or less entirely the work of the worker and owns from the outset the products of that labour), then I think this statement is true. It is also precisely what I am arguing when I say that art is a product of unalienated labour.

William Morris was unaware of Marx's theory of alienation and had, by his own admission, a decidedly limited knowledge and understanding of Marxism. But he became a committed revolutionary socialist, and he outlined, in his own language, a view of art that in important respects prefigures that presented here. Morris believed in the capacity of 'all men' to engage in creative labour and that prior to the development of capitalism they habitually did so:

> So much is now known of the periods of art that have left abundant examples of their work behind them, that we can judge of the art of all periods by comparing these with the remains of times of which less has been left us; and we cannot fail to come to the conclusion that down to very recent days everything that the hand of man touched was more or less beautiful: so that in those days all people who made anything shared in art, as well as all people who used the things so made: that is, ALL people shared in art.[32]

With the arrival of capitalism, however, the memory of this was lost. '[I]n short the whole civilised world had forgotten that there had ever been an art made by the people for the people as a joy for the maker and the user.' Art, he maintains, '*is man's expression of his joy in labour*' (original emphasis), adding, '[T]he chief accusation I have to bring against the modern state of society is that it is founded on the art-lacking or unhappy labour of the greater part of men.' Thus Morris argues that artistic labour was typical of the Middle Ages (i.e., of feudal society), marginalised under capitalism by the spread of wage labour, but that it will be restored, collectively, by socialism:

> [A]ll through the Middle Ages from the 12th to the end of the 16th century . . . the middle class was being formed from the enfranchised serfs, yeomen, and craftsmen of the guilds. Throughout that period, at least, all manufactured goods, everything that admitted of ornament was made more or less beautiful; nor was the beauty charged for as a separate article, for all craftsmen were more or less artists, and could not help adding beauty to the goods they made. It is easy to see that this could not have happened if they had been

> working for the profit of a master. They worked, on the contrary, under such conditions that they themselves were masters of their time, tools, and materials, and, for the most part, their goods were exchanged by the simple process of the user buying from the maker. Under these circumstances it was a matter of course that a man, being master of his work should choose to make it pleasanter to himself by exercising on it that love of beauty which is common to all men till it is crushed out of them by the mere bitter struggle for life called competition for wages, and by subjection to a master who also is struggling for profit against other competitors. This system of a man working for himself leisurely and happily was infinitely better, both as regards the worker and his work, than that division of labour system which the profit-grinding of rising commercialism supplanted it by; but of course it is impossible to go back to such a simple system, even if it would not involve, as it would, a return to the whole hierarchical, or feudal state of society. On the other hand it is as necessary for the existence of art as it is for the well-being of the people otherwise, that the workman should again have control over his material, his tools, and his time only that control must no longer be of the individual workman, as in the Middle ages but of the whole body of workmen. When the workers organise work for the benefit of the workers, that is to say of the whole people, they will once more know what is meant by art.[33]

Like Morris, Leon Trotsky would appear not to have read Marx's *Economic and Philosophic Manuscripts of 1844* (published in Russia in 1932) or to have been aware of Marx's theory of alienation. But he was much engaged in questions regarding art and literature and wrote on these issues with great intelligence and sensitivity. In particular, he was concerned to defend artistic freedom against rising Stalinist authoritarian control, and in the course of this defence he made an argument which bears on the definition under discussion. In his 1936 *The Revolution Betrayed*, he writes:

> Spiritual creativeness demands freedom.... Personal relations, science and art will not know any externally imposed 'plan', nor even any shadow of compulsion. To what degree spiritual creativeness

> shall be individual or collective will depend entirely upon its creators. . . .
>
> In 1924, on the threshold of the new period, the author of this book thus formulated the relation of the state to the various artistic groups and tendencies: 'while holding over them all the categorical criterion, *for* the revolution or *against* the revolution, to give them complete freedom in the sphere of artistic self-determination.'[34]

Trotsky is most insistent on this and returns to it again and again. In 'Art and Politics in Our Epoch' (1938), he writes:

> The October revolution gave a magnificent impetus to all types of Soviet art. The bureaucratic reaction, on the contrary, has stifled artistic creation with a totalitarian hand. Nothing surprising here! Art is basically a function of the nerves and demands complete sincerity. . . .
>
> Art, like science, not only does not seek orders, but by its very essence, cannot tolerate them. Artistic creation has its laws – even when it consciously serves a social movement. Truly intellectual creation is incompatible with lies, hypocrisy and the spirit of conformity. Art can become a strong ally of revolution only in so far as it remains faithful to itself. Poets, painters, sculptors and musicians will themselves find their own approach and methods.[35]

And in the 'Manifesto: Towards a Free Revolutionary Art', which he wrote that same year with André Breton and Diego Rivera, Trotsky quotes the passage from the young Marx cited above – about the writer not living and writing to make money – and comments:

> It is more than ever fitting to use this statement against those who would regiment intellectual activity in the direction of ends foreign to itself. . . . In the realm of artistic creation, the imagination must escape from all constraint and must, under no pretext, allow itself to be placed under bonds. To those who would urge us, whether for today or for tomorrow, to consent that art should submit to a discipline which we hold to be radically incompatible with its nature, we give a flat refusal, and we repeat our deliberate intention of standing by the formula: complete freedom for art. . . .
>
> No authority, no dictation, not the least trace of orders from above![36]

If Trotsky was right on this point and it was not possible to produce worthwhile or genuine art according to the orders of a dictatorial (in this case Stalinist) state, then it is also not possible to produce it according to the orders of a capitalist business. The making of art requires that it be determined and controlled by the makers themselves.

Finally, I want to cite observations made by John Berger in the course of a critical review of Nicos Hadjinicolaou's *Art History and Class Struggle*. Hadjinicolaou was an Althusserian Marxist who proposed the foundation of a 'science' of art history based on the idea that paintings were essentially expressions of class visual ideology (independent of the artists who produced them). Berger rejected this, arguing:

> The culture of capitalism has reduced paintings, as it reduces everything which is alive, to market commodities, and to an advertisement for other commodities. The new reductionism of revolutionary theory, which we are considering, is in danger of doing something similar. What the one uses as an advertisement (for a prestige, a way of life and the commodities that go with it), the other sees art only as the visual ideology of a class. *Both eliminate art as a potential model of freedom*, which is how artists and the masses have always treated art when it spoke to their needs.[37]

In the same review Berger also refers to the Marxist art historian Max Raphael, saying that '[w]hereas Hadjinicolaou begins with the work as an object . . . Raphael believed that the explanation had to be sought in the process of production itself.' He quotes Raphael, to the effect that '[a]rt and the study of art lead from the work to the process of creation' and that '[t]he work of art holds man's creative energies in crystalline suspension'.[38]

What is it that makes art 'a potential model of freedom' (remember that Marx used composition as an example of 'really free working'), and what does it mean to say 'art holds man's creative energies'? In the proposition that art is produced by unalienated labour, we have the answer to these questions.

Objections

Among the reactions I met with when I first put forward this definition of art in 1998 were, from some Marxist colleagues whose general outlook I shared, a mixture of certain misunderstandings and substantial objections. I will first try to clear up the misunderstandings so as, hopefully, to avoid their recurrence.

The main misunderstanding occurred in the idea that I was arguing either that artists were somehow unalienated as people or that artistic production existed in a sort of asocial bubble, unaffected by the alienation that pervaded the rest of capitalist society. It is, of course, the case that many artists have exhibited manifest signs of being highly alienated individuals – Richard Dadd, Arthur Rimbaud, Andy Warhol, Oscar Wilde and Jack Kerouac spring to my mind – and for anyone with any understanding of Marx's general theory of alienation, it would clearly be literally impossible for art in the capitalist era to be unaffected by it. After all, Marx argues that as a result of alienated labour, human beings are alienated not only from the products of their labour (that come to dominate them and stand over them as alien forces) but also from themselves, from each other and from nature. This is a total social process that affects everybody and everything in capitalist society, including artists and their art. Whether or not this makes unalienated labour impossible we will come to in a moment, but manifestly all artistic production is 'influenced' or 'affected', and in many ways damaged, by this general alienation, by the role of the capitalist market and by the continual transformation of artworks of all kinds into commodities and private property. The history of modern art, in particular, is replete with examples of artists, from Gustav Metzger and 'auto-destructive' art to graffiti and street art, who have grappled with these problems in various ways. Moreover, numerous artists have, more or less explicitly, made human alienation a major theme of their work – Eliot, Kafka, Beckett, Giacometti, Bacon, Camus, Ginsberg and so on. My argument is only about the nature of *artistic labour* (which is why the Marx quote about Milton, in which he says *Paradise Lost* is 'an expression of his own nature' later sold for five pounds, is important); I am not arguing that art cannot be commodified or produced 'for the market'. Again, I will return to this.

The two more substantial objections were (1) that alienation is so all-pervasive in capitalist society that unalienated labour is impossible, and since there is no 'space' for it, it cannot be the case that art is produced by unalienated labour; and (2) that it is indisputable that large amounts of alienated labour go into the production of artworks (e.g., the labour of a technical crew in making a film), so therefore this cannot be the basis for a definition of art.

Let me deal first with the 'impossibility' of unalienated labour. If what is meant by this is that under capitalism it is impossible to engage in labour in which the process and content of the work is controlled and determined by the worker/labourer – work which is not sold or made over (the old literal meaning of 'alienated') to another, work which is voluntarily undertaken and through which the worker affirms and/or expresses herself and her purposes (what I mean by 'unalienated labour') – then this is not true. Clearly, despite the overweening power of capital, the pervasiveness of capitalist social relations and the hegemony of capitalist ideology, people – not only artists, but all sorts of people – engage in such work and activity on a large scale.

To argue that this is not so is especially problematic for socialists and Marxists since it negates the possibility of resistance and revolutionary work, either theoretical or practical. If there is not a qualitative difference between the labour of writing *Capital* and hack journalistic work, or between organising a strike (maintaining a picket is hard work) and work performed for and under the control of a boss, if Marx was not really in control of the content of *Capital* and the pickets are not voluntarily and purposefully organising the picket line but are still more or less completely dominated by alienation in this work, then changing the world becomes impossible. And if Marx determined and controlled the writing of *Capital*, why should the same not apply to James Joyce writing *Ulysses* or Pablo Picasso painting *Guernica* or John Coltrane composing or playing *A Love Supreme*?

Certainly it is possible to reply that Marx was affected by alienation when writing *Capital*, by poverty and poor housing conditions and ill health and all sorts of difficulties, that strikers wouldn't need to go on strike or organise picket lines, and so on, if it were not for alienation. This is true, but it is not what I am arguing. To those who insist there can be no unalienated labour under capitalism, I would say, 'Alright, keep your word, but do you not accept there is a real difference between work controlled by the worker/artist and work controlled by a boss/employer? My argument is that the former is the basis of art in our society.'

This whole argument does, however, raise the possibility that the pressures of capitalism, of the need to be 'commercial', may not just affect the artist but so 'capture' her/him as to determine the content of her/his work so that what in formal terms appears to be unalienated artistic labour is in reality alienated, externally controlled work. This undoubtedly happens on a very large scale in our society (I will return to this), and when it does, the artistic character of the work is more or less destroyed and the artist ceases to be an artist. Intermediate cases also often arise as a result of these pressures, either in the art category where the art is damaged, or in intermediate, semi-artistic categories. But it is only possible to understand and analyse these intermediate cases if we start from understanding the qualitative difference between the two poles of alienated wage labour and unalienated artistic labour.

The argument that large quantities of alienated labour are involved in making much art, such as a film or a play, is manifestly true. I would go further and say that in capitalist society, *all* art without exception rests on alienated labour: not only did Michelangelo depend on quarry workers in Carrara to produce his block of marble for the *David* and other labourers to transport it to Florence, but any painter requires paints and canvas,[39] and even the lonely poet in his garret uses pen and paper produced by alienated labour. But the key point is that whether we are talking about a film or play or sculpture or novel, it is the unalienated, self-directed labour of the artist or artists (director, composer, author, sculptor, etc.) that determines the character of the work as art. Without that, the work of the quarrier, the film technician, the carpenter who constructs scenery, the printer or the papermaker is simply wage labour producing stone, film, furniture, books and so on.

However, noting the combination of alienated and unalienated labour in the production of artworks, especially inherently collective works such as plays, films, operas, ballets, concerts and the like, again raises the question of transitional and intermediate cases. Consider the performance of a play, say *Waiting for Godot*. This is a collective enterprise involving a spectrum of different kinds of labour. At one pole of this spectrum, we have the unequivocally creative labour of the playwright, Samuel Beckett. At the other pole, we have the alienated wage labour of workers in the box office, ushers, cleaners and others (not to speak of the construction workers who built the theatre or the print workers who print the programmes). Between these poles we have the work of the producer/director of the play, of the lead actors, minor actors,[40] set designers, costume designers and so on – roles which contain more or less 'artistic' elements. The issue of such intermediate cases needs further exploration.

Intermediate Cases

I said at the start of this chapter that '*all* definitions, even the most apparently precise, have a tendency to fray at the edges' and that 'there are bound to be problematic transitional cases between art and nonart'. I shall now examine some of these transitional cases – though not all, because there are too many – conscious that in doing so I am putting the definition I have advanced to a significant test.

Let's begin with the huge field of 'Western popular music'. I'm using the term as broadly as possible here, excluding only non-Western music and classical music, but including jazz, blues, rock, soul, pop, punk, folk, hip-hop and all other genres. This field comprises a vast array of roles – singers, songwriters, composers, session musicians, arrangers, sound engineers, record company executives, roadies, promoters, security guards and so on. If we apply my definition to this whole field, we find, as with the example of the play given above, a spectrum of more and less artistic activities. This spectrum includes a pole of singers, songwriters, composers and musicians who control their own musical work and invest it with a unity of form and content; it therefore qualifies definitely as art. Here is a somewhat arbitrary list of people whose work seems to me to fall into this category: George Gershwin, Cole Porter, Louis Armstrong, Duke Ellington, Bessie Smith, Billie Holiday, Robert Johnson, Charlie Parker, Woody Guthrie, Bob Dylan, Leonard Cohen, Ewan MacColl, Edith Piaf, Chuck Berry, Shane MacGowan, Paul Simon, the Beatles, Marvin Gaye, Janis Joplin, Nirvana, Amy Winehouse. At the other end of the music spectrum we have manufactured pop stars and boy bands (the likes of Tommy Steele, Billy Fury, the Monkees, Take That, Westlife, One Direction, etc.) and the composition of advertising jingles, where commercial considerations not only influence the music but totally determine it from start to finish, such that the element of self-determined, creative labour more or less disappears.

Of course, the names I have listed are famous and, generally speaking, masters of their craft, but I want to stress that I'm not making a judgment of quality here, nor saying that only great or excellent art counts as art. Many less well-known (and maybe less outstanding) musicians – for example, Irish 'trad' musicians in the Cobblestone pub in Dublin – meet my criteria for producing art, just as my poet friends Tim Evans and Phil Knight and my artist friends Hector Lopez-Kern and Anna Paczuska are not Dylan Thomas or Joan Miró, but they, and thousands like them, are producing real art. Nor am I making a judgment about different genres, such as for jazz and against rock. The dividing line, or more accurately, the transition zone, lies within genres, not between them. Flamenco, for example, contains unambiguous art (and of a very high order) as well as completely manufactured and commercialised 'shows', based on highly alienated labour, for tourists.

However, the proportion between art and nonart does differ among different genres or 'art forms'. In filmmaking, for example, there is a relatively high proportion of alienated labour, both in terms of technicians, camera operators, extras and the like, and in terms of the preponderance of films totally subordinated to market forces and containing minimal elements of art: for instance, James Bond movies, CGI superhero series or pornography. Nevertheless, this doesn't entirely prevent artistic work, in terms of screenwriting, direction and acting, being done even within the framework of Hollywood, as well as in film worldwide. In TV there is also a strong tendency – probably even stronger – to marginalise artistic production, although I would say some definitely exists (for example, *The Wire*, *The Handmaid's Tale* or the TV plays of Ken Loach, David Mercer, Trevor Griffiths and Stephen Potter). In TV production, unalienated labour, insofar as it exists, is probably more prevalent in the areas of current affairs and documentary, but these may fail to meet the criterion of fusion of content and form. Of course, it should also be noted that TV is a medium for broadcasting art (as in films, plays, concerts or ballets) that was originally made outside the TV industry, as well as programmes about art.

In literature, as opposed to writing as such, the balance is somewhat different. The role of the novelist's and poet's self-determined artistic labour, with its concomitant goal of fusing content and form, remains more entrenched. At the same time, there clearly exists a substantial layer of 'pulp fiction', in which the writer may have formal control over their own labour while in reality having completely internalised the requirements of the publisher for formulaic hackwork: for example, the romances published by Mills & Boon. And between the unequivocally artistic novels or poetry – say, of Gabriel García Marquez or Pablo Neruda – and outright pulp fiction, there is a substantial transitional layer with elements of both, for example, the detective fiction of Agatha Christie.

The sphere of visual art (painting, sculpture, drawing, etching, and now installations, video art, performance art, relational art, etc.), where much of the 'What is art?' debate has been concentrated, is also configured somewhat differently. Alongside what is often called 'fine art', there are the adjacent and related categories or disciplines of graphic design, product design, interior design and illustration.[41] While there are many areas of overlap in practices, techniques and skills between all these areas, there are nonetheless real distinctions between them and 'fine' art, in terms of the criteria we are using. In all of them, the element of control of the work and imposition from above, primarily by the commissioning company, is more detailed and directive than in fine art, and in the design categories (though not in illustration) there is a relative absence of content/meaning compared with art. For these reasons, these areas seem to me to be best considered transitional, with a spectrum within each of them, between art and nonart.

I want now to consider advertising. John Berger, who devoted the last section of *Ways of Seeing* to the analysis of advertising (which he called 'publicity'), began by noting that '[i]n the cities in which we live, all of us see hundreds of publicity images every day of our lives. No other kind of image confronts us so frequently.' This was written in 1972. Today, the extent and density of advertising, in the West and throughout the world, has grown enormously.

Advertising parallels and integrates all the different forms of art to an extraordinary degree, combining at will still visual images, photographs, film, music, drama and dance. Moreover, this combination is effected with large amounts of inventiveness, humour, pathos and 'creativity', and is all-pervasive in our society: it is on every billboard, in every cinema, surrounding almost every TV programme, in every newspaper and right across the internet. If advertising is art, then it is the dominant art form of our day by a long way. This has, indeed, been suggested in the past, by Germaine Greer. Berger demonstrated in detail the relationship between publicity/advertising and the tradition of oil painting. He argued:

> Publicity is the culture of the consumer society. It propagates through images that society's belief in itself. There are several reasons why these images use the language of oil painting.
>
> Oil painting, before it was anything else, was a celebration of private property. As an art-form it derived from the principal that *you are what you have*. It is a mistake to think of publicity supplanting the visual art of post-Renaissance Europe; it is the last moribund form of that art.[42]

I would go further than Berger's formulation. Advertising is not a 'moribund form of art'; while it is alive, well and spreading, it is *not* art. It is a caricature and mockery of art – art's shadow, its dark side – because it is, to the nth degree, the product of alienated labour in which the content of advertising images are determined 100 per cent by the commissioning 'client' and the pursuit of profit. This condition is inherent to advertising. Everyone who works in advertising knows this to be true; if it were not, advertising agencies, beginning with Charles Saatchi, would simply manufacture art on an industrial scale, without the troublesome need for artists at all.

What this discussion of intermediate cases shows is that the definition of art I have offered, in terms of unalienated labour and the fusion of content and form, works in practice to delineate the contours and limits of 'art' in our society, understanding that those limits are not absolute or impermeable but are nonetheless real.

Conclusions

Thus far I have set out my case for a definition of art in the capitalist era, outlined its roots in the Marxist tradition, considered a number of possible Marxist objections and tested it against the complexity of intermediate cases. Now I want to summarise the conclusions that follow from this definition.

First, it follows that almost all the works around which the 'But is it art?' controversies have raged, for the last century or so, are indeed art: Picasso's *Les Desmoiselles* and cubist works, Malevich's *Black Square*, Duchamp's *Fountain*, Brâncuși's *Bird*, Pollock's drip paintings, Rothko's colour fields, Warhol's *Brillo Boxes*, Lichtenstein's *Whaam!*, Andre's *Bricks* (*Equivalent VIII*), Richard Long's *A Line Made by Walking*, Hirst's shark, Whiteread's *House*, Emin's *My Bed* and the rest.

Second, it follows that art in general represents within capitalist society a positive human value – a 'model of human freedom', as Berger put it – to be supported and nourished. I do not mean by this that all art is 'good' or beneficial to humanity. Some may indeed do more harm than good, such as Rudyard Kipling's colonialist poem 'The White Man's Burden', D. W. Griffith's Civil War drama *Birth of a Nation*, Leni Riefenstahl's Nazi propaganda film *Triumph of the Will*, or many of the paintings of Balthus. But overall, art is a benefit to mankind. The comparison I would make is with medicine and education. Clearly some medicines, some doctors, some schools and some teachers do harm (a few abuse and even kill people), but overall, medicine and education are to be supported and expanded. This is the common position of all socialists and progressives – the same applies to art or 'the arts'. On balance, the word 'art' is used in our culture as an honorific. My definition and analysis explains why this is so.

Third, it follows that in capitalist society art exists and will continue to exist in a state of siege. This state of affairs is not conjunctural but permanent. It includes direct attacks, like cuts to funding in times of austerity, and, under authoritarian regimes, censorship and state repression; but most fundamentally it consists of the antagonism that exists between capitalist social relations and production processes and artistic production. Capitalism, by its nature, always puts artistic labour and artists under pressure, attempting or threatening to damage, limit or destroy artists' necessary autonomy, their control over their own creative labour and the content of their work. This pressure is exercised continually with both sticks and carrots – the sticks of poverty, isolation and marginalisation, and the carrots of recognition, fame and wealth.

This does not mean that art is going to be extinguished; the human impulses towards creative labour are far too universal and powerful for that. Even under extreme fascist and authoritarian regimes, art survives in numerous nooks and crannies of society; this has been the case even in concentration camps. But as individuals, artists all experience the struggle in one way or another and are often defeated by the difficulties. Often their art is damaged or compromised or stunted: How many actors who aspired to play Hamlet or Cleopatra end up earning a living doing voiceovers for adverts? How many painters who dreamt of being Picasso end up surviving by teaching art in school or college with little practice of their own – or simply give up? Of course, as with any struggle, the traffic goes both ways: Andy Warhol made it from commercial illustrator to world's most famous artist, Salman Rushdie from advertising copywriter to *Midnight's Children*. Orson Welles, after *Citizen Kane*, made sherry adverts to finance his films but often failed to complete his projects.

Socialists who understand the antagonism between capitalism and art should, in general terms, sympathise with and defend art and artists against the system in the same way we defend the health service. Art, in its many forms, is a kind of spiritual health food which contributes to the development of the human personality, especially among working-class people – that is, when they can overcome the numerous economic, social and psychological barriers to accessing it.[43]

Politically, therefore, there is an objective basis, a potential, for an alliance between the Left and art. Not that all artists are left-wing; far from it. Many are reactionaries and some – Ezra Pound, some of the Italian futurists, perhaps Dalí – are fascists, but the predominant trend in art over the last two hundred years has been to the left. Take one area, visual art: the list of left-leaning artists, including many avowed socialists and communists, far exceeds that of reactionaries: Géricault, Courbet, Pissarro, Repin, Seurat, van Gogh, Munch, Morris, Picasso, Léger, Kollwitz, Grosz, Heartfield, Dix, Malevich, Goncharova, Rodchenko, Lipchitz, Ernst, Miró, Siqueiros, Orozco, Rivera, Kahlo, Andre, Herman, Guttuso, Moore, Yeats, Shahn, Pollock, Golub, Spero, Basquiat, Beuys, Kiefer, Kelly, Tàpies, Art and Language, Wallinger, Banksy, Ballagh and many others. And that is only an off-the-cuff selection from among the famous. Among the young and less successful, the left tendency is probably even more pronounced.

The realisation of this alliance in practice involves combatting the notion, cultivated by the bourgeoisie when it suits them, that art is or should be nonpolitical – a truly nonsensical idea for anyone who has any knowledge of art history or the history of literature or music. But it also involves combatting the idea which exists on the left that art is only of interest when it is overtly political and radical, or that it falls to the Left to prescribe themes, subjects or methods of work to artists, writers and the like. Trotsky is probably the most eloquent and persuasive of Marxists on this question, and essentially, I believe that what he wrote on it in *Literature and Revolution*, 'Class and Art' and elsewhere stands today. Alliances between the Left and art must be based on mutual respect and are most likely to take the form of a multitude of episodic collaborations rather than a formal arrangement or structure. But there is very considerable historical experience, from the Russian and German revolutions to the surrealists and the Mexican muralists to May '68 and Rock against Racism, as well as the recent experience of Occupy Wall Street (discussed in the final chapter of this book) to show that it can be done.

Finally, it follows from the nature of art as unalienated human labour that the overthrow of capitalism and the initiation of the transformation of society into a socialist one will produce a complex dialectical development of art. It will, in the first place, unleash the creative energies of large sections of the population and generate, as it started to do (even in the most desperate of circumstances) in Russia after 1917, a huge wave of artistic enthusiasm, innovation and experiment which will reach layers of society hitherto largely untouched by artistic culture. On the other hand, as the transition to socialism becomes fully realised, 'art' as a separate category, defined by its opposition to the predominant alienated labour, will cease to exist because alienated labour will cease to exist. This does not mean people will cease painting, writing, making music and so on, but that these activities will exist alongside other activities not separated into a distinct sphere. As Marx and Engels put it in *The German Ideology*, 'In a communist society there are no painters but at most people who engage in painting among other activities.' And, as I wrote twenty years ago:

> Capitalist society, with its division of mental and manual labour, its fragmentation and alienation, gives rise to a separation of art and the artist from the mass of people on the one hand, and from productive work on the other. Moreover, both these separations reinforce each other. Art becomes a privileged arena in which the minority express themselves creatively while the majority are condemned to mechanical, non-expressive, non-creative labour. Art, reflecting society's division into classes, divides into 'high art' and 'low art'. The 'high' artist becomes a member of an elite, administering to an elite.
>
> Socialism will overcome these separations, not by forcing artists to be 'popular', or even simply by raising the cultural level of the majority – though this will happen of course. Rather socialism will make all work a creative activity, so that every producer becomes in a sense an artist. Likewise the skills of painting, design, architecture, writing – of all the art forms – will become integral elements in the collective work of shaping the human environment.

Just as the producer becomes an artist, so the artist will become a producer.[44]

CHAPTER 2

How We Judge Art

Let us start with the fact that judgment is more or less inescapable. Some people may profess themselves uninterested in this question, but in practice most people, including those who deny it and including those whose interest in visual art is minimal, do make some judgments of the merits of various artworks. Even the statement 'I don't know much about art but I know what I like' is a judgment of sorts. And regardless of what individuals do, it is clear that society as a whole has no choice but to make a series of such assessments. Far more art is produced than is going to survive, so decisions have to be made as to what will be preserved and what will be discarded and destroyed. Within what is preserved, another multitude of decisions arise as to what will be displayed and where. Which works will hang in the Louvre or the Uffizi? Which statues will be placed in the main square or in front of the presidential palace? Which examples will be featured in the art books? Which artists merit monographs? Which works and which artists will feature in the educational curriculums and the slideshows of professors? Which will be bought and sold by dealers and collectors, and at what prices?

And if judgment is unavoidable, this raises the questions of how the judgment is made, by whom and on the basis of which criteria. This chapter is predominantly concerned with the third of these questions, but I will start by saying something about the first two. The process of judgment is often imagined by people to be largely personal or individual, but this is not really so. Just as people often tell themselves that the clothes they wear are a purely personal decision when in fact they are heavily determined by quite strict social norms, occupational rules, dress codes, fashion and all sorts of social influences, so it is with art.

Both the average person and the so-called art lover are heavily influenced by what they have heard and read. They don't stand in front of a painting they've been told is by van Gogh and look at it with the same eyes as they look at one by an unknown artist. This applies just as strongly, perhaps even more so, to 'the expert' – the art historian or professional critic – on whom there is social pressure to 'appreciate' the Vermeer, whereas the layperson might just say, 'It does nothing for me'.

So the judgment of art is a social process. It operates through a range of institutions and strategically placed individuals within those institutions. The process changes over time. It was not at all the same in the Renaissance as it was in nineteenth-century France or is in the world today. No judgment is wholly innocent, original or final. Whereas in fourteenth-century Florence or eighteenth-century Russia the process may been relatively simple and transparent, involving a small number of readily identifiable aristocrats, royals, popes and burghers, it is now highly complex and, in a sense, mysterious.

One reason it seems mysterious is that it involves the art market, which works, to a considerable extent, anonymously. Another reason is that many of the key decisions are made in secret and never publicly explained. If the Tate Modern decides to commission a work for its Turbine Hall or hold a 'blockbuster' exhibition for a certain artist, this will undoubtedly boost that artist's reputation. But why that artist is chosen and not another – why Ai Weiwei and not Tracey Emin, or why Joan Miró and not Salvador Dalí – need never be publicly articulated. Then there is the fact that the process is simultaneously national, continental and global, with different judgments made at different levels. Jack Yeats is 'big' in Ireland, with a room dedicated to his work in the National Gallery, but he is little celebrated in Europe or the United States and almost unknown in India or China. Very few artists have generated truly global reputations, and, for obvious historical reasons, they have been overwhelmingly European.

Another point that needs to be made is that judgments are not unanimous. There is no absolute consensus. I have known seriously engaged and knowledgeable 'art world' people who thought Michelangelo vastly overrated or totally disparaged Francis Bacon.[1] Salvador Dalí and David Hockney are both 'popular' and 'successful', especially in market terms,[2] but would be less highly rated by scholarly opinion. The same divergence would be even more the case with the work of Jack Vettriano. However, the absence of absolute consensus does not render the collective judgments of the 'art world' and its key players ineffectual. On the contrary, they have real social and economic force.

When it comes to the operation of the art world today,[3] it is possible to identify the following actors in the formation of aesthetic judgments: critics (journalistic and academic), historians, museum and gallery directors and curators, dealers, collectors, the art-engaged public and artists themselves. Obviously the identification of their relative influence cannot be an exact science, though it might make an interesting ethnographic study. In the absence of that, I'm merely offering some impressionistic observations which may, however, be useful.

Of the categories listed, the critics may appear to play the central role, especially because their judgments are public. But in my view their influence is generally overrated. Much more important are museum directors, dealers and, above all, collectors: they have much greater institutional and economic power, and we should not ignore the extent to which the critics actually depend on them, economically and culturally, rather than shape them. Here we should note that most of the ruling class (the bourgeoisie) do not concern themselves much with visual art, and certainly not in any serious way, but they are aware of its cultural significance and either 'delegate' some of their number to ensure their overall hegemony in this field (as in all fields of cultural life) or select certain people as their trusted intermediaries.

The role of big capitalists – the Rockefellers, Whitneys, Guggenheims, Gettys and so on – in promoting 'modern' art is indisputable, and we know that the CIA consciously intervened to deploy abstract expressionism as an ideological weapon in the Cold War[4] (a manoeuvre which also had the effect of raising the movement's aesthetic standing). Check out the patrons of any major gallery and one will see a list of big corporations and significant members of the bourgeoisie. At certain moments in time, it is possible to identify particular individuals as having exceptional influence: Alfred H. Barr Jr at MoMA in the 1930s; Clement Greenberg as 'top' US critic in the fifties and sixties, along with Kenneth Clark in Britain; Charles Saatchi and Nicholas Serota in the nineties. But none of them stood alone or were unchallengeable. Behind Barr was the Rockefeller family, and he was sacked as MoMA director in 1943 by a businessman, Stephen Carlton Clark of the Singer Sewing Machine Company, who was chairman of MoMA's board of trustees. Greenberg was rivalled as a critic by Harold Rosenberg, and his influence waned dramatically as art changed in a direction Greenberg had not foreseen.

The role of 'the public' should also be mentioned here. Of course, the public is not undifferentiated. There are vast swathes of the world's population who take little or no interest in the art world and whose influence on the process of aesthetic evaluation is close to zero. But even if we restrict consideration to those who visit museums and galleries, purchase art books and reproductions and so on, their influence on critical judgment is small. Their lack of funds prevents them having any serious weight in the art market, and they have almost no institutional mechanisms (except via attendance figures at exhibitions) for expressing their views. Most of the time they are far more influenced by art world 'movers and shakers' than they are influencing. Nevertheless, it would be wrong to discount the art-engaged public altogether. For example, Tracey Emin's intense popularity with a certain layer (mainly of young women) has, I think, had an influence on directors and critics (see the discussion of Emin later in this book).

Finally, we should consider the influence of artists themselves. Again, this cannot possibly be measured in any way exactly, but when we look at art history it would appear to have been a factor. Many times the leading artists of a period have gravitated to each other's company, in Montmartre or Soho or the Cedar Tavern. In Florence, Michelangelo and Leonardo da Vinci were rivals, knowing each other to be the key players. In Paris in 1906, the same seems to have applied to Picasso and Matisse. In London in the fifties it was Bacon and Freud, and in the late eighties, Damien Hirst, Sarah Lucas, Tracey Emin et al. They, the artists themselves, probably have the clearest idea out of any of the groups listed as to who are the best artists of their time, and their opinions do have an impact on wider aesthetic tastes. The reason they have an effect is that although it is ultimately the bourgeoisie (or its cultural wing) who have the most influence on the establishment of the art canon (past and present), as part of their overall project of class hegemony, they nevertheless want to do so on the basis of hegemonising *great art* and *great artists*, rather than promoting the merely second- and third-rate. In the second half of the nineteenth century, the bourgeoisie and aristocracy made historical fools of themselves by backing the wrong horse, by supporting the academic art of the Salon against the emerging avant-garde – for instance, William-Adolphe Bouguereau versus Paul Cézanne. They, the more intelligent ones at least, do not wish to repeat this error. Therefore they need to find out what should be considered good, which they learn, at least in part, from artists whose company they cultivate.

At this point I want to move beyond the sociology of aesthetic evaluation to the criteria on which it can be based. Here I propose to look first at the main criteria which have been used, and are used today, to make judgments of quality. I will then look at what Marxism has to add to this conversation, in the process shifting from a consideration how judgments are actually made to how I think they *should* be made.

The Criteria of Judgment

There has long existed a tendency within art criticism to argue that aesthetic evaluation is a matter of 'intuition'. This goes back at least to Clive Bell in 1914, and his 'aesthetic hypothesis' that 'the starting-point for all systems of aesthetics must be the personal experience of a peculiar emotion'.[5] Its foremost proponent has been Clement Greenberg, who believed that no aesthetic philosopher had been able to advance a coherent set of rules or criteria for judging art and that in the end it all came down to 'the eye', to whether it 'sits right' – in other words, to intuition.[6]

In my opinion there is a strong element of upper-class snobbery in this view. There used to be a TV advert for Croft Sherry which featured a Bertie Wooster–type character delivering the slogan, 'One instinctively knows when something is right.' Similarly, in the play *Educating Rita*, working-class Rita asks her Open University tutor, Frank, how he knows that one book is 'literature' and that another, which she has been reading, is not. Frank replies, 'I suppose one has always just known.'

Nevertheless, I am not dismissing the idea of intuition out of hand. As a chess player, I know that a great player like Mikhail Tal or Garry Kasparov can play blitz or lightning chess in which they produce profound and brilliant sequences of moves at a speed that precludes the possibility that they have been thought through or calculated. The same applies to many other fields of human activity: the ace striker in the penalty area; the boxer on the ropes; the political leader calling for a quick decision in the critical moment[7] or, indeed, Picasso painting on glass. So there is no reason why it should not be applied to an art critic standing in front of a Piet Mondrian or a Jackson Pollock – provided, that is, that we understand by 'intuition' or 'instinct' not some mystical or innate gift, miraculously bestowed on the likes of Bell or Greenberg or Kasparov, but the concentrate of an immense accumulation of knowledge and experience. And if this is how we understand the 'aesthetic emotion' of Bell or the 'eye' of Greenberg, it should be possible to unpack, at least approximately, the criteria or values guiding and underlying the innumerable evaluations that have formed these and other 'good eyes'.

This leads to the first argument I want to present about how people judge art – not about how they *should* but about how they *do* – which is that it is based on an amalgam, and largely an unsystematised amalgam, of criteria and values that have been developed over centuries. These judgments are commonly expressed in terms of approval or disapproval scattered through descriptive, explanatory and interpretive texts – 'stunning', 'masterly', 'superb', 'fine', 'exquisite', 'interesting', 'challenging', 'seminal' or 'pathbreaking', versus 'banal', 'derivative', 'clumsy', 'illustrative', 'uninteresting', 'problematic' and so on. Which adjectives are chosen – 'masterly' or 'pathbreaking' – are indicative of different underlying criteria, but these criteria are not usually made explicit. Here I want to examine certain criteria which, in the Western tradition, have underpinned aesthetic judgments over the centuries: mimesis, skill, beauty, the sublime, morality, emotional power and expression, realism, innovation and critique.

Mimesis

The criteria of mimesis or imitation (or 'naturalism') is, of course, ancient, going back to Plato and Aristotle. The concept is well illustrated by the story of the fifth-century BCE Greek artist Zeuxis, whose painting of grapes was so lifelike that birds came down to peck at it. Interestingly, Plato criticised art, especially poetry, for being mere mimesis and thus at two removes from 'the truth', which is the 'ideal form' underlying the physical embodiment which is copied by the artist. In contrast, the more materialist and empirical Aristotle praised art for its mimesis. Nevertheless, they both assumed that was essentially what art did.

In terms of the Western art tradition over the centuries, it is clear that mimesis has continued to play an important role, especially between the fourteenth and mid-nineteenth centuries. When Ernst Gombrich, in *The Story of Art*, titles his chapter on Italy in the fifteenth century 'The Conquest of Reality', what he means, at least in part, is the mastery of mimesis. When Masaccio and Mantegna, with their increase in plasticity, and Uccello and della Francesca, with their development of perspective, are seen as an advance on Giotto, it is in terms of an advance in mimesis.

In *Ways of Seeing*, John Berger argued that the preeminence of oil painting in the Western tradition rested on its mimetic qualities in the depiction of ownable and consumable objects and materials. Even the emergence of impressionism in the 1870s could be seen as a shift from one form of mimesis – that of the tactile – to another – light effects. For much of the time mimesis has been seen as a secondary quality, subordinate to the achievement of beauty, the sublime or morality. Works which were purely mimetic, such as Dutch trompe l'oeils, were seen as merely technical exercises of relatively little interest. Nevertheless, mimetic skills of a high order were a prerequisite for the artistic prowess of a Holbein, Titian, Constable or Ingres.

Today all of this persists in popular discourse about art, in that works which entirely lack mimetic qualities are, even now, often considered not to be art, while others will be praised on the grounds that they make you feel 'as if you were there' or 'can touch that velvet'. However, it is clear that since the invention of photography and its successors, the criteria of mimesis has declined in importance, although it made a kind of return with photorealism in the late sixties and still survives residually in the evaluation of some works.[8]

Skill

Etymology is frequently a poor basis for analysis, but in this case the fact that the Latin for 'skill' is *ars* or *artis* is of significance, and the apparent absence of skill has frequently figured prominently in the refusal to grant the status of art to works such as Duchamp's *Fountain* and Carl Andre's *Equivalent VIII*. The criteria of skill has long been closely associated with that of mimesis, but it is not necessary that it should be. Skill or technique may be required for and manifested in many nonmimetic works. To paint a work like Pollock's *Lavender Mist* required great skill in controlling the distribution of paint over the canvas, but the outcome was nonmimetic. Whether or not Damien Hirst's shark, *The Physical Impossibility of Death in the Mind of Someone Living*, is mimetic is highly debatable, since it is/was a real shark, not a sculpture of one, and while its construction clearly involved a multitude of skills, those skills were not mimetic ones in the sense traditionally understood.

If, however, we define skill not as the ability to represent appearances in paint, stone or bronze but as the ability to achieve desired effects, then it remains a valid criteria – if, like mimesis, a subordinate one – for the assessment of art, from Giotto or van Eyck to Emin and Eliasson.

Beauty

Like mimesis and skill, 'beauty' has been a fundamental criterion for judging works of visual art ever since ancient Greece and Plato. Obviously any deployment of the term 'beauty' raises the question of its meaning, and, as with all the concepts discussed here, there have been numerous theories. Herbert Read, writing in 1931, stated that 'there are at least a dozen current definitions of beauty'.[9]

However, for many centuries the concept of beauty that predominated in the judgment of works of visual art was one that derived basically from Aristotle. In his *Poetics*, Aristotle wrote of beauty as 'a matter of size and order', 'unity and wholeness' and 'a certain order in its arrangement of parts'.[10] The evolution of this conception of beauty as essentially harmony between the parts and the whole can be traced down the ages through Giorgio Vasari – who wrote of Michelangelo's *David* that '[t]he grace of this figure and the serenity of its pose have never been surpassed, nor have the feet, the hands, and the head, whose harmonious proportions and loveliness are in keeping with the rest' – via William Hogarth, Edmund Burke, Gotthold Lessing and Immanuel Kant to the likes of Read, who argued:

> [M]an responds to the shape and surface and mass of things present to his senses, and that certain arrangements in the proportion of the shape and surface and mass of things result in a pleasurable sensation, while the lack of such arrangement leads to indifference or to even positive discomfort and revulsion. The sense of pleasurable relations is the sense of beauty; the opposite sense is the sense of ugliness.[11]

There is a strong implication in Read's statement that this 'sense of beauty' is innate in humans – that we are, in some sense, hardwired with it. Aestheticians writing today would lay much greater stress on the role of socialisation and, therefore, the cultural relativism of all standards of beauty. Be that as it may, it is the former conception which has exercised the predominant influence in the evaluation of art in the Western tradition. Indeed, there have been periods when beauty thus understood was so predominant as a value that it was widely held to be the very essence of art, or its defining characteristic. This, broadly speaking, was the case from about the fifteenth to the nineteenth century, and gave rise to the view that artists such as Raphael and Leonardo de Vinci constituted the highest summit of human achievement in visual art.

The course of art over the last several centuries has, I think, rendered that position unsustainable – we need think only of Goya's *Disasters of War* series or Warhol's cans of Campbell's soup or, indeed, a lot of Picasso – but 'beauty' as one possible criterion of judgment out of many remains in current use. If a contemporary art critic or historian (or, indeed, a layperson) refers to a painting or sculpture as beautiful or states that Turner's atmospheric effects or Matisse's uses of colour are 'beautiful', that is still significant praise.

We should also note, before moving on, that the criteria of mimesis and skill (*techne*) had a connection and complementarity with the criterion of beauty, in that skill in producing an accurate imitation of reality – as in the rendering of skin tones and muscles or cloth and furs – could be seen as a means to the end of producing a work that was beautiful as a totality. It is easy to see how this would apply to, say, da Vinci's *Virgin of the Rocks*, Botticelli's *Primavera* or Velázquez's *Rokeby Venus*.

The Sublime

The sublime is another evaluative concept dating back to the Ancient world, in this case to a Roman-era Greek work of literary criticism, *On the Sublime*, of uncertain authorship.[12] This used 'the sublime' to refer to literary work of exceptional power, involving 'great thoughts, strong emotions, certain figures of thought and speech, noble diction, and dignified word arrangement'. As a general superlative 'sublime' has, of course, operated as part of everyday discourse and continues to do so. In terms of art history and criticism, however, it only really becomes important in the eighteenth century with Edmund Burke's *Philosophical Enquiry into the Origin of Our Ideas of the Sublime and Beautiful.*

For Burke 'the sublime' designates feelings of awe and terror evoked by great forces, especially natural forces. He lists a number of qualities or characteristics associated with the sublime: darkness, obscurity, deprivation, vastness, magnificence, loudness, suddenness. After Burke, the concept was further discussed and debated by Johann Joachim Winckelmann, Lessing (in his *Laocoön*) and Kant.

In my view it has largely functioned as a subdivision of the beauty criterion, but also as its necessary complement, to deal with obviously aesthetically powerful works, such as Michelangelo's *The Last Judgment* or Turner's *The Fall of an Avalanche in the Grissons*, which failed to fit into the conception of 'beauty as harmony'.

In the latter part of the nineteenth century, it receded in use – it did not sit well with impressionism and post-impressionism – but it was revived in the twentieth century, particularly in relation to the large canvasses of some of the abstract expressionists (Rothko, Pollock, Still, Newman),[13] and today it could be applied to some work by Anish Kapoor, Antony Gormley, Richard Serra and Olafur Eliasson.

I should say that in my opinion 'the sublime' can easily be invoked to praise or legitimate second-rate works on the basis of their size or subject matter, but this criticism does not change the fact that within the art world it continues to operate as a category and standard of judgment.[14]

Ethics/Morality/Politics

There is an argument that ethics or morality (or politics) should be irrelevant to the assessment of art *as* art.[15] In fact, ethical virtue, or moral or political rectitude, has 'always' (i.e., very frequently) operated as a criterion of aesthetic evaluation. In Christian art prior to the Renaissance, it was generally assumed that it was made 'for the glory of God', and one of the principal functions of painting was to illustrate Bible stories for the moral/religious education of the populace. The rise of humanism in the Renaissance pushed this criterion back somewhat, but it returned with a vengeance in the Counter-Reformation with the Council of Trent (1545–63), which explicitly required that art should serve the propagation of Catholic doctrines.[16]

With the onset of the Enlightenment, Western art became increasingly secularised (though this process had already begun in the Renaissance and in Dutch art of the Golden Age), and the demand that art should be ethically edifying waned. Nevertheless, morality remained as a kind of backstop which could be invoked in condemnation of work that offended established moral codes. Amusingly, Marcel Duchamp records that one of the grounds given for the rejection of his *Fountain* in 1917 was that '[s]ome said it was immoral'.[17] In the twentieth century, moral concerns increasingly merged with political ones. The Far Right have fairly consistently attacked modern art as both communistic and immoral, with the Nazis famously condemning 'degenerate art' and the Republican Right in the United States in the eighties and nineties waging a campaign of denunciation known as the 'culture wars'.[18] This was paralleled in Stalinist Russia and, consequently, on some of the Stalinist-influenced Left by both a rejection of modernism as a whole and by an insistence on 'realism' and, within Russia, on so-called 'socialist realism'. Since the late 1960s there has been a widespread tendency to criticise art and, in some ways more importantly, art world institutions on grounds of sexism and racism.

The question of the relationship of politics to the aesthetic evaluation of art is complex and requires further discussion (which it will receive later in this chapter), but it should be noted here that there has been a strand within Marxism, epitomised by Leon Trotsky, that has rejected any straightforward application of political criteria. It is also worth noting that issues of 'morality' have not disappeared, even if the morals in question have changed. In 1997 there was a 'moral outcry' over the inclusion in the famous *Sensation* exhibition of Marcus Harvey's painting *Myra*, which depicted the serial child murderer Myra Hindley. I myself critiqued some of the work of the Chapman brothers in that show for its paedophiliac tendencies,[19] and much of the work of Balthus and the photography of Sally Mann has been condemned for similar reasons. If one were to observe that many of the photographs of Diane Arbus are 'cruel', would this be a 'moral' criticism? I think probably it would. Moral/political questions have reemerged in a new way with the twenty-first-century 'social turn', in which art projects involve both the participation of 'nonartists' and the ethics of the process by which the work is made – is it sufficiently egalitarian? Is it elitist, authoritarian or even sadistic?

Finally, a distinction can be made between the extrinsic and intrinsic deployment of moral and political criteria. By 'extrinsic' criteria, I mean the argument that however great the 'artistic' merit of a work or works by an artist, this is or should be outweighed by the moral/political offence which they commit. Literary examples are easier to give than visual art ones (e.g., 'Ezra Pound was a great poet, but his work should be rejected because he was a fascist.'), though this could be applied to Emil Nolde and Salvador Dalí. By 'intrinsic' criteria, I mean the argument that *because* X is racist/sexist/fascist et cetera, and this is expressed in their art, therefore the art is bad. In practice this distinction is often blurred because of the tendency of critics to mask moral and, especially, political judgments as aesthetic ones and, more importantly, because the argument can be presented in mediated form, as in: 'Y's misogyny affects their novels by limiting their ability to create rounded female characters and therefore damages their quality as art.'[20] I think a criticism on these lines can be made of much of Picasso's work, though this does not obliterate his overall greatness, and of Renoir. Should the now well-established feminist critique of the tradition of the female nude in the European art tradition[21] be regarded as a moral, political or aesthetic criticism, or as all three?[22]

Emotional Power and Expression

Lionello Venturi, in his *History of Art Criticism*, tells us that in 1719 the Abbé Du Bos stated: 'The first aim of Painting is to move us. A work which moves us greatly must be excellent on the whole. For the same reason the work which does not move us . . . is worth nothing.'[23] Clearly the criterion of emotional power can be applied retrospectively, even if it was not used by art writers of the time, to numerous works such as Grünewald's *Crucifixion*, Michelangelo's *Pietà*s and *Slaves*, Gentileschi's *Judith Slaying Holofernes* and Rembrandt's late self-portraits.

However, it was primarily in the late nineteenth century and early twentieth century, with the emergence of the concept of expressionism, that this criterion really came to the fore. For Tolstoy, art was essentially a means of communicating emotions,[24] and Matisse said in his 'Notes of a Painter,' 'What I am after, above all, is expression.'[25] Herbert Read's *A Concise History of Modern Painting* postulated two main strands in the development of modern art: an art of 'determined relations' deriving from Cézanne (and leading to Mondrian), and an art of 'inner necessity' (i.e., self-expression) deriving, above all, from van Gogh.

I should note here that while in recent times the assumption has overwhelmingly been that the 'expression' involved will be *self*-expression, this need not necessarily be so. A work of art may give powerful expression to emotions that are not the artist's own, or that are collective emotions. In any case, it is easy to think of huge numbers of works, from the aforementioned van Gogh to Munch, Rothko and Bacon, which have been valued particularly, if not exclusively, for their ability to express emotions and move the viewer.

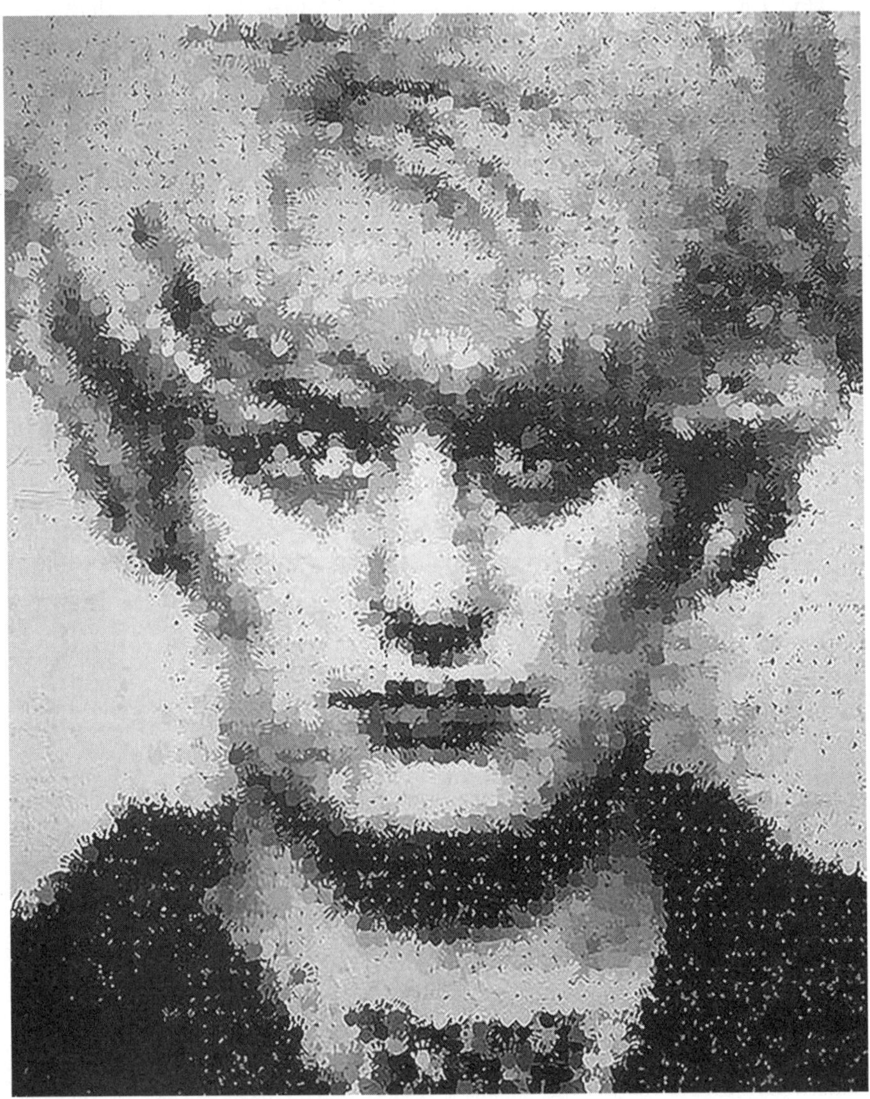

Marcus Harvey, *Myra* (1995)

Realism

The concept of realism as a major positive value makes its appearance in art history with Gustave Courbet and the realist school (Millet, Corot, Daumier, etc.) in France, in the wake of the 1848 Revolution. Emerging in opposition to the romanticism and neoclassicism that preceded it, realism was a response to democratic and proletarian aspirations. It signified neither mimesis nor naturalism, but instead the attempt to depict social realities; as seen in Courbet's *The Stone Breakers* and *A Burial at Ornans*, or Millet's *The Gleaners*, its themes centred on everyday life rather than kings, queens, religion or mythology.[26] It has also been called social realism.

Picked up on by Frederick Engels and later elaborated by the influential Georg Lukács, as well as by the Communist International in its mid-1930s 'Popular Front' period, realism was adopted by wide sections of the Left as the key criterion by which art of all kinds should be judged. For Engels realism famously meant 'besides truth in detail, the truthful reproduction of typical characters under typical circumstances'.[27] For Lukács it signified the representation of the social relations of a given society as an integrated whole or totality. For both Engels and Lukács, this concept of realism was literary in origin, and for Lukács its main exemplars were the great nineteenth-century novelists – Honoré de Balzac, Stendhal, Leo Tolstoy and Charles Dickens, among others.

Clearly the representation of social relations as a totality lends itself much more readily to the novel, and drama, than it does to painting and sculpture, though photography and, particularly, cinema are more suitable.[28] Nevertheless, there are a number of artists from the past who can be particularly valued for their realism in the Lukácsian sense – for example, Bruegel, Hals, some Velázquez, Hogarth, Goya, Manet, Repin – and a few from the twentieth century, such as Diego Rivera, Edward Hopper and Jack B. Yeats. If the definition of realism is relaxed and broadened, the second list can doubtless be expanded (Kollwitz, Nash, Grosz, Heartfield, Guttoso, maybe even Warhol). But even so, its paucity points to the difficulty of trying to make 'realism' into the principal concept of artistic evaluation: it simply excludes far too much art, from Cimabue, della Francesca and da Vinci to Picasso, Matisse, Ernst, Miró, Mondrian and Pollock, not to speak of the innovators of today.

One way of extending the range of realism as a criterion is to deploy a subcategory of 'psychological realism,' as this draws in portraiture. John Berger was right, I think, to deny that the overwhelmingly majority of portraits offer any special insight into the psychology of their sitters. But some do, especially what might be called a social psychological insight; think of Velázquez's portrait of Pope Innocent X, of Rembrandt's late self-portraits, of Géricault's studies of mad people, and of many of the portraits of Lucian Freud. And even if neither social nor psychological realism, any more than mimesis or beauty, are viable as master categories of art criticism, they nonetheless continue to relate to genuine qualities which can be recognised and assessed.

Innovation

The concept of originality has a dual meaning in art history and criticism. On the one hand, it refers to provenance, to whether it can be established that a particular work is by a particular artist. Is this a genuine Vermeer or an actual Rembrandt? Given the central role played in the art world by the notion of 'genius', this question makes an immense difference to the likely evaluation of a work in both monetary and aesthetic terms. However, leaving provenance and prices aside, originality also refers to the extent to which an artist or a work is seen as pioneering, as breaking new ground – that is to say, as innovative.

During certain periods, notably the Middle Ages, painters and sculptors have been seen primarily as artisans working in a tradition in which they attempt merely to achieve the standards of previous 'masters' of the craft. This starts to change with the Renaissance, which reflects the birth of capitalism and its concomitant individualism, and already in the writings of Giorgio Vasari we find praise for artists as 'the first' to do this or that. For instance, Giotto 'made a decisive break with the crude traditional Byzantine style and brought to life the great art of painting as we know it today, introducing the techniques of drawing accurately from life';[29] and Masaccio 'gave a beginning to beautiful attitudes . . .

rendering relief in a new way that was characteristic and natural and that no painter had ever before attempted'.[30]

As capitalism develops and the pace of social and cultural change speeds up, until with the Industrial Revolution we enter the 'maelstrom of modernity' in which, to use the language of Marx and Marshall Berman, 'all that is solid melts into air', this emphasis on originality and innovation intensifies to the point where it becomes one of the most important hallmarks of modern art. Édouard Manet's paintings, in the narrative of Clement Greenberg, become 'the first Modernist ones by virtue of the frankness with which they declared the surfaces on which they were painted'. Claude Monet was the founder of impressionism, Georges Seurat of 'pointillism' and Picasso and Georges Braque initiated cubism; Wassily Kandinsky painted, it was long supposed, the first abstract painting (it is now clear that 'honour' belongs to the relatively little-known Swedish female artist Hilma af Klint in 1906–7);[31] Duchamp produced the first readymade, Pollock invented drip painting and Richard Hamilton is widely credited with the first work of pop art, while Joseph Kosuth pioneered conceptual art, and so on.

The pursuit of originality and innovation comes to permeate the culture of modern art for artists, dealers, collectors and critics alike. It is manifested in the concept of 'the avant-garde', in the so-called 'march of the isms' and in the emergence of the artist's manifesto as a literary form in its own right. It is there in artists' more or less conscious quest for their unique 'signature', which can range from Miró's very distinctive visual language[32] to Lucio Fontana's cuts in the canvas, or trademark 'gimmicks' such as Chris Ofili's use of elephant dung. And it pervades the language of art writing with the proliferation of terms such as 'cutting edge', 'pathbreaking' and 'seminal', while 'derivative' becomes, along with 'uninteresting', a major put-down.

Critique

As radical artist Martha Rosler points out, critical art, 'stepping outside the ambit of patronage or received opinion without losing one's livelihood or, in extreme circumstances, one's life, became possible for painters and sculptors only a couple of hundred years ago'.[33] Certainly it is possible to identify implicit social critique or critical elements in the work of earlier artists, for example Rembrandt and Hals (or even Holbein), but I would say that explicitly and consciously critical art on any scale appears only in the mid-nineteenth century: Courbet is the key figure,[34] followed by Manet.[35] It is produced by the parallel development of two social forces: on the one hand, a 'democratic', disaffected middle class able to provide an audience, if initially only a very small one, for critical art; and, on the other, the challenge presented by an emergent industrial proletariat which has its theoretical expression in socialism and Marxism. And for a period the whole of 'advanced' or 'nonacademic' art in France 'emigrates', as Clement Greenberg puts it, 'to Bohemia'[36] to resist, if only temporarily, the clutches of aristocratic and government control.

At any rate, the emergence of critical art predates, as is often the case, the appearance of 'critique' or 'critical' as a term of approval in the vocabulary of art critics, which only becomes widespread in the twentieth century.

The concept of 'critical' art as something praiseworthy contains two strands. The first relates to art which critiques the existing social conditions and the existing political order or dominant ideas within that order; examples would range from Käthe Kollwitz and George Grosz to Banksy. The second strand relates to art which critiques past or present art; for example, implicitly, the work of the later Cézanne or, explicitly, Dadaism and Marcel Duchamp, the abstract expressionists and minimalism such as that of Carl Andre. Sometimes the two forms of critique are combined, as in the art of the recent 'social turn', which is both anti-capitalist in intention and directed against the elitism and individualism of previous modernist art practice: for example, Jeremy Deller's reenactment of the Battle of Orgreave or the Global Ultra Luxury Faction (GULF) action of 29 March 2014, when thousands of notes of pseudo-currency were thrown into the rotunda of the Guggenheim Museum in New York.[37]

In discussing the concept of critique, we should note first its relation to and centrality for Marxism. The Marxism of Marx begins with his critiques of Hegel's philosophy of right, alienation, the young Hegelians and Feuerbach's mechanical materialism. It develops through the critique of classical political economy (Smith and Ricardo) and culminates in the critique of capitalist production.[38] The Lukács of *History and Class Consciousness* identifies 'the standpoint of the proletariat' as the uniquely privileged ground for the critique of reified capitalist social relations and 'the antinomies of bourgeois thought'. The later Lukács counterposes 'critical realism' to both naturalism and Stalinist 'socialist realism'. The Frankfurt school of Adorno, Horkheimer et al. identify their project as 'critical theory', and Adorno writes, 'Even in the most sublimated work of art there is a hidden "it should be otherwise"',[39] and that 'art becomes social by virtue of its opposition to society itself'.[40] Trotsky writes, '[A] protest against reality, either conscious or unconscious, active or passive, optimistic or pessimistic, always forms part of a really creative piece of work.'[41]

Second, we should note how Greenberg, in his important article 'Modernist Painting', identifies critique as central to modernism and rooted this in Kant:

> Western civilisation is not the first to turn around and question its own foundations, but it is the civilisation that has gone furthest in doing so. I identify Modernism with the intensification, almost the exacerbation, of this self-critical tendency that began with the philosopher Kant. Because he was the first to criticise the means itself of criticism, I conceive of Kant as the first real Modernist.[42]

In his earlier 'Avant-garde and Kitsch', Greenberg referenced Marxism as foundational for modernism. Now in 'Modernist Painting' he references Kant. This goes hand in hand with his shift away from a materialist focus on the social context of artistic development to an idealist account, in which modernism develops under its own inexorable logic. The first essay was written in 1939, the second in 1960. Between the two lay, among other things, McCarthyism, which drove Marxism and socialism to the absolute margins of American cultural and political life and made any public reference to Marx or Marxism a serious risk to career, reputation and even freedom. For Greenberg's disciple Michael Fried, the reference point was the, again explicitly idealist, Hegelian dialectic.[43]

But if we move from these rather rarefied theoretical heights to the language of everyday art critical journalism, of gallery notes and art school education, we find that in recent decades 'critical' has become for many, through a kind of trickle-down effect, the buzzword of choice, often combined with 'challenging'. Unsurprisingly, it is often applied rather indiscriminately to work that in reality offers little challenge to either the existing social order or the existing practices of art and the art world, or offers a challenge/critique on a very narrow and limited basis.

How These Criteria Can Be Used

I said at the outset that the list of criteria discussed here is not exhaustive – it could easily be extended to include, for example, 'authenticity', 'purity' and 'autonomy'. Moreover, each criterion merits chapter- or even book-length analysis, and it is arguable that I should also have given consideration to more of the terms that are commonly employed in art writing to convey merit, such as 'vital' or 'fresh' or 'provocative',[44] or the opposite, such as 'illustrative', 'jaded' or 'stale'. But I want now to move on to look at how these criteria can actually be used to make concrete assessments and then explain what I believe Marxism can add to this whole process.

Let us begin by comparing two works: Peter Paul Rubens's *A View of Het Steen in the Early Morning* and David Hockney's *Garrowby Hill.* My reasons for choosing these are (a) that they depict somewhat similar subject matter – landscapes which stretch into the distance; (b) that they come from very different historical periods – the early seventeenth century and late twentieth century; and (c) that they are, to my mind, of very different quality. Considered in light of the criteria outlined, it is clear that the Rubens outdistances the Hockney in almost all of them. In terms of imitation of nature and technical skill, the difference is vast; in terms of beauty, the gap is equally wide with the Rubens, through the effect of great distance which it achieves, touching on the sublime; the Rubens, by virtue of the mood of serenity it creates, is expressive of the artist's contented retirement towards the end of his life, and possesses emotive power entirely lacking in the Hockney. As far as social realism is concerned, the Rubens is at least suggestive of the social position of the hunters in relation to the lord's chateau, whereas there is nothing evocative of social relations in the Hockney. Neither work can really be seen as innovative or critical, so those categories do not apply. It could, of course, be objected that the difference in quality between the two works is 'obvious'. I have no quarrel with that, but would argue that my brief analysis helps to explain *why* it is 'obvious'.

Now let us turn from the comparison of two individual works to the comparison of two artists: Frida Kahlo and Diego Rivera. My comments here will be very brief and general, and merely suggestive – this is not the place for a detailed analysis.

The first thing to note is the huge shift that has occurred in their relative reputations. Eighty to ninety years ago, Rivera was a major international artist, supported by Alfred H. Barr Jr of MoMA and receiving big commissions from both the Mexican government and the Rockefellers. Trotsky cited him as a key exemplar of a true revolutionary artist and coauthored with him and André Breton the *Manifesto for an Independent Revolutionary Art*. Frida Kahlo's work, though appreciated and claimed for surrealism by Breton, was by comparison little known. Forty years ago this state of affairs would still, broadly speaking, have been the same. Today, however, Frida Kahlo is a world-famous 'feminist icon' who is not only better known than Rivera but also widely claimed to be a 'greater' or 'more important' artist.

The explanation for this shift is ultimately social and political – crudely, the decline of 'communism' and the rise of feminism and identity politics[45] – but how this is expressed in art critical terms and in terms of the criteria I have outlined is not mainly a matter of their different evaluation with regard to each criteria, but one of a different *weight* being attached to the relative importance of those criteria.

Thus, in terms of mimesis and technical skill, both Kahlo and Rivera are skilled practitioners, though not comparable to 'Old Masters' such as Holbein or Titian in this regard; but the nature of their work does not require this. In terms of social realism, however, there is a huge gap. Rivera's achievement here is massive and contains a new element. He was able, in his great murals, to present with immense power not just an image of contemporary Mexican society but also the whole historical development of the nation. In contrast, Kahlo's work displays enormously more personal, intimate 'psychological realism'.[46] She finds, for example, in *The Broken Column* and in *The Wounded Deer*, powerful objective correlatives for her personal physical and emotional feelings which also connect strongly to – 'speak' to – the emotions and feelings of millions round the world, especially millions of women. In terms of innovation and critique, both artists can be highly valued but in different ways. Rivera brought to large-scale social realist painting many of the 'techniques' or methods of pictorial representation which he learned from cubism in Paris. This had not been done before and distinguished his work from the other Mexican muralists, José Clemente Orozco and David Alfaro Siqueiros. Kahlo's work realised and achieved the dramatic representation of an individual's, especially a woman's, feelings in a way that was unprecedented. Rivera's work contained an explicit critique of capitalism and imperialism, Kahlo's a more implicit, but nonetheless powerful, critique of gender relations and issues of disability and personal alienation.

What this example illustrates is that the criteria I have identified cannot be used mechanically, as some kind of measuring grid, but rather can serve as a way into thinking about and interrogating how specific artistic judgments actually get made.

Finally, I think it is important to test the criteria against a completely abstract work.[47] Here I am going to look at Barnett Newman's *Vir Heroicus Sublimis* (Man, heroic and sublime) from 1951, which is about as abstract as one can get, more so in some ways than even Mondrian or Pollock.[48]

Let us start by acknowledging that if realism is held up as the master category of art evaluation, as it was by Lukács and other 'communist' critics from the late twenties onwards, this painting must be judged effectively worthless or even a negative quantity. But the same would apply to the whole development of abstract art from the early twentieth century onwards or before.[49]

Setting aside this view and rejecting not realism as such but realism put forward as an obligatory quality for all works of art, what of the other criteria we have been considering? One of the main objections to paintings like this, and to many similar abstract works, is that they require no skill. Now, if by 'skill' is meant skill in mimesis (such as was possessed, perfected even, by the likes of Holbein, Titian and Velázquez), then this is clearly true. But if we actually consider the making of *Vir Heroicus Sublimis*, it is by no means clear that no skill was involved. It is certainly the case that a considerable number of decisions were involved: the size and shape of the canvas; the existence or not of a frame or border; the exact colour of the panels; the exact density and texture of the paint and the nature of the surface; the location and dimensions of the 'zip(s)' If any of these decisions are altered or clumsily executed, it will alter the whole visual effect of the painting.[50]

Therefore, whether or not the painting displays skill depends on our judgment in relation to the other criteria: Is the painting beautiful, sublime, emotionally expressive, innovative, critical and so on? Now, we know from Newman's own writing that he had set himself the goal of achieving the sublime (see his 1948 article 'The Sublime Is Now')[51] and that he considered his work both artistically and politically critical, and for 'the end of all state capitalism and totalitarianism'.[52] Are these claims justified?

In my view they essentially are. I think *Vir Heroicus Sublimis* is both beautiful and evokes the sublime: for me its scale, colour and composition conjure up a lone individual, the viewer, ('the first man') standing before and defying immense, awe-inspiring forces and in that sense expressing, very powerfully, the idea of freedom. This is not a fanciful interpretation: it is strongly suggested by the title and by Newman's own statements, as well as by the ideological climate of the time.[53] What I am saying here is that Newman's painting works for me, has these aesthetic and emotional effects on me. Obviously this can be dismissed as a purely subjective judgment which cannot be proved or substantiated. But then it also cannot be *proved* that Botticelli's *Primavera* or Raphael's *Madonnas* are beautiful either, except that we know that large numbers of people have found them so over a substantial period of time, and that the same can be said (if not yet to the same degree) about *Vir Heroicus Sublimis*. And this fact does substantiate, if not prove, my, and others', subjective judgment. It also confirms that this work involves a serious amount of skill. To this can be added that Newman's distinctive 'style' was innovative – no paintings like this had ever been made before.

In an article on 'abstract expressionism', Charles Harrison, an art historian of great theoretical sophistication, says that '[i]n the three years 1949–51 Newman painted some of this century's greatest paintings'.[54] Harrison makes a sustained and detailed analysis of how Newman's paintings work but does not explicitly justify this assessment. The analysis I have made, using the criteria I have outlined, shows how such a judgment or other similar judgments of abstract or non-figurative art can be supported – not, of course, conclusively or definitively, but at least reasonably coherently and potentially persuasively.

The Marxist Contribution to Aesthetic Judgment

I now want to turn to what I see as the specifically Marxist contribution to this question. I use the word contribution rather than 'theory of' because I think it builds upon and adds to all the criteria developed over the centuries that we have been discussing, rather than replacing them. As my examples would indicate, I accept that these criteria, inherited from the past, have been and can be used to make valid and effective aesthetic judgments. However, I am now shifting to considering how I think we, as Marxists, *should* assess art – not just how people actually do assess it. But I do so on the understanding that while these Marxist assessments may differ from what might be considered the traditional academic or bourgeois canon, this will certainly not be the case in every instance. In other words, we should not expect that because mainstream art history approves of Piero della Francesca, Velázquez and Rembrandt, Marxist art history will reject them.

This will not be a survey of the views of Marxists who have contributed to the question of aesthetic value: even naming them produces an excessively long list.[55] I will first deal briefly with the question of politics and art and, even more briefly, once again with 'realism' and then set out my own view.

It is widely assumed that Marxism advocates and entails the assessment of an artwork's merit, mainly or partly, on the basis of its politics. As literary critic Stuart Sim puts it, 'Marxism is the prime example of a politically motivated aesthetic theory', and 'underneath both crude and sophisticated Marxism lies a similar compulsion to situate artworks within a political context.... Art's value to a Marxist, therefore, is to be politically determined.'[56] Sim, in his essay, repeats this idea on numerous occasions – but this does not make it true. The 'therefore' in the above sentence is especially illegitimate in that it does not follow from 'situating art in a political context' that its value is 'politically determined'. But there is more involved here than that particular piece of poor logic.

Certainly it is true that for Marxism art is ultimately subject to assessment by political criteria, but, and this is crucial, only in the final analysis; it is the case only in the sense that everything – food, medicine, science, sport, all human activities – are subject to politics, because politics is about the general governance of human society, and (Marxist) politics is about the survival and liberation of humanity. This does not mean that Marxists can or should judge whether or not della Francesca's *The Baptism of Christ* or Bacon's 'Screaming Pope' is a good painting by either the political views of the artist or what we deem to be the political/ideological message expressed in the painting.

Some care is needed to explain precisely what I mean here. I do not mean that some works of art are 'nonpolitical' or nonideological. All works, without exception, exist in a social, ideological and political context, and are permeated by ideology; and all ideology is political in the broad sense. Nor do I mean that the analysis of works of art should ignore their ideological and political content, focussing only on their 'form'. I mean that a Marxist cannot read off the aesthetic evaluation of a work on the basis of the extent to which that work's worldview is 'progressive', 'radical' or corresponds to Marxism.

In the seventeenth century, Rubens was the principal artist of the Catholic/aristocratic counterrevolution, and this profoundly shaped the form and content of his work. But this does not mean that Marxists can, on this account, write him off or deny his greatness as an artist. His work displays far too many outstanding qualities for that, and part of his greatness was precisely the skill and élan with which he expressed the outlook and visual sensibility of that counterrevolution compared to numerous mediocre works of the day. Another example would be

George Grosz, who was a member of the Communist Party of Germany (when it was a revolutionary socialist organisation, not yet corrupted by Stalinism), and whose work was explicitly anti-capitalist, predominantly comprising savage attacks on the German bourgeoisie. It does not follow from this that for a Marxist, Grosz is a greater artist than, say, the much less radical Matisse or Mondrian. It is possible to argue that the greatness or merits of an artist's work are damaged or limited by the artist's ideological standpoint, but this argument has to be made concretely and demonstrated in the work; it cannot be read off or assumed.[57]

Of course, it must be recognised that many would-be or self-proclaimed Marxists have attempted or even insisted on the mechanical application of political criteria to art. Mainly, if not exclusively, this is associated with Stalinism in its various forms,[58] but it was not the practice of the classical Marxism of Marx, Engels, Lenin, Trotsky, Luxemburg and Gramsci, to which I adhere, or of most serious Marxist art historians and critics. The most well-rehearsed examples are Marx's advocacy of the conservative Balzac (along with Aeschylus, Shakespeare and the like) and Trotsky's polemics on this question in the early years of the Russian Revolution.

To identify the distinctive Marxist contribution to aesthetic evaluation, we have first to go back to basics. According to historical materialism, art is a component of the superstructure which arises on, and is conditioned by, the economic base which comprises the forces and relations of production. In his 1859 preface to *A Contribution to the Critique of Political Economy*, Marx wrote:

> In the social production of their existence, men inevitably enter into definite relations, which are independent of their will, namely relations of production appropriate to a given stage in the development of their material forces of production. The totality of these relations of production constitutes the economic structure of society, the real foundation, on which arises a legal and political superstructure and to which correspond definite forms of social consciousness. The mode of production of material life conditions the general process of social, political and intellectual life.[59]

Speaking at Marx's graveside, Engels restated, as he did on many occasions, this basic idea:

> Just as Darwin discovered the law of development or organic nature, so Marx discovered the law of development of human history: the simple fact, hitherto concealed by an overgrowth of ideology, that mankind must first of all eat, drink, have shelter and clothing, before it can pursue politics, science, art, religion, etc.; that therefore the production of the immediate material means, and consequently the degree of economic development attained by a given people or during a given epoch, form the foundation upon which the state institutions, the legal conceptions, art, and even the ideas on religion, of the people concerned have been evolved, and in the light of which they must, therefore, be explained, instead of vice versa, as had hitherto been the case.[60]

The truth of the proposition that art is 'conditioned' by the economic base of society, its forces and relations of production, is, I think, obvious. The art of the Paleolithic Age, of the Middle Ages, of the Renaissance, of nineteenth-century Europe, and of the twenty-first century is hugely different, and much of this difference is accounted for by the fact that Paleolithic society rested on stone tools and cooperative foraging, that of the Middle Ages on agriculture and feudal land ownership and nineteenth-century Europe on industrial capitalism and wage labour; and today, we live with globalised late capitalism in decay. The art of da Vinci, Michelangelo or Rembrandt would have been literally impossible in the Paleolithic or even the early Middle Ages, and that of Tracey Emin and Ai Weiwei equally impossible in the nineteenth or even early twentieth century. Of course, the relationship between base and superstructure is not mechanical or automatic. As Engels put it:

> We regard the economic conditions as conditioning, in the last instance, historical development.... The political, legal, philosophical, religious, literary, artistic, etc., development rest upon the economic. But they all react upon one another and upon the economic base. It is not the case that the economic situation is the *cause, alone active*, and everything else only a passive effect. Rather there is a reciprocal interaction with a fundamental economic necessity which *in the last instance* always asserts itself.[61]

But, even with Engels's proviso, there is more to be said when it comes to understanding and judging art. The core social relations of production (slave owner and slave, lord and peasant, capitalist and worker) generate and are surrounded by a host of other social relations: between monarchs and subjects, husbands and wives, lovers, children and parents, brothers and sisters, masters and servants, bartenders and customers, entertainers and audiences, officers and soldiers, judges and prisoners, prostitutes and clients, popes, priests and their flock, almost ad infinitum; they also generate a no-less-extensive set of social relations between people and things and people and nature; people and their food and drink, their houses, their other possessions, their animals, their land, their transport, the mountains, the sea, the trees, flowers and sky. These relations are just as much social relations, ever-changing and products of historical development as the relations between people. A hunter-gatherer and an eighteenth-century squire do not have the same relationship to a horse or a bull. The different meaning of trees to Hobbema, van Gogh and Mondrian is as much a social change as the difference between Titian's and Manet's views of a courtesan/prostitute.

These social relations occupy a social space, as it were, between the economic base and the political and ideological superstructure, and they are shaped by both in an ongoing dialectical interaction. Moreover, they are the stuff of art. By this I mean not only that art depicts these relations, which it does a great deal of the time, but also that it expresses them and responds to them. The last point is important. Because art, as I argued in the previous chapter, is a product of creative human labour, it constitutes not just a passive reflection of social relations but also an active, sometimes positive, sometimes negative, response to them. There are times when this is starkly obvious – van Eyck's *Arnolfini Portrait* or Hals's group portraits of the *Regents* and *Regentesses of the Old Men's Almshouse* or Léger's *Cyclists* or Warhol's *Campbell's Soup Cans*; other times it is much more indirect – a Constable landscape, a Turner storm, a Mondrian abstract, Emin's *My Bed*. But always the expression and response to social relations is there, and always it constitutes the core, the animating spirit of a significant work of art.

Here we have a further and overarching criterion for the evaluation of art, and one that is distinctively Marxist in that historical materialism offers the most convincing and effective basis for the analysis and understanding of social relations.

Works of art are good or great, insofar as and to the degree that they give powerful and insightful expression to social relations and, especially, to new and changing social relations. The other criteria I have considered here – mimesis, technical skill, beauty, emotional power, realism and so on – are not negated or replaced by this criterion but subsumed under it. They become possible means – each important in its own right – to achieving a unity of content and form through which the powerful expression of social relations is achieved.

All the critical essays that follow in the body of this book argue this case in relation to their respective subjects – from Michelangelo to Yasser Alwan – but for the sake of clarity I will give some examples here.

Holbein's *Henry VIII* is a great portrait not simply because it achieves an accurate likeness (we assume) or because it deploys immense technical skill in the rendering of attire, but because these and other qualities, for example the composition, all combine to achieve a powerful representation of what it meant to be an absolute monarch in the sixteenth century, to have the power of life and death over not only his wives but over everyone in the kingdom. Absolute monarchy, of course, is not a quality that inheres in the personality of the individual ruler but is a condensation of class and social relations; and this portrait expresses brilliantly the relationship between the king and his subjects. The same general point can be made about other great portraits, such as Bellini's *Portrait of Doge Leonardo Loredan* and Velázquez's *Portrait of Pope Innocent X* or, obviously in a different way, van Gogh's *Portrait of Postman Joseph Roulin.*

Grünewald's *Crucifixion* powerfully evokes the suffering of Christ on the cross, in a way that distinguishes it from the numerous Renaissance, mannerist or Baroque crucifixions. But this is an expression of the more personal and intimate view of the relationship between the individual and God that was a key element in the Protestant Reformation, which was in turn a reflection of new 'bourgeois' social relations arising with the first stirrings of capitalism.

Seurat's *Bathers at Asnières* is one of the greatest paintings of the nineteenth century because of its originality in combining with fine compositional and painterly skill the achievements of Manet and impressionism to give pictorial expression to a new social relation: the emergence and 'solidification' of a factory proletariat.[62] It was the combination of this content and this form, classical and monumental, that made the painting so initially unacceptable.

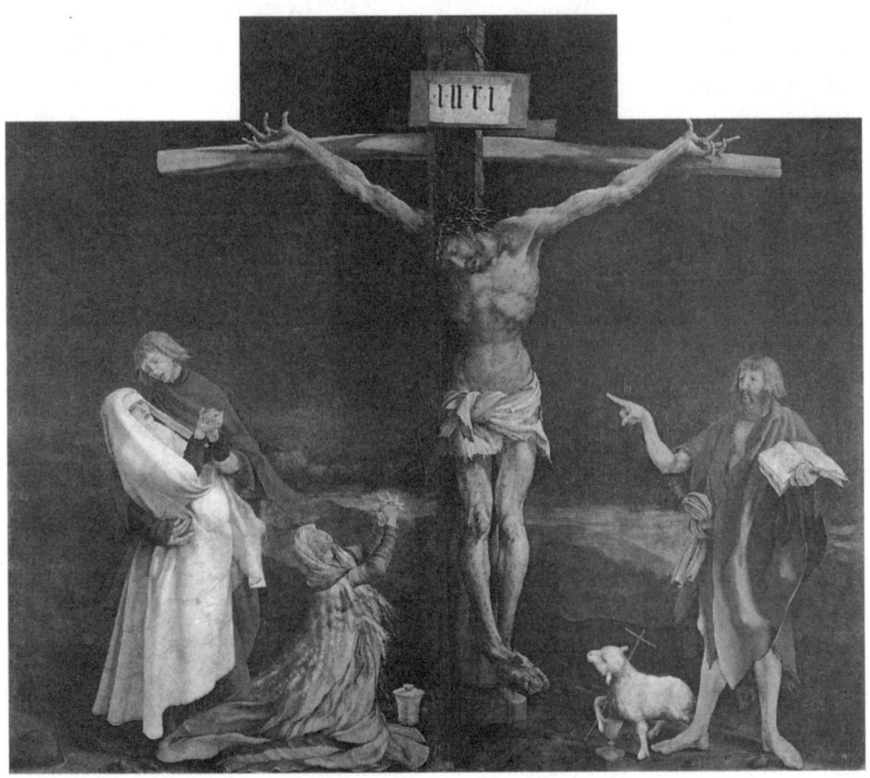

Matthias Grünewald, *Crucifixion* (1512–16)

In this context I want to mention one of John Berger's finest essays, 'The Moment of Cubism' (which builds on his analysis in *The Success and Failure of Picasso*), in which he demonstrates how the development of cubism was a response to the massive transformation in social relations in the specific conjuncture of Europe before the First World War. This is an exceptionally rich example of the kind of Marxist analysis I am advocating.

Mondrian's trademark abstracts of the twenties and thirties – compositions with blocks of primary colours within a grid of black lines on a white or pale background – are great works not because (as he himself imagined) they express fundamental natural or mystical forces, but because they are a response to a 'pure' aesthetic distillation of one aspect of the modern city environment – the bourgeois city of steel, glass and straight lines – hence their affinity with Bauhaus and modernist design and architecture. His *Broadway Boogie Woogie* builds on this work, but moves beyond it, in response to the experience of the dynamism and energy of Manhattan skyscrapers, automobiles and street life.[63]

It is clearly necessary that this approach should work not only for demonstrating the merits of various works and artists, but also for making comparative and negative judgments – that is, for explaining why other works and artists are much less good. Compare, for example, the French Academy nudes of the nineteenth century such as the *Birth of Venus*, or paintings by Alexandre Cabanel and William-Adolphe Bouguereau, with Manet's contemporary *Le Déjeuner sur l'Herbe* and *Olympia*. It is not just that Manet is undoubtedly original and 'critical' in formal terms; it is that Manet gives expression to important developments in social relations in a way that is absent from Cabanel and Bouguereau, whose works tell us nothing about lived and changing social experience, other than constituting 'evidence' of the persistence of a lazy and familiar sexism.

Two other examples I would give are Salvador Dalí and Anish Kapoor. Dalí is one of the most famous painters of the twentieth century, and certainly the most famous surrealist, but his art, despite its mimetic surface facility within fairly conventional naturalist representation (of 'surrealistic' fantasy scenes), says little or nothing of power or insight about mid-twentieth-century social relations. Essentially, it is superficial sensationalism. Anish Kapoor is much less meretricious, but most of his work, while visually attractive, consists primarily of mere visual tricks and effects. It expresses nothing significant about social relations and is therefore not significant or important art.

There are many other comparisons we can make using this approach. Compare the sculpture of Henry Moore and Alberto Giacometti – two very important artists of the mid-twentieth century. Moore is certainly highly skilled and probably more 'beautiful' than Giacometti, but which artist's work speaks more powerfully and profoundly to the social relations of the age? In my view the answer would be Giacometti. His art expresses with great intensity the individual isolation and alienation of human beings under capitalism. True, it is a one-sided expression – for there is much more to contemporary social relations than isolation and alienation – but in art, intense one-sided insight is more valuable than well-balanced but shallow reflection. By contrast, Moore, for all his formal power, offers uncritical expression of conventional social relations (principally of the nuclear family) and tries to render them profound by 'naturalising' them. To me this makes Giacometti the greater artist.

Now let us look at Francis Bacon and Lucian Freud. There are obvious parallels between the work of these two artists, who hailed from the same time and place and knew and painted each other.[64] I would rank Freud higher than Bacon in terms of technical skill, realism and psychological insight, but whose work makes the more powerful statement about human social relations in the twentieth and twenty first centuries? In my view the answer is Bacon, which is why, without in any way dismissing Freud (whom I admire), I would consider Bacon the greater artist.

Finally, this Marxist criterion is highly appropriate for assessing the recent work of relational art, participatory art and 'the social turn' – more appropriate, at any rate, than criteria which focus on qualities inhering in the art 'object', such as mimesis, harmonious beauty, or even realism. Nicolas Bourriaud famously defined relational aesthetics and art as 'a set of artistic practices which take as their theoretical and practical point of departure the whole of human relations and their social context, rather than an independent and private space'.[65] What I am saying is that, ultimately, all aesthetics should be 'relational aesthetics' (albeit not in the narrow sense of involving audience interaction) and that, again ultimately, the same standard applies for judging the *Mona Lisa* and *Guernica* as for Carsten Höller's *Test Site*.

Höller's *Test Site* was an installation in the huge Turbine Hall space of the Tate Modern in 2006. It consisted of five massive metal tubes or slides stretching from the upper floors to ground level, which visitors were invited to use. One of the key characteristics of relational art is that the viewer is asked to participate in the work, and their participation 'completes', as it were, its making. In this respect *Test Site* is exemplary. But how can it be evaluated aesthetically?

Höller called his work 'a sculpture that you can travel inside' but maintained it could be observed as a sculpture in its own right without sliding down it. In this respect it is possible to assess it in terms of all the different criteria outlined earlier in this chapter – its technical skill, beauty, sublimity, emotive power and so on. However, his main pitch was that it offers, to those who take the slide, 'a device for experiencing an emotional state that is a unique condition somewhere between delight and madness'.[66] It is also possible to see the work as 'art critical' in that it critiques and challenges the traditional space of the gallery as highly elitist, stuffy, silent or temple-like, and certainly makes it more child friendly.[67] But to what extent and how powerfully does *Test Site* express and respond to social relations in the wider society? It can be reasonably argued that the work offers an implicit critique of existing (alienated, utilitarian, commodified) social relations by evoking and involving people in the experience of 'utopian' relations of play, conviviality, pleasure and so on.

Thus, on all these grounds, *Test Site* can be considered a work of some merit, but the merit, in my judgment, is limited. As sculpture it is not outstanding (compared say to that of Brâncuși, whom Höller references), nor especially beautiful, sublime or emotionally powerful, and the same could be said of the 'experience' it offers the participant. The critique of the gallery space is valid and useful, but the critique of wider social relations is indeed utopian and rather lightweight, bland even; and this points to an objection that can be made to much of the relational art championed by Bourriaud.

The question of relational art – how it has developed further and been further politicised in 'the social turn' – will be taken up again in the final chapter. At this stage, however, I have demonstrated how the criteria of aesthetic evaluation we have been considering are and can be deployed, especially within a historical materialist framework, to assess art across its full range, at least in the Western tradition.[68]

CHAPTER 3

Michelangelo and Human Emancipation

First published in International Socialism *128 (Autumn 2010)*

Michelangelo stands at the very summit of human fame, or celebrity as we now call it. His position is secure among that very small band of individuals – Aristotle, Shakespeare, Goethe, Mozart, da Vinci and so on[1] – who seem to tower over history, much as one imagines the Colossus of Rhodes, and whose status is commonly given a universal, transcendental character.

Remarkably, he attained this pinnacle within his own lifetime, as a glance at Vasari testifies, when he was ranked even higher than da Vinci in the genius stakes (though I think it is fair to say that da Vinci has subsequently outdistanced him a little, thanks to helicopters, the *Mona Lisa* and Dan Brown), and it is probably now close to unassailable as far as the wider culture is concerned, as opposed to the specialism of art history.

Such a reputation is, of course, a decidedly mixed blessing. One downside of it, becoming the object of endless banality, has been fixed forever in a single line by T. S. Eliot in 'The Love Song of J. Alfred Prufrock': 'In the room the women come and go / Talking of Michelangelo.' And it is almost enough to deter one from even attempting to write on the man. Another is the indignity, shared with van Gogh, of being Irving Stoned (in *The Agony and the Ecstasy*) and then being played in the film of the same name by Charlton Heston (a fate van Gogh was mercifully spared) opposite Pope Rex Harrison. Naturally such appropriation by the world of capitalist kitsch has brought with it a corresponding rejection from the avant-garde. An elderly and very austere artist friend of mine, a systems painter from the sixties, tells me he detests Michelangelo's grandiloquence and much prefers Verrocchio. According to Robert Hughes, Barnett Newman once said, 'I thought our quarrel was with Michelangelo', prompting Hughes's riposte: 'Well, bad luck, Barney. You lost.'[2]

Nevertheless, despite Eliot's implied warning and despite the vast amount of guff written on the subject, it is precisely this question of Michelangelo's exalted standing that I wish to investigate in this essay, not in order to challenge or undermine it, for as we shall see I basically think it is justified, but in order to help explain it and place it on a less transcendental, more solid, more earthly, more historical foundation. The investigation will focus on, and move between, several related questions: (1) What explanations can be offered as to the causes and nature of Michelangelo's reputation and his artistic achievement? (2) What is the relation between Michelangelo's art and history? (3) What is the nature of Michelangelo's response to that history as seen in his art? Which amounts to offering a certain 'interpretation' or way of looking at that art. Obviously no attempt or claim is made to offer complete or definitive answers to any of these questions – one of them alone would require a book – but it is hoped that these tentative and rather speculative observations can nonetheless move the discussion on to more fruitful ground.

The existing ground is not very fertile. The story begins, of course, in Renaissance Florence with the widely expressed view that Michelangelo's achievements were attributable to, and explicable in terms of, divine inspiration. How literally this was believed is hard to tell, but Vasari spells it out in some detail:

> While industrious and choice spirits, aided by the light afforded by Giotto and his followers, strove to show the world the talent with which their happy stars and well-balanced humours had endowed them, and endeavored to attain to the height of knowledge by imitating the greatness of Nature in all things, the great Ruler of Heaven looked down and, seeing these vain and fruitless efforts and the presumptuous opinion of man more removed from truth than light from darkness, resolved, in order to rid him of these errors, to send to earth a genius universal in each art, to show

> single-handed the perfection of line and shadow, and who should give relief to his paintings, show a sound judgment in sculpture, and in architecture should render habitations convenient, safe, healthy, pleasant, well-proportioned, and enriched with various ornaments. He further endowed him with true moral philosophy and a sweet poetic spirit, so that the world should marvel at the singular eminence of his life and works and all his actions, seeming rather divine than earthly.[3]

But unless one believes in this kind of personally interventionist God, this is not very helpful (and if one does, further explanation, certainly of the kind I shall attempt, seems superfluous). Three hundred and fifty years later and the level of analysis had not advanced: 'Each supreme artist whom God hath sent into the world with inspiration and a particle of the imperishable fire, is a law unto himself. . . . Michelangelo belongs to the genus of deep, violent, colossal, passionately striving natures; not like Raffaello . . . to the smooth . . . calmly perfect tribe.'[4]

In the second half of the twentieth century, Ernst Gombrich, unable or unwilling to invoke God, simply substitutes genius and throws up his hands:

> The beginning of the sixteenth century, the Cinquecento, is the most famous period of Italian art, one of the greatest periods of all time. This was the time of Leonardo da Vinci and Michelangelo, of Raphael and Titian, of Correggio and Giorgione, of Dürer and Holbein in the North, and of many other famous masters. One may well ask why it was that all these great masters were born in the same period, but such questions are more easily asked than answered. One cannot explain the existence of genius. It is better to enjoy it.[5]

If we are not getting very far in terms of explaining Michelangelo's existence, maybe we can do better when it comes to establishing the nature of his achievement. We can again go back to Vasari, and this time we find not religious mysticism but fairly clearly defined technical criteria:

> Design is the imitation of the most beautiful things in Nature in all forms, both in sculpture and in painting, and this quality depends on having the hand and the skill to transfer with great accuracy

> and precision everything the eye sees to a plan or drawing . . . and the same is true for relief in sculpture. And then the most beautiful style comes from constantly copying the most beautiful things. . . .
>
> Neither Giotto nor those early artisans did this. . . . But the man who wins the palm among artists both living and dead, who transcends and surpasses them all, is the divine Michelangelo Buonarroti, who reigns supreme not merely in one of these arts but in all three at once.[6]

Unpick this statement and we find three definite claims: (1) Michelangelo is supreme by virtue of his technical skill; (2) technical skill consists in the classical notion of 'mimesis', accurately copying nature; (3) the key thing is to copy, 'imitate', beautiful things. That Gombrich, essentially, follows this view can be seen from the fact that he entitles the chapter of *The Story of Art* dealing with the early fifteenth century (Brunelleschi, Masaccio, Donatello, van Eyck, etc.) 'The Conquest of Reality' and that on the early sixteenth (da Vinci, Michelangelo, Raphael) 'Harmony Attained', and we must remember that Gombrich spoke for whole generations of art historians in this.

Moreover, it is clear that in these claims and in this narrative there is an important element of truth, both about the development of art as a whole at this time and, specifically, about Michelangelo. I for one would think it close to impossible to stand before the *David* in the Academia or the *Moses* in San Pietro in Vincoli – these giant statues carved from single blocks of marble – and not be awestruck at the level of sheer technical skill involved in their creation. Has any human ever lived more adept than Michelangelo in the carving of stone? However, it is equally necessary to question aspects of this account and to reject the notion that it is anywhere near the whole story.

First of all it is necessary to question whether Michelangelo's prodigious skill in shaping stone (and paint) according to his will was in fact skill in 'imitating' nature or representing 'reality'. So hegemonic, in Western culture, has been the Renaissance view of these matters and so accustomed have we become to the element of truth in its claims to naturalism (for example, single-point perspective and plastic shading) that we generally 'miss' or leave unsaid the numerous really obvious ways in which this art is not naturalistic at all. For instance, the *David* is an eighteen-foot-high stone object which does not and cannot resemble in any way – dimensions, colour, texture, mobility, – a sixth-century BCE shepherd boy, of whose actual appearance we have no knowledge whatsoever, and whose very existence is likely mythical. Likewise *The Creation of Adam:* of what could this possibly be a 'naturalistic' or 'realistic' representation? Even Adam's muscles and God's beard are idealised. When it comes to Baudrillard's hyperreality, his simulacrum of a simulacrum with no underlying referent, Michelangelo beats CNN and the Gulf War any day.

But even if we set those sorts of considerations aside, and adopt the conventional usage of naturalism, neither Michelangelo's own artistic trajectory nor his standing can satisfactorily be accounted for in these terms. On his deathbed, aged eighty-eight, Michelangelo is reputed to have said, 'I am dying just as I am beginning to learn the alphabet of my profession.' Yet, clearly, as he got older he moved further and further away from 'technique' in the naturalist sense and more and more towards a 'freer' and more 'expressionist' handling of the stone. Compare an early and late work on a similar subject – the *Pietà* in St Peter's, Rome, made in his early twenties, with the *Pietà* (or *Deposition*) in the Florentine Duomo, made in his eighties. The first is a technical virtuoso piece, staggering in its ability to render the folds in Mary's raiment and the veins on the back of Christ's hand. The second is rough hewn and 'unfinished', and Christ is strangely missing his right leg. Yet, to my eyes the later work has an artistic power and merit that far exceeds that of the earlier one. If Michelangelo's artistic achievement rested primarily on technique and so-called naturalism, he would stand with Holbein or Hals, not, as he does, with Rembrandt, Shakespeare and Bach.

Thus we are compelled to leave the supposedly safe and objective waters of technical skill for the apparently subjective and dangerous waters of 'interpretation'. We have to attempt to confront and deal with what Michelangelo, or rather his work, is actually saying. For understandable reasons many art historians and critics shy away from this in relation both to Michelangelo and art in general, but some fools rush in where angels fear to tread, and there is no doubt some wonderful nonsense has been written on this score. For example, Rolf Schott, in the Thames & Hudson monograph on Michelangelo, writes:

> The pressure of everyday existence has dimmed, for our generation, the memory of mankind's divine origin. Michelangelo's work is a visual statement of what the world has lost – the sense of wonder aroused by the mystery of human existence and human form.
>
> As an artist, Michelangelo is impersonal. His visual work tells us nothing about the man himself or his environment.[7]

These lines make no sense even in their own terms, never mind as an interpretation of Michelangelo. Assuming 'the world' once had a 'sense of wonder aroused by the mystery of human existence and human form', when did it have it and when was it lost? Was it around in the High Renaissance for Michelangelo to make a visual statement of it? Is it only our generation that has mislaid it, and was this really due to 'the pressure of everyday existence'? How can it possibly be true that 'his visual work tells us nothing about the man himself or his environment'? If the *only* thing Michelangelo's work told us, and it is not, was that the artist was very interested in the male body, that would be of some considerable significance.

The only reason for quoting Schott here (and Gombrich, and Symonds) is that it seems to me that such writing, often high flown but vacuous, sets the tone for how Michelangelo is perceived and received in our culture. Apart from seeing Michelangelo as primarily a 'naturalist', the other major difficulty has been caused by seeing him as primarily a religious artist. Obviously he was a 'believer', a sincere Christian, and obviously much of the work was commissioned by the church and had overtly religious themes or subject matter – all of that went with the territory and the time. But it does not follow from this that the driving force of Michelangelo's art was some pure and lofty spirituality, any more than piety was the dominant quality of Chaucer's *Canterbury Tales.* In my opinion, there are few artists for whom Marx's insights that '*man makes religion*, religion does not make man' and that 'the earthly family is . . . the secret of the holy family' are more apposite and more essential.

Take, for example, the *David.* This is based on a Bible story, but its motivation was thoroughly secular and 'political'. It was commissioned in 1501 by the Operai of Santa Maria del Fiore (a sort of committee of public works) on behalf of the new republican government of Florence to celebrate the recent ousting of its Medici rulers and its independence from Sforza Milan and the Roman papacy. The symbolism is obvious. In that the work also has a 'deeper', more universal reference and resonance, this is because it is a humanist statement about 'man'. (Clearly any such claim needs to be unpacked, and this will be – a little later.)

Then there is the so-called *Dying Captive* or *Dying Slave*, which stands now in the Louvre. The titles are posthumous attributions, not Michelangelo's, and the work itself contains no indication that the young man is a slave or captive, except in some metaphorical sexual sense – a 'love slave'? – or that he is dying, except in the sense of an orgasmic *petit mort*. De Tolnay, an esteemed Michelangelo expert, says he is 'a dreaming adolescent shaking off the bonds of sleep', and Sala, following de Tolnay, but edging a little further, says, 'In fact this figure is not dying at all, but rather absorbed in a dream-like state . . . somewhere between the languorous sensuality of an adoloscent ephebe and the wistfulness of a captive restrained none too convincingly.'[8] These are degrees of evasion. The capacity of art historians not to see what is literally in their faces never ceases to amaze me, for this is blatantly a work of homoeroticism. I do not say that homoeroticism is all that it is about, but it is *manifestly* its driving force. And indeed the moment one casts aside the taboo and the four-centuries-old veil of hypocrisy, it is manifest that homoeroticism is a major driver of Michelangelo's art as a whole.[9] Not only is the naked male body overwhelmingly the predominant motif, but there are several works which are not far off being mass orgies of male flesh (e.g., *Battle of the Centaurs*, parts of *The Last Judgment*), and there are others, ostensibly religious in theme, where male nudes appear, in numbers, with no conceivable narrative or theological justification – there are four frontal male nudes in the background to *The Holy Family*, and more than twenty in the interstices of the Sistine ceiling. This essay cannot possibly do justice to the role of homoeroticism in Michelangelo's work but I raise the issue simply to reinforce the point that religious subject matter does not guarantee or correspond to religious content. And no matter how pious the artist, it does not preclude the art serving as a means to express thoroughly earthly concerns.

At this point I need to move swiftly from the negative to the positive, from what Michelangelo's work was not, to what it was. To do so I believe it is essential to see Michelangelo in relation to his times. By his times I do not mean, principally, events but the broader and deeper social forces at work in the society in which he lived. Some major works are occasioned by specific events – Picasso's *Guernica* is the obvious example, but Picasso's cubism and his whole way of painting and representing the world was conditioned by the social relations of capitalism in its imperialist phase, as was demonstrated by John Berger in his book *The Success and Failure of Picasso* and his article 'The Moment of Cubism'. When Hyacinthe Rigaud painted Louis XIV, he was painting not just the features or personality of the Sun King but also the whole social institution of absolute monarchy. Moreover, it is necessary to understand those times, those social forces, in a Marxist (i.e., historical materialist) way. Only the Marxist theory of history, that is, a theory that sets out from the development of the forces and relations of production and their expression in class struggle, is able to identify correctly the underlying forces at work in a society and to which artists in general, but especially great artists, respond.

It is, I suppose, necessary to insist at this point that this methodology is not a reductionist or economic determinist one. The artist – Michelangelo or whoever – is not denied their creativity, originality or personal vision, based on their unique experience. Least of all are they seen as simple vehicles or ciphers for class interests or class ideologies. (It is true that the Althusserian Nicos Hadjinicolaou propounded a view close to this in his *Art History and Class Struggle*, but this not the kind of Marxism or the kind of art history I propose). The artist is an individual human being who not only reflects the wider society but also actively responds to it, often critically, but what the artist responds to has to be part of the analysis, and, generally speaking, the greater the artist the more profoundly they will engage with the deep social forces, rather just superficial appearances, of their moment in history.

In the case of Michelangelo, the best starting point for grasping his situation is a quotation from Frederick Engels in what may seem an unlikely location, namely the introduction to *Dialectics of Nature* – Engels is discussing the birth of modern science, not art, but it remains extraordinarily relevant:

> Modern natural science dates, like all more recent history, from that mighty epoch which we Germans term the Reformation, from the national misfortune that overtook us at that time, and which the French term the Renaissance and the Italians the Cinquecento, although it is not fully expressed by any of these names. It is the epoch which had its rise in the last half of the fifteenth century. Royalty, with the support of the burghers of the towns, broke the power of the feudal nobility and established the great monarchies, based essentially on nationality, within which the modern European nations and modern bourgeois society came to development.... In the manuscripts saved from the fall of Byzantium, in the antique statues dug out of the ruins of Rome, a new world was revealed to the astonished West, that of ancient Greece: the ghosts of the Middle Ages vanished before its shining forms; Italy rose to an undreamt-of flowering of art, which seemed like a reflection of classical antiquity and was never attained again. In Italy, France, and Germany a new literature arose, the first, modern literature; shortly afterwards came the classical epochs of English and Spanish literature.... The dictatorship of the Church over men's minds was shattered; it was directly cast off by the majority of the Germanic peoples, who adopted Protestantism, while among the Latins a cheerful spirit of free thought, taken over from the Arabs and nourished by the newly-discovered Greek philosophy, took root more and more and prepared the way for the materialism of the eighteenth century.
>
> It was the greatest progressive revolution that mankind has so far experienced, a time which called for giants and produced giants – giants in power of thought, passion, and character, in universality and learning. The men who founded the modern rule of the bourgeoisie had anything but bourgeois limitations. On the contrary, the adventurous character of the time inspired them to a greater or

> less degree. There was hardly any man of importance then living who had not travelled extensively, who did not command four or five languages, who did not shine in a number of fields. Leonardo da Vinci was not only a great painter but also a great mathematician, mechanician, and engineer.... Albrecht Dürer was painter, engraver, sculptor, and architect, and in addition invented a system of fortification.... Machiavelli was statesman, historian, poet, and at the same time the first notable military author of modern times. Luther not only cleaned the Augean stable of the Church but also that of the German language.... The heroes of that time had not yet come under the servitude of the division of labour, the restricting effects of which, with its production of onesidedness, we so often notice in their successors. But what is especially characteristic of them is that they almost all pursue their lives and activities in the midst of the contemporary movements, in the practical struggle; they take sides and join in the fight, one by speaking and writing, another with the sword, many with both. Hence the fullness and force of character that makes them complete men.[10]

I apologise for the length of the quote, which I have cut as much as possible, but which, without mentioning Michelangelo's name, nonetheless fits him like glove, even down to the building of fortifications, which he did for Florence in 1529. The key points are: (1) that the Renaissance is part of the birth of capitalism, or more precisely, an episode in the transition from feudalism to capitalism; (2) that the transition from feudalism to capitalism is a lengthy and complex international process (not a series of separate national processes).

Capitalist production and capitalist social relations develop, at first slowly, within feudalism – in its interstices, as Marx put it, primarily in the medieval towns – and its social bearer, the bourgeoisie (originally the burghers or 'townsmen') are literally the middle class, subordinate to the feudal nobility, who are the dominant class, but superior to the peasants, artisans and fledgling proletarians or wage labourers. The bourgeoisie develops economically and culturally before it achieves political (i.e., state) power. The fairly prolonged period in which bourgeois power more or less rivals that of the aristocracy sees the rise of the absolute monarchs, who raise themselves above the contending classes, playing them against each other but ultimately preserving the old feudal regime. The bourgeoisie's conquest of state power and establishment of full-blown capitalist states involves a series of struggles, revolutions and wars, in which there are victories and defeats, steps forward and steps back, over several centuries. The most important victories are the Dutch Revolt (and establishment of the Dutch Republic) at the end of the sixteenth century, the English Revolution of 1642–7, the American Revolution of 1774–6 and the French Revolution of 1789–93. The French Revolution, together with the contemporaneous Industrial Revolution in Britain, is decisive. The bourgeoisie will now rule the world, though mopping-up operations continue well into the twentieth century.

The place of Florence in the early part of this story has been extensively documented by Frederick Antal in the first chapter of his classic study *Florentine Painting and Its Social Background*:

> The great economic power of Florence . . . grew up chiefly in the twelfth century and expanded during the thirteenth and fourteenth centuries to dimensions unparalleled elsewhere in Italy or indeed Europe. Its foundations were threefold; the textile industry, the trade in textiles and other products, and banking. . . . In all these industries it was no longer the master-craftsman but the capitalist entrepreneur, who disposed of the wares to the customer. . . . The industry of Florence, particularly the cloth industry and the international trade connected with it, was undoubtedly the most important enterprise of an early capitalist character in the whole of the later Middle Ages. . . . The same Florentine citizens who were the world's greatest industrialists and merchants were also its chief bankers.[11]

This was the economic foundation of the Renaissance, Early and High, and it should be noted that the association of artistic 'golden ages' with periods of spectacular wealth is common in the history of art – Venice just after Florence, Antwerp and then Amsterdam in the late sixteenth and seventeenth centuries, Paris in the nineteenth and early twentieth, New York post–World War II and, even, in a small way, London in the 1980s and '90s are all examples. Arnold Hauser puts it thus:

> The new artistic culture first appears on the scene in Italy, because this country also has a lead over the West in economic and social matters, because the revival of economic life starts here, the financial and transport facilities of the crusades are organised from here, free competition first develops here, in opposition to the guild ideal of the Middle Ages, and the first European banking system arises here, because the emancipation of the urban middle class takes place here earlier than in the rest of Europe.[12]

To properly outline the interconnections between this economic development and the specific art of Cimabue, Giotto, Masaccio, Uccello, Donatello, della Francesca, Botticelli and so on is beyond the scope of this essay, but certain general features can be outlined. The most fundamental thing is that this art of the fourteenth and fifteenth century achieves – I'm tempted to say *wins* or *forges*, for you can see it developing painting by painting, artist by artist – the three-dimensional space within and behind the picture frame, within which can be depicted urban and rural spaces, solid objects and, above all, human actions and human personalities. This is an optimistic art characterised by 'freedom and effortlessness of expression . . . grace and elegance'[13] which serves as a visual accompaniment to the rise of humanist philosophy. The sense in which the work of da Vinci, Raphael and the younger Michelangelo constitutes the culmination of this process is clear.

Overall, the birth of capitalism in its early stages (and this is true in Italy, in the Netherlands, in England, in America and in France) is experienced by the mass of people, and especially the middle and lower-middle classes, from which most artists and intellectuals spring, as a massive expansion in human freedom, a liberation from the restrictions, bonds and superstitions imposed by the church and the feudal aristocracy, who were, of course, close ideological and practical allies, and thus a huge emancipation of the human personality. Two works by Michelangelo, the *David* and *The Creation of Adam*, express this more clearly, more powerfully and more beautifully than, perhaps, any others in European history.

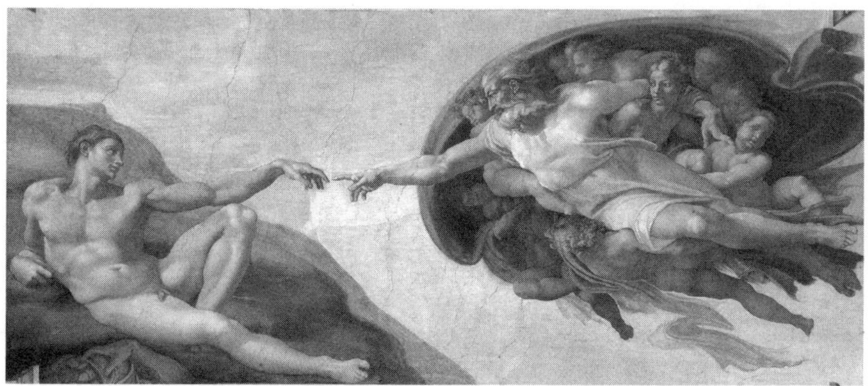

Michelangelo Buonarotti, *The Creation of Adam* (1508-12)

As we have already noted, the *David* was commissioned as a work celebrating political liberty in a quite definite sense, but just as Picasso's *Guernica* was painted in response to a particular war crime but has emerged as a statement about the crime of war in general, so the *David* has been pretty generally read as a statement about 'man'. The 'perfection' of the body and its sheer scale guarantee that is seen as a celebration, but there is more to it than that. Unlike his predecessors in sculpting this subject, Donatello and Verrocchio, who show David after the defeat of Goliath with the giant's head at his feet, Michelangelo shows David before the battle, thus providing a basis in the narrative for David's frowning forehead and making it a work which looks to the future in anticipation of the decisive struggle. Moreover, the *David* is not in fact in 'perfect' proportion; the head and hands, especially the right hand holding the stone, are slightly too large, and this has the effect of making David a brain as well as a body, and a doer and maker as well as an object of desire. Thus what the *David* celebrates is not 'man' as he is, but a vision of the whole man that he has the potential to become. As Gramsci says: 'In putting the question "what is man?" what we mean is: what can man become? That is, can man dominate his own destiny, can he "make himself", can he create his own life?'[14]

The Creation of Adam depicts the moment God brings Adam to life, but visually it is Adam, not God, who is the 'star' of the painting and indeed of the whole Sistine ceiling. This is very much a humanist creation. The predominance of this panel over all the others, visually as well as in historical reputation, is both because of its content (the 'moment' of creation) and because it is the panel with the most sky and therefore the most light, and because of the clarity of its forms in their semi-symmetrical composition. This semi-symmetry also hints at the potential always latent in the biblical notion of God creating man in his own image, namely the materialist (Feuerbachian, then Marxist) reversal whereby man creates God in his own image. But 'man' who creates God is 'man who has either not yet won through to himself, or has already lost himself again' (Marx), and the God he creates is a dream, an idealised fantasy of what he might become. When God (Michelangelo) creates man, he creates him as a young man in his prime, and when man (Michelangelo) creates God, he creates him as a wise and benevolent old man.

The possibility of a homoerotic reading of this scene is, or should be, obvious. God and Adam yearn for each other. But this homoerotic element actually contributes to the 'universality' of the image. In Michelangelo (and up to now I have simply reflected this without comment), the male figure/'man' represents or 'stands for' humanity. This could hardly be otherwise in such a male-dominated society and was indeed general practice, at least linguistically, until well into the 1970s. However, when I look at *Adam* (and this also applies, though less strongly, to the *David*) I think Michelangelo's homoeroticism has 'softened' his depiction. He is a beautiful, but not a macho, man. There is Hegel's profound dialectic of slavery at work here. The slave is freer than the slave owner. Mankind is represented by the despised gay man.

However, as we move from the Sistine ceiling to the wall behind the altar, namely *The Last Judgment*, we enter a different emotional world. The frescos on the ceiling participate in the same humanist optimism as da Vinci or even Giotto before them. *The Last Judgment* is a work of extreme anguish. Only a quarter to a third of the fresco, the top, least visible part, shows those raised up by Christ to heaven, and no particular attempt is made to depict their eternal joy. Two-thirds of it focusses on the torments, mainly mental, of the damned. Hauser writes:

> It is no longer a monument of beauty and perfection, of power and youth, that arises here, but a picture of bewilderment and despair,

> a cry for redemption from the chaos which suddenly threatens to swallow up the world of the Renaissance....
>
> *The Last Judgment*... is the first important artistic creation which is *no longer* 'beautiful' and which refers back to those medieval works of art which were not yet beautiful but merely expressive.[15]

Nor is *The Last Judgement* a one-off. All Michelangelo's major artworks that follow it – *The Conversion of Saul* and *The Crucifixion of St Peter* frescos, the Florentine *Pietà* and his last work, the *Rondanini Pietà*, share a similar gloomy, perhaps tragic, atmosphere. By Renaissance standards these pieces might be judged wanting – they are not beautiful depictions of beautiful things, and they certainly lack 'perfection' or 'harmony' – but I think they are among his finest art. I see affinities here with the Shakespeare of *King Lear* and *The Tempest*, and the Rembrandt of *The Jewish Bride* and the late self-portraits.

The question, however, is what produced the profound change in mood. For those disposed to the biographical approach to art history, there is an obvious answer: the onset of old age and the approach of death. And there is clearly some truth in this, especially in the case of the *Rondanini Pietà*, on which he was working to within days of his death. It cannot, however, be anything like the whole story, because, as Hauser has shown, Michelangelo's shift in style is part of a much wider shift in style in Italian and, to some extent, European art – the move to mannerism.[16] We need therefore to look again to the wider society, to history.

What happened between the ceiling (1508–12) and the wall (1535–41)? Lots of 'events' certainly. Many great artists died: Botticelli, da Vinci, del Sarto, Giorgione, Giovanni Bellini, Raphael, Correggio (as well as Holbein, Dürer, Grünewald and Bosch, outside Italy). In 1512, Cardinal Giovanni de' Medici, with the aid of papal troops, restored Medici rule in Florence, ending a period of republican democracy under Piero Soderini (and Niccolò Machiavelli). In 1527, the forces of the Habsburg Holy Roman Emperor Charles V defeated Rome and sacked the city, after executing one thousand of its defenders. Faced with this development, the citizens of Florence seized the opportunity to overthrow their Medici rulers for the second time (the first was in 1494), and to reestablish their republic. Michelangelo rallied to their support and in

1529 accepted a commission to design the city's fortifications. But Pope Clement VII made a deal with Charles V to use the emperor's troops to recapture Florence and return it to Medici hands. In 1533, Alessandro de' Medici was made Duke of Florence, bringing an end to the republic and inaugurating two hundred years of hereditary Medici rule. The sacking of Rome and the defeat of Florence effectively brings the Renaissance to an end (except for the late Titian in Venice). While all this is happening in Italy, Luther has launched the Reformation in Wittenburg in 1517, and this has led to the German Peasants' War of 1525, in which Luther sided with the aristocracy in ferociously crushing the peasant revolt he had himself called forth. In response to the Reformation came the Counter-Reformation: humanism was eclipsed, Pope Paul III revived the Holy Inquisition (1542) and convened the Council of Trent (1545–63) to repel the Protestant threat. And, most importantly in the long run, the opening up of the Americas, following Columbus, combined with the Ottoman threat in the eastern Mediterranean, following the fall of Byzantium, moved the economic centre of gravity of Europe from the Mediterranean to the northwest and the Atlantic seaboard.

But it is not so much the events as their wider import that is crucial here. Let us recall that it was Florence's (and Italy's) role as pioneer of capitalism in Europe that was the economic and social foundation of the Renaissance. Then let us also recall that Italy did not at all maintain its leading position, economically or socially. Italy did not produce a bourgeois democratic revolution, did not make the transition to a fully fledged capitalist state, did not even find the 'leader' that Machiavelli called for in *The Prince* to unify the nation, until the Risorgimento in the mid-nineteenth century, and it consequently experienced centuries of relative cultural decline – Giotto, da Vinci and Michelangelo gave way to Canaletto and Canova – while economic and cultural supremacy passed north to the Netherlands and England. The early sixteenth century was thus a crucial turning point in the history of Italy, and also Germany, as Marx and Engels were to explain – and therefore of Europe and the world. It was one of those moments when the door of history begins, tantalisingly, to open, inviting us to step through into a golden future, only to slam shut in our faces. The closest parallel I can think of is the 1920s and '30s, when the hopes aroused by the Russian Revolution were dashed and ended in the nightmare of Stalinism and Fascism. Michelangelo's late works were produced in the early modern 'midnight in the century' (the phrase is Victor Serge's). In fact, the next major wave of the struggle, the international struggle of the bourgeoisie against feudalism, was only a couple of decades and a few hundred miles away; the Dutch Revolt began two years after Michelangelo's death, but neither he, nor anyone else, could possibly have had any sense of this at the time.

This raises the question, how much of the history I have been talking about would Michelangelo have been aware of and how would it have influenced his work? Clearly, in the terms that I have been using (feudalism, capitalism, bourgeoisie, etc.), he could not have been conscious at all – this kind of analysis only becomes possible with Marx. Moreover, Michelangelo was a professional artist who depended, to live and to work, on commissions from Medicis and popes and who, in order to survive, had often to keep his counsel and sometimes make his excuses and leave. But we do know where his sympathies lay. We know that the young Michelangelo was sympathetic to Savonarola, the Dominican priest and popular democrat who led Florence from 1494 till he was deposed by the pope and the Medicis and burned at the stake in 1498. We know that he was often in conflict with his Medici and papal masters and that he supported the Florentine Republic of 1527, leaving the city in disgust when Medici rule was restored. We know that in later life his 'platonic' friendship with Vittoria Colonna in Rome involved much discussion of 'Lutheran'-type ideas, which were regarded as heretical by the papacy. He would therefore most certainly have been sensitive to the changed political, moral and cultural climate. After all, it resulted in the painting over of the genitals in *The Last Judgment* on the orders of Pope Paul IV in 1559!

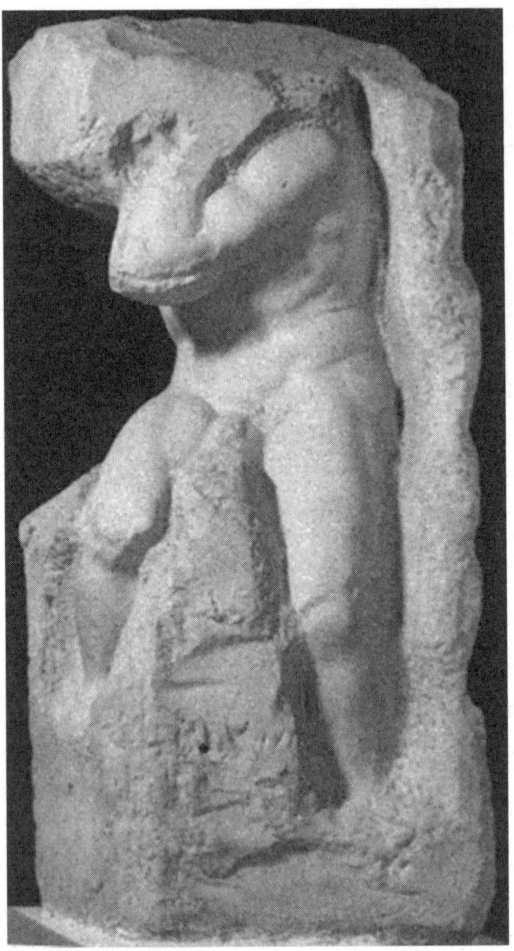

Michelangelo Buonarotti, *The Atlas Slave* (1525-30)

But it so happened that Michelangelo produced, during these years, a series of major works, among the greatest in his whole output, which express with exceptional intensity this moment in history. These works are the so-called 'slaves' or 'captives'. The first two, the *Dying Slave* and the *Rebellious Slave*, both from 1513, are still close in form and spirit to the *David* and *Adam*. But then, between 1519 and 1533, came *Atlas*, the *Young Slave*, the *Bearded Slave* and the *Awakening Slave*, who in age, size and physique are nearer to the Christ of *The Last Judgment*. They were all intended for the tomb of Julius II, whose centrepiece was to be the awesome *Moses*, and they are all left 'unfinished'. Their unfinished character gives rise to one of those art historical disputes that has not been, and probably cannot be, conclusively resolved. Why are they unfinished? Are they unfinished because Michelangelo was obliged, by circumstances beyond his control, to leave them that way? Did he consciously, or unconsciously, choose not to finish them? In which case are they really unfinished? If he really wanted to produce finished work, why did he not finish one of the series before starting on the next? My personal inclination is to believe they were deliberately left as they are because they are so powerful that way.

Anyway, conscious or unconscious, intended or unintended, the effect is the same – four giant figures struggling for freedom from the stone but still held captive by it. And they do not just capture the essence of that moment; they also make a powerful statement about human history and the struggle for human emancipation as a whole. For today, nearly five hundred years later, we are still slaves fighting for our freedom, and still gripped by the rock of class society, alienation and 'the muck of ages'.

Now the question posed at the beginning of this essay – on what does Michelangelo's status as a giant of human history and culture rest? – has received an answer. It is by no means a comprehensive answer; many aspects of Michelangelo, such as his architecture, and many of his works, have been neglected, but hopefully it grasps the main point. In his work as a whole, Michelangelo expressed, more than any other artist, the hope and the dream of the Renaissance and the despair and misery of the betrayal and crushing of that dream. And as always, the art that penetrates most deeply into, and responds most powerfully to, the social relations and forces of its time is also the art that achieves the greatest 'universal' appeal and validity.

CHAPTER 4

Rembrandt and Revolution

From Rembrandt and Revolution *(London: Redwords, 2002)*

Anyone writing about visual art has to come to terms with a basic problem – the inadequacy of writing in the face of the art. Just as the meaning of a poem, if the poem is any good, cannot be rendered in prose, so the 'meaning' of a good painting cannot be fully conveyed in words – otherwise what is the point of poetry or painting?

This general problem is particularly acute where Rembrandt is concerned because of his peculiar 'eloquence'. His work 'speaks' to us – emotionally, psychologically – with a directness unmatched even by masters such as Holbein and Titian. If you want to know how Rembrandt felt about his wife, Saskia, or his lover, Hendrickje Stoffels, or his religion, or beggars, looking at the paintings, etchings and drawings will tell you more than any words, including the words in this essay.

So what is the justification for writing about art? What functions does it perform? In my opinion, writing about art has three main useful functions. The first is that of a signpost – it is akin to the humble but vital guidebook or museum plan. It says: 'This way lies an important visual experience. Out of all the visual images with which you are bombarded, this is something worth really looking at.' The second is like that of a viewing platform from which to survey a natural or urban panorama – it provides a context or vantage point favourable to seeing the artwork clearly. It does this primarily by supplying information (technical, biographical and, especially, sociohistorical) relevant to the work's production and reception. For example, Géricault's *The Raft of the Medusa* is a mighty painting in itself, but it is easier to 'see' it properly, to grasp its power, if one is provided with the information that it was painted in response to an actual shipwreck which was controversial in the way that the 1999 Paddington rail crash and the sinking of the *Herald of Free Enterprise* at Zeebrugge were controversial. The third is as part of a wider argument about culture, society and history, as when Marx observed that 'Rembrandt painted the Mother of God as a Dutch peasant woman' in order to make a point about ideology and material conditions in a debate about freedom of the press.

In this essay I am concerned with all three of these functions, but especially with the second. Regarding the first, Rembrandt is hardly in need of my recommendation, but every little helps. Regarding the third, I hope that effective treatment of Rembrandt will serve as a demonstration of and recommendation for the method which I have endeavoured to use, namely historical materialism. But mainly my hope is that the wonder and depth of Rembrandt's art will appear all the more clearly when it is seen in its true historical context.

* * *

The subject of this study is the revolutionary art of Rembrandt van Rijn. Rembrandt's art, I shall argue, is revolutionary in three senses. First, Rembrandt was a revolutionary artist who pioneered a new way of painting (and of seeing) which overturned previous norms and conceptions of this art. Second, his art – a product of an actual social and political revolution in Holland during the second half of the sixteenth century – gave strong expression to many of the themes of that revolution. In this respect Rembrandt could be said to parallel Jacques-Louis David's relationship to the French Revolution. Third, his art was the product of a radical critical attitude to the outcome of a revolution that was probably the world's first properly constituted capitalist society. In this I think Rembrandt stands alone.

We should begin with the paintings.

The Revolutionary Character of Rembrandt's Art

Rembrandt is thought of above all as a portrait painter, and portraiture is one of the three or four most important genres in the history of European painting. What kind of portraits were painted before Rembrandt?

To answer this question look at one of Holbein's great portraits, *Portrait of Henry VIII* (1539), or his even greater dual portrait of *The Ambassadors* (1533), or look at Giovanni Bellini's magnificent *Portrait of Doge Leonardo Loredan* of Venice, or Titian's extraordinary *Portrait of a Man* (ca. 1512), which is possibly a self-portrait and certainly the most magnificent portrait of a sleeve in the history of the world. What kinds of portraits were painted by the greatest of Rembrandt's contemporaries? Look at van Dyck's huge equestrian portrait of Charles I (1638), or any of Velázquez's paintings of Philip IV of Spain or, one of his greatest masterpieces, so admired by Francis Bacon, the *Portrait of Pope Innocent X* (1650).

These paintings are not chosen at random or for their typicality. They are put forward because, in my opinion, they represent the very best in the way of portraiture that European art had to offer in the sixteenth or early seventeenth century. Technically, they are literally of the highest quality imaginable. Is it possible to conceive of painting that would achieve a higher degree of verisimilitude in the rendering of fur, silk or velvet than is found in these masterpieces? Is there in the whole of European art any work with greater command of precise significant detail than *The Ambassadors*? Was the dignity and sagacity of a ruler ever more convincingly depicted than in Bellini's *Portrait of Doge Leonardo Loredan*? Have the shrewdness and cunning of power ever been more subtly revealed than in Velázquez's pope?

Yet set any or all of these great works alongside a major portrait by Rembrandt – for example that of Jacob Trip or that of his wife, Margaretha de Geer (both ca. 1660), both of which hang in the National Gallery – and it is immediately apparent that with Rembrandt we are entering a different world. One key characteristic common to all the aforementioned pre-Rembrandt portraits is the concern to emphasise – through expression, pose and, above all, attire – the social status and position of the sitter. This is the function of the supreme elegance of the Doge's hat, of the sensuous tangibility of Titian's sleeve, of the perfection of the sheen on Innocent X's red cape. In the Rembrandt portraits there is none of this. The clothes of both Jacob Trip and Margaretha de Geer are painted in such light and sketchy fashion that they simply merge into the dark background of the chiaroscuro without conveying any sense of grandeur or luxury, and the viewer's attention is focussed overwhelmingly on the subjects' faces (and secondarily on their hands). Moreover, in both works there are specific formal devices to reinforce this effect. In the de Geer portrait it is the delicately but unobtrusively painted white ruff and cuffs which make her face and hands stand out, and in the case of Jacob Trip it is the combination of the plain headband and scarf which isolate and emphasise the face. In other words, in these paintings our attention is concentrated on the individual personality, one might say 'the soul', of the sitter to the virtual exclusion of everything else. It is not that the Trips were poor or even not rich. On the contrary, they were immensely wealthy and powerful, and their huge town mansion, the Trippenhuis, still stands today on the Klovenierzburgwal Canal in the Old Centre of Amsterdam. It is that Rembrandt has deliberately chosen to present them this way.

The technical device most characteristic of Rembrandt's portraiture (though he does not use it in every case), and most associated with his painting as a whole, is a deep chiaroscuro which casts the majority of the picture in shadow while illuminating a small section of the canvas from a single light source. In Rembrandt's hands this device is used to screen out everything which is nonessential while focussing on the psychological or spiritual core of the person or scene that is being depicted.[1]

The result, again and again, is portrait painting with a degree of personal psychic intensity unprecedented in the history of European and probably world art.

Even more striking evidence of the revolutionary character of Rembrandt's art is afforded by his treatment of the female nude. Let us adopt the same procedure as with the portrait and begin by considering some outstanding examples of the female nude in the European tradition prior to and contemporaneous with Rembrandt. Think of Botticelli's

The Birth of Venus (ca. 1485) (which inaugurated the whole tradition), Giorgione's *Sleeping Venus* (ca. 1510), Titian's *Venus d'Urbino* (ca. 1538), Tintoretto's *The Origin of the Milky Way* (ca. 1575–80), Rubens's *The Three Graces* (1639) and, most relevant of all, Velázquez's *Rokeby Venus* (ca. 1648).

In all of these works, without exception, and in innumerable similar paintings pre- and post-Rembrandt, the nude woman is presented as an idealised figure of erotic beauty (as Venus or some other mythological figure) posed as an object of display for the male gaze. In short, the woman is presented as an abstract sex object. This tendency, present in all these paintings, reaches an extreme in Velázquez's *Venus*. Despite the brilliance of this work in its handling of colour, depiction of flesh tones and other formal qualities, it is clear that almost every aspect of its composition – the presence of the mirror as a symbol of vanity, the absence of feet, hands and face (except as a very blurred reflection in the mirror),[2] the positioning of the body as a whole with its behind literally in the viewer's face – combines to reduce this image to an impersonal object of desire.

Now look at Rembrandt's *Bathsheba* (1654), painted within a few years of the Velázquez. What a complete contrast! In place of an idealised impersonal body, an actual whole person – a real woman – painted with deep love.

It is helpful in looking at this painting to know the Bible story on which it is based. King David desired Bathsheba, who was married to and pregnant by Uriah. David arranged for Uriah to be sent into battle and killed. The painting depicts the toilet of Bathsheba as she is prepared for the king, whose summons she holds in her right hand. There is thus the potential for intense poignancy built into the scene.

However, this is not at all the key factor in shaping the nature and feeling of the painting. In the Amsterdam Rijksmuseum there is a painting of the very same scene, *The Toilet of Bathsheba* (ca. 1594), by Rembrandt's fellow countryman Cornelis Cornelisz van Haarlem (1562–1638), which lacks any of the qualities of the Rembrandt and is much closer, in spirit if not in quality, to Titian or Tintoretto. Of greater significance is the fact that the model for Rembrandt's Bathsheba is Hendrickje Stoffels, Rembrandt's lover and companion from about 1650 until her death in 1663, and the strength of his feeling for her is evident in the work. But what is crucial, and what conveys that personal feeling, is the way in which Rembrandt has painted Bathsheba.

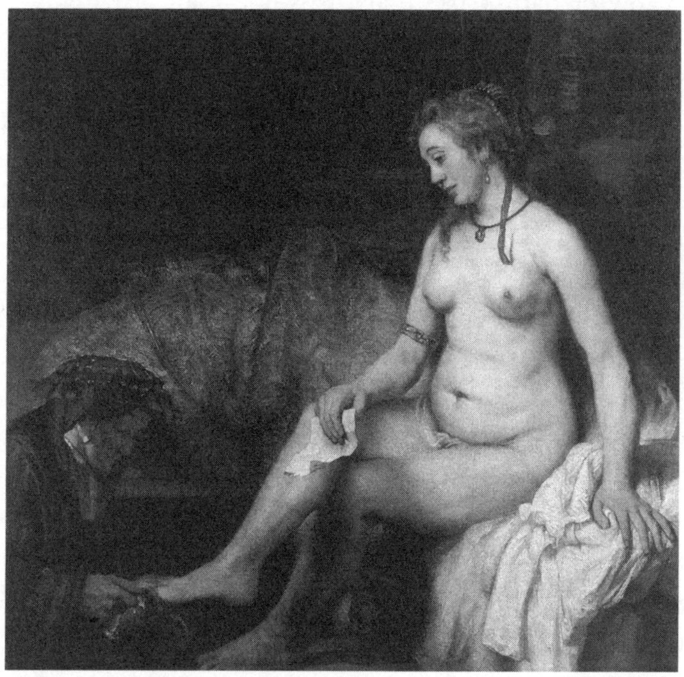

Rembrandt van Rijn, *Bathsheba* (1654)

This is not easy to express in words. There are compositional elements involved – the presence of, indeed the emphasis on, Bathsheba's feet and hands which works to particularise her, the positioning of her body where she sits straight-backed rather than reclining, which conveys strength and dignity. There is the expression on her face, neither coquettish nor pouting nor falsely coy, but an air of deep sadness and resignation entirely appropriate to the situation. There is the peculiarity of her slightly overlong left arm, explanation of which can only be speculative but which I believe is expressive of heaviness and reluctance, which is important because it is symptomatic of Rembrandt painting Bathsheba not from the standpoint of an observer but from, as it were, inside Bathsheba's body. (There is a parallel here with the way in which

Michelangelo exaggerates the size of David's right hand as it rests on his thigh, this being the hand that holds the stone that will strike down Goliath.) Above all there is the utterly exceptional sensitivity of the handling of the paint in the depiction of every curve, every highlight and every shadow of Bathsheba's body. It is not at all that Rembrandt has given us an asexual or unerotic image of Bathsheba/Hendrickje. On the contrary, it is intensely sexual, suffused with desire, but it is concrete desire for a concrete independent woman – desire that can be and is reciprocated, desire that is an integral part of a loving relationship.

It is very hard to overstate how rare an achievement this is in the European art tradition both before and after Rembrandt – only Rubens's study of Helena Fourment as Venus (ca. 1636–8) and one or two of Picasso's *Nude Woman in a Red Armchair* paintings of Marie-Thérèse Walter come to my mind as in any way similar, and they are plainly not really comparable. Yet it is by no means an isolated or unique example when it comes to Rembrandt's oeuvre. *Woman Bathing in a Stream* (ca. 1654), which hangs in the National Gallery and is also probably modelled for by Hendrickje Stoffels, possesses the same qualities and is equally breathtaking. When one considers the potential for titillation of the pose – the young woman lifting her chemise to the top of her thighs as she steps into the water – it is extraordinary how not an ounce of titillation or voyeurism attaches to this work. Then there is a remarkable series of portraits of Hendrickje, especially *Hendrickje Stoffels Leaning against a Door* (ca. 1656–7), which has its own particular combination of love, kindliness, strength and independence. Nor are we talking only about images of Hendrickje Stoffels (though clearly she was the most important inspiration in this direction). The *Danaë* (ca. 1636), in the Hermitage Museum in St Petersburg, for whom the model was probably his first wife, Saskia, exhibits a warm, open sexuality that is drawn from the same well. Even Rembrandt's earliest drawings and etchings of anonymous nude women eschew any conventional idealisation or sexualisation. Finally on this theme, there is the etching depicting sexual intercourse called *The French Bed* (1646). In one sense the work is an extremely simple and straightforward naturalistic representation of the sexual act, yet it is also amazing because it manages to be neither biological nor prurient, but warm and human.

I keep using words like 'amazing', 'exceptional' and 'extraordinary' to describe these paintings because that is what they are. There is simply nothing or almost nothing in the history of European art to compare with them – a sexual but nonsexist representation of nude or seminude women.

Portraiture and the nude are by no means the only genres of visual art in which Rembrandt transformed existing modes of representation and, indeed, ways of seeing, as we shall see in the course of this study. Nevertheless, I have already said enough to substantiate my claim regarding the revolutionary nature of Rembrandt's art, and can therefore now move on to the question of how that art came about and what made it possible.

Rembrandt as Bourgeois Artist

So where does Rembrandt stand in relation to Dutch art and Dutch society? In some respects he is its supreme representative, the bourgeois artist par excellence.

Born in Leiden, the ninth son of a miller and his relatively prosperous wife, his background was classically petty bourgeois, the typical class position of the artist under capitalism.[3]

His talent showed itself early, and by the age of twenty he was established as an independent painter. At twenty-three he was spotted by a man of power, Constantijn Huygens, secretary to Stadtholder Frederick Henry, and by his late twenties he was a highly successful, probably the most successful, painter in Amsterdam.

Judging by his output at the beginning of his career, Rembrandt's original intention was to be a history painter, that is, a painter of action scenes from the Bible and classical mythology (traditionally regarded as the highest form of painting). Approximately two-thirds of his known paintings from the period 1625 to 1629 are history paintings.

Thereafter, roughly coinciding with his recognition by Huygens, the proportion of history paintings declines abruptly to about one in five, remaining roughly at that level for the rest of his life. Instead Rembrandt turned to portrait painting, and portraits (including group portraits and self-portraits) make up two-thirds or more of his subsequent work.[4] Of these a substantial proportion, and the main means by which Rembrandt earned his very considerable living, were commissions to paint portraits or group portraits of members of the Dutch bourgeoisie, and for the most part these were paintings which the clients would have been pleased to receive.

This does not mean that these were inferior or hackworks. On the contrary, most of them are extremely good of their kind, executed with exemplary technical skill and acute psychological insight. Let us take for example the 1634 portrait of Maerten Soolmans (one of a typical marriage pair with wife Oopjen Coppit). Soolmans is clearly a fashionable man about town and a flashy dresser. Rembrandt makes this the occasion for a tour de force of lace painting, particularly with regard to the outrageous rosettes on Soolmans's shoes. There is, one suspects, a slight element of irony or mockery in Rembrandt's portrayal of this self-satisfied young man, but it is unlikely that a man who could wear such rosettes would detect it.

Rembrandt produced many such society portraits, and they are far from being his greatest work. Nevertheless, besides exceptional naturalistic technique and verisimilitude, they also usually have built into them an inner dynamism or movement in the pose and the contrast of light and dark which distinguishes them from the average, rather wooden, portrait of the day.

An outstanding example of these qualities is *The Anatomy Lesson of Dr Nicolaes Tulp* (1632). It is clear that the group portrait had a special place in the culture of the ascendant Dutch bourgeoisie – Schutterij (paintings of militia companies like *The Night Watch*), regents of almshouses and charitable boards (like the aforementioned works by Hals), burgomasters and guild masters, surgeons' anatomy lessons; all these were established conventions of Dutch painting. In them, the Dutch burghers sought to find themselves reflected as strong, confident, united, moral, dignified, learned, austere, the epitome of whatever Protestant and bourgeois virtues were appropriate for the role and occasion.

It is also clear that Rembrandt's *Anatomy Lesson* exists within these conventions. It was his first commission for a large group portrait, indeed one of his first commissions of any kind, and it seems likely that he wished to please his clients, the Amsterdam Guild of Surgeons. Yet the painting is a masterpiece of social and psychological observation – each surgeon so similar but different – and of formal composition. The angle of each head and each hand, the line of each nose and point of each beard, the light on each forehead and each ruff forms a living pyramid looming over the pallid laid-out corpse and its red flayed arm. The subject matter of the painting allows for much speculative interpretation regarding 'the body as text', the social role of surgeons and science, the development of anatomical knowledge and the treatment of criminals (the body is that of Adriaen Adriaensz, known as 'the child', a hanged criminal). But this is secondary to my point, which is that despite the fact that the painting lacks 'soul' or intensity of feeling and is basically a publicity painting, it still puts most group portraits of the time, or any other time, in the shade by virtue of its inner dynamism.

On those occasions when Rembrandt finds something genuinely admirable or moving in his sitters, he achieves even greater wonders within the framework of the commissioned portrait. The marvellous portraits of Jacob Trip and Margaretha de Geer discussed at the beginning of this study fall into this category, though they break with some of its conventions. So does the extraordinary *De Staalmeesters* or *The Sampling Officials* (1662). This has all the merits of *The Anatomy Lesson* raised to a higher level, to virtual perfection. The arrangement of the six figures round the table is apparently natural and straightforward but in reality is a masterpiece of subtle calculation designed to bring the whole group to life as a differentiated totality.

The miraculously painted red tablecloth bathes the whole canvas in warm light. And for all their evident dignity and stature, Rembrandt captures the hardness in the sampling officials' characters required for their role but, as with the portrait of Maerten Soolmans, with so deft a touch that men of such character could hardly take offence. In my opinion it is the greatest painting of its genre in history.

Two other examples of this kind are the portraits of the Amsterdam merchant Nicolaes Ruts (1631) and of Jan Six (1654). *De Staalmeesters* is the work of an ageing master, displaying all his accumulated craft. The *Portrait of Nicolaes Ruts* is work of a young virtuoso – Rembrandt was only twenty-five – but it still shows great maturity as well as brilliant technique. If the technique is seen in the rendering of the velvet hat and fur coat, it is first and foremost the pose – the grip of the right hand, the slight forward inclination of the body, the hint of the braced shoulders, the angle of the head across the body, the implied statement or question in the left hand holding the note – which lends the figure its dynamism. This is complemented by the facial expression, with its clear piercing eyes. As Simon Schama has pointed out, the fur also tells an interesting story:

> For Nicolaes Ruts is literally wearing his stock in trade: sable. No fabric of any kind – not Persian silk, not Indian calico, not French-worked damask – was more precious than sable . . . the fur that was used by the Muscovite Tsars as diplomatic gifts and treaty-sweeteners. . . . And yet for all the unparalleled magnificence of the coat that sits on the shoulders of the fur trader, Rembrandt has managed to avoid the least impression of vanity or idle opulence. . . . He is the epitome of the entrepreneur-as-man-of-action – not a complete fiction, since the Muscovy fur trade [out of Arkhangelsk] was certainly one of the more heroically risky of the 'fine' trades.[5]

Schama goes on to say it is no wonder that the painting was later bought by J. P. Morgan since there has never been 'a better portrait of the businessman as hero'.[6]

Jan Six, who was for a period Rembrandt's friend, was an even richer and more prominent merchant than Ruts. Six inherited his wealth from his grandfather's textile business and retired from business in 1652 to devote himself to poetry, art collecting and various state duties, serving as maritime commissioner in 1659 and mayor of Amsterdam in 1691. He was without doubt one of the most distinguished representatives of the Dutch ruling class in the Golden Age. Yet Rembrandt's portrait of him is distinguished by its extremely effective combination of bright colours (red, yellow and grey), and even more so by the exceptional freedom and looseness of the brushwork, especially on the hands, the buttons and the scarlet cloak with its yellow braid. In its handling of paint, the portrait looks forward to Goya, 150 years later, and even Manet, two hundred years later.

But the point is that this was an age in which a painter of Rembrandt's sensitivity could paint a businessman as hero and a member of the ruling class in the manner of Goya or Manet without satirising him, and not just because the voyage to Arkhangelsk was fraught with peril or because Jan Six was a man of taste, but because the Dutch bourgeoisie were the makers and products of a heroic revolution. It was not an age that was to last long.

This history of art shows that there are periods when certain kinds of paintings are possible and then periods when they cease to be possible. If one compares Piero della Francesca's *The Baptism of Christ* or his *Resurrection* with Stanley Spencer's *Resurrection in Cookham*, or Mathias Grünewald's *Crucifixion* with Salvador Dalí's *Christ of St John of the Cross*, it is clear that the time of great Christian art is over and cannot be restored by any act of will. Velázquez could produce a masterpiece like his *Pope Innocent X*. For Francis Bacon to make serious art of this material it had to come out as the 'Screaming Pope'. Holbein could paint a great portrait of Henry VIII. All recent portraits of British royalty are complete rubbish. The era when a great artist could paint a great portrait of a businessman or ruler did not last long and came to a definitive end in the mid-nineteenth century, about the time of the 1848 revolutions. Jacques-Louis David, who during the French Revolution voted for the death of Louis XVI, could glorify Napoleon in *Napoleon Crossing the Alps* (1805). Picasso, despite being a member of the Communist Party and willing to try, could do nothing with Stalin.

Rembrandt was the supreme bourgeois artist, not only in his portraits of the Dutch bourgeoisie, but also in his portraits of himself. Many artists – Dürer, Titian, Rubens et cetera – produced individual self-portraits before Rembrandt, but never in such numbers. Rembrandt produced more than seventy, and he produced them at every stage of his career. For no artist before Rembrandt, and none after until van Gogh, was the self-portrait so central to their output. Nearly all these self-portraits were displayed in a magnificent exhibition at the National

Gallery in 1999. In an unparalleled visual documentation of a life, they recorded Rembrandt's passage from brilliant prodigy to mature master to broken – or is it unbroken – old man. Together they constitute one of the wonders of world culture, taking further, almost to the limit imaginable, the visual representation of personality, of 'self' or of 'soul', that we have already noted at the beginning of this study as a distinctive and revolutionary feature of Rembrandt's art, and which also corresponds to one of the key social and intellectual themes of the rise of the bourgeois epoch, namely the rise of the individual and of individualism.

In *Rembrandt by Himself*, the book accompanying the National Gallery exhibition, this view is rejected. Ernst van de Wetering, in the keynote article, argues that 'the prevailing view of the self-portrait as a means for "self-examination" is an anachronism when applied to the period before 1800',[7] because the notion of the 'self' to be explored dates only from the romantic period (roughly the French Revolution and its aftermath) and was not available to Rembrandt in the seventeenth century. Instead van de Wetering attributes the proliferation of self-portraits to 'the strength of the demand from collectors for these works . . . which were seen as representative of his art and of the techniques for which he was most famous.'[8] This argument links Rembrandt's self-portraits to the rise of capitalism via the art market and the demand of 'consumers' rather than via the consciousness of the artist, and I see no reason to deny the existence of this link, but nor do I see this connection as ruling out or invalidating the kind of explanation I have put forward.

Establishing the reasons for a certain commission or for the demand for certain kinds of works of art does not in itself explain exhaustively the nature of the artist's response to the commission or demand. Ferdinand VII's reasons for commissioning Goya to paint him clearly do not coincide with Goya's motives in carrying out the commission. In 1937, the Spanish Republican government commissioned Picasso to produce 'a work' for the Spanish pavilion in the Paris Exhibition. This is not enough to 'explain' the painting of *Guernica* (though it is part of the explanation).

Also I do not find the claim that 'self-exploration' is anachronistic for Rembrandt a convincing one. A trend towards individuation and individualism is discernible in the art of the Renaissance, both in terms of the representation of individual personalities in the painting (compare Giotto with Giovanni Bellini, or Fra Angelico with Raphael or Titian) and in terms of the status and reputation of the artist with the transition from anonymous artisan to master craftsman to 'divine' genius (Michelangelo).[9]

The Reformation provides a further development of individualism in that it replaces the idea of a relationship with God mediated by the social institution of the church with the idea of a personal relationship with God through the Bible. And is it not the exploration of self in Shakespeare's *Hamlet* which has made it such an archetypal play for the bourgeois epoch? Then there is the fact that Descartes is a coresident with Rembrandt in Amsterdam when he makes *Cogito ergo sum* ('I think, therefore I am') the starting point of his philosophy. Bertrand Russell comments: 'Descartes' fundamental certainty, "I think, therefore I am", made the basis of knowledge different for each person, since for each the starting point was his own existence, not that of other individuals or of the community.... Most philosophy since Descartes has had this intellectually individualistic aspect in a greater or less degree.'[10]

Finally, there is the evidence of the works themselves. There are a number of works which appear to be publicity pieces or may well have been undertaken in response to market demand – for example *Rembrandt and Saskia* (ca. 1635), the *Self-Portrait Wearing a Hat* (1632), the *Self-Portrait* (1634), and the famous *Self-Portrait* (1640) in the National Gallery, where the pose is derived from Titian's *Portrait of a Man*, mentioned earlier. However, there are many others where market forces are simply not a plausible explanation for their production. There are the 'tronies', tiny etchings in which Rembrandt has used his own face as a model for 'heads' depicting certain emotions, such as the 1630 series of four (*'Self-Portrait' Wide-Eyed*, *'Self-Portrait' with Angry Expression*, *'Self-Portrait' Smiling* and *'Self-Portrait' Open-Mouthed*). Some art historians regard these tronies as purely technical exercises, practice for the depiction of emotion in history painting, but these striking little works contain a lively sharpness and a darkness which suggests an element of personal identification and self-expression. Then there are the very informal pen-and-ink drawings of himself at work such as *Self-Portrait Seated* (ca. 1636), where he is shown with short, tousled hair and a very casual open shirt, and the beautifully simple full-length *Self-Portrait* (ca. 1650) in which he stands with arms akimbo in his working clothes. Or there is the *Model Sheet with Self-Portrait* (ca. 1651), where a single sheet shows an etching of a beggar, a self-portrait next to it, and beneath the portrait – at a ninety-degree angle – a mother and child. Or the self-portrait *Drawing on an Etching-Plate* (ca. 1658) in which the self-representation is so unflattering as to exclude the possibility that it was primarily market driven.

Above all, there is the series of self-portraits from near the end of his life. From the final decade (1659–69) there are twelve full-size paintings, and from the last year at least three. Just as *De Staalmeesters* is the greatest painting of its kind, so these are the finest of all self-portraits, and they immediately confront the writer with the difficulty referred to in the preface to this study – the inadequacy of anything one can write in the face of the works. Yet faced with the argument that such masterpieces are simply a response to market demand, one has to say something, even if what is said is not the kind of thing that can be supported by documents or proved by evidence other than the paintings themselves. The *Self-Portrait with Beret and Turned-Up Collar* (1659) is an unsurpassed masterpiece of humane realism. Standing before the original in the National Gallery exhibition, I felt I was seeing a living presence looming from the surface of a darkened pool. The final four self-portraits – the *Self-Portrait with Two Circles* (1665–9) which hangs in Kenwood House in north London, and the three from 1669 itself – are like a summing up of the artist's life. The Kenwood portrait shows us the old artist, battered by life's woes but still standing firm and strong, monumental in his craft and his defiance. The next two, *Self-Portrait at the Age of Sixty-Three* in the National Gallery and *Self-Portrait* in the Uffizi, Florence, show unmistakeable signs of decline – not decline in the artist's powers but of something starting to fail inside the man. The process seems more advanced in the Uffizi portrait than in the National Gallery one. By the time we get to what is probably the very last of the series, the *Self-Portrait* in the Hague Mauritshuis, the man's mainspring has gone. Yet the painting constitutes a kind of amazing paradox in that someone this broken down by life ought not to have been able to paint this picture. We enter here the territory which the American poet William Carlos Williams attempted to describe when he wrote, 'Everyone in this life is defeated, but a man, if he be a man, is not defeated.'[11]

Of course, all this can be dismissed as fanciful speculation, but unless some communication of this kind is possible in art (however imperfectly or inaccurately I may have expressed it), it is hard to see any point in taking it seriously. The view that the profusion of self-portraits in Rembrandt's oeuvre is explicable in terms of consumer demand is not only false, but also a reflection within art history of the ideology of the supremacy of the consumer and the omnipotence of the market. Greatly preferable is Arnold Hauser's formulation that '[i]t was only in a bourgeois period of art, such as the Dutch seventeenth century, that the subjective conception of painting was possible which produced the flood of self-portraits of Rembrandt'.[12]

The Anti-Capitalist Rembrandt

It is a dialectical principle that any tendency pushed to its extreme turns into its opposite. So it is with bourgeois individualism – a product, indeed a great achievement, of the rise of capitalism. Individualism, taken beyond a certain point, comes into conflict with capitalist society (we should not forget Marx's description of communist society in the *Communist Manifesto* as 'an association in which the free development of each is the condition for the free development of all'). This is what happens with Rembrandt's self-portraits. Analysing the 1669 Uffizi *Self-Portrait*, John Berger writes:

> In [this] painting he has turned the tradition against itself. He has wrested its language away from it. He is an old man. All has gone except a sense of the question of existence, of existence as a question. And the painter in him – who is both more and less than the old man – has found the means to express just that, using a medium which has been traditionally developed to exclude any such question.[13]

The tradition of oil painting to which Berger refers is a tradition obsessed with the visible representation of property, commodities and status, 'not so much a framed window open on to the world as a safe set into the wall, a safe in which the visible has been deposited'.[14] This is the tradition Rembrandt contests with weapons forged by the tradition.[15] The late self-portraits are implicitly anti-capitalist in the double sense that they are a sympathetic representation of someone who has been broken down by the vicissitudes of life in capitalist society, and that they embody an intense humanism which is incompatible with the values and norms of a society based on production for profit, not human need.

Of course the word 'implicitly' must be heavily stressed here. There can be no question of attributing to Rembrandt some kind of conscious anti-capitalist ideology or critique of capitalism. Some 150 years before Babeuf's Conspiracy of the Equals in the French Revolution, two hundred years before the utopian socialists and the Chartists, never mind Marx and Engels, and with no equivalent in the Dutch Revolt of Thomas Müntzer or Gerrard Winstanley, Rembrandt could not possibly have held a coherent anti-capitalist political position. But he could rebel, spontaneously and intuitively, against the experience of capitalist social relations, against the way capitalism treated people, and unlike most such spontaneous and intuitive rebels, he had a means of expressing his rebellion in his work.

In fact, rebellious, critical and implicitly anti-capitalist elements are not at all confined to Rembrandt's last works or even to the period of his own financial difficulties and relative lack of success after 1656. On the contrary, they are present throughout his career, including during the period of his early success, even if only in latent form and even if they remain subordinate to the dominant bourgeois elements. Their most basic manifestation is in what Rembrandt does not paint. Of the various genres of Dutch art, it is noticeable that Rembrandt produces almost no still lifes – he has no interest in trompe l'oeil effects or the naturalistic rendering of food and other commodities for its own sake – and no paintings of sea battles or marine paintings of any kind, and virtually nothing that was in any way militaristic, except the special case of *The Night Watch*, which will be discussed shortly. Either Rembrandt had no interest in matters naval, colonial and martial, or he received no such commissions because the authorities in these areas had no interest in his style of painting, or both.

In sharp contrast there is his remarkable predilection for depicting the outcasts and outsiders of Dutch society. In his career as a whole, Rembrandt etched or drew more than twenty-five images of beggars and several others of poor people whose situation was not far removed from beggary, such as the etchings of *The Rat Killer* (1632), *The Spanish Gypsy* (ca. 1642) and *Peasant Family on the Tramp* (1652). Of these, sixteen or seventeen were done before he reached the age of twenty-five in 1631, and it seems reasonable to suppose that many of them were drawn from life in Leiden, where pauperism was particularly intense. I have already described the treatment of, and prevailing attitude towards, beggars in the Dutch Republic. In such a context, Rembrandt's studies are an act of defiance. Here we encounter the leper with his clapper, the beggar with a wooden leg, the seated beggar warming his hands, the seated beggar with his dog, the blind fiddler led by his dog on a string, the gaunt mother begging with a child in her arms (the contemporary resonance is unmistakeable). Of course, it is not the subject matter itself but its treatment that determines the nature of the work. It has always been possible to picture the poor sentimentally or voyeuristically or as curiosities, but there is no trace of these attitudes here.[16] Kenneth Clark refers to Rembrandt's 'sympathy for poor people'[17] and provides documentary support in the form of testimony from a contemporary, Joachim von Sandrart, who complained that Rembrandt 'did not at all know how to keep his station, and always associated with the lower orders'.[18] But sympathy is not quite the right word for the standpoint of these works. Identification and solidarity are nearer the mark, as evidenced by what is perhaps the most extraordinary of all this series, namely the etching *Beggar Seated on a Bank* (1630), where he portrays himself as a beggar.

Another marginal group who were frequently the focus of Rembrandt's attention were the Jews. The Amsterdam Jews benefitted from the unique religious tolerance operating in Dutch society – that is why they came there from Spain and central Europe – but they remained outsiders nonetheless, and were subject to a degree of oppression.[19] It is sometimes said that Rembrandt was attracted to the Jews as subjects because he saw in them the people of the Old Testament. Be that as it may, personal association and friendship also played a major part as Rembrandt's house in Amsterdam, until forced by poverty to move in 1658, was located in Sint-Antoniesbreestraat (today Jodenbreestraat – the Jewish Broad Street) in the heart of the Jewish quarter. The Jewish community was divided into Sephardim from Spain known as *marranos* (swine) who fled the Inquisition, and Ashkenazim from Germany who fled the Thirty Years War. The Sephardim were few in number but tended to be wealthy and educated. The Ashkenazim were more numerous but poorer and less cultured.

Rembrandt painted and etched them both. Of the Sephardim, who were freer in their attitude to graven images, we get named and commissioned portraits such as *The Jewish Physician Ephraim Bueno* (1647) and the etching of the famous Rabbi Menasseh ben Israel. Of the Ashkenazim we get studies of anonymous figures such as the *Portrait of a Young Jew* (1661) and the highly unusual etching of *The Synagogue* (1648). Then there is the equally unusual series of portraits of Christ with Jewish features (I count nine). All in all, Fowkes calculates that 'of two hundred male portraits . . . which the artist made, thirty-seven, nearly one-fifth, are identified as Jews: a remarkably high number since Jews represented little more than 1 per cent of the city's population'.[20]

To this we can add Rembrandt's portrayal of blacks – there are about six works in all, including a wonderful double portrait, *Two Negroes* (1661), which contains not a hint of racial stereotyping – and his interest in people, art and things Asian. Not only do we have three paintings of men in oriental costume, all strongly sympathetic, but also a number of copies of miniatures from Moghul India including, fascinatingly, a drawing of Shah Jahan (who 'built' the Taj Mahal). Regarding the Indian miniatures, K. G. Boon comments, 'He was probably the first European to recognise their unique beauty.'[21] Finally, there is Rembrandt's deeply affectionate representation of old people, which begins in his early twenties, and his uniquely anti-sexist portrayal of women, discussed earlier.

Running through Rembrandt's depictions of the oppressed is one of the most distinctive characteristics of his art – the ability to paint or draw from 'inside' the mind and body of his subjects. As John Berger has said, this is contrary to the dominant tradition of European oil painting, which is one of exteriorisation. Normally the artist paints with the eye of the observer – the voyeur or perhaps lover in most nudes, the prostitute's client (in Manet's *Olympia* and Picasso's *Les Demoiselles d'Avignon*), the visitor to the house in a de Hooch interior, to the estate in Gainsborough's *Mr and Mrs Andrews*. The reversal of this relationship is a 'political' characteristic – it is 'solidarity in paint'. It is not present in all Rembrandt's works, in many of the society portraits, even in the masterpieces like *The Anatomy Lesson* and *De Staalmeesters*, or his paintings of Saskia as Flora, for instance, but it is a key factor in some of the 'oddities' we find scattered through his oeuvre, moments of disturbance which often upset or puzzle the art historians because they are so 'different'.

I shall give four examples. First, *The Rape of Proserpine* (ca. 1628–9). The abduction of Proserpine by Pluto, king of the underworld, was a well-known classical theme from Ovid, also treated by Rubens and others. In Rubens, Proserpine is shown with her arms dramatically flung back over her head. In Rembrandt, she is clawing at Pluto's face. Kenneth Clark comments:

> [Rembrandt's] sense of truth would not allow him to accept the ineffectual eloquence of those flung-back arms, with which, by classical convention, Sabine women and other heroines of antique legend convey the information that they are being raped. What in fact would a decent young Dutch girl do in the situation? Kick and scratch: scratch his eyes out.[22]

Clark notices the key difference but misunderstands and makes light of it. It is not about down-to-earth Dutch realism – it is about identification. Rembrandt is 'with' Proserpine – Rubens and Clark are not.

Second, *The Rape of Ganymede* (1635). Once again the story comes from Ovid, who tells how Jove 'burned with love' for the young Ganymede and transformed himself into an eagle to whisk him off to be his servant and plaything on Olympus. Rembrandt's dark and dramatic painting is clearly derived, but also different, from an engraving by Beatrizet which is taken from a lost original by Michelangelo. In the Beatrizet/Michelangelo version, Ganymede is a beautiful young man who submits ecstatically to the grip of the great bird-god. In Rembrandt Ganymede is a young child, almost a baby, who screams and urinates in terror at his sudden seizure. The contrast has occasioned much debate, with the Rembrandt being called, absurdly, 'a comedy' and 'a grotesque parody', and by Kenneth Clark 'a protest not only against antique art, but against antique morality', and 'a protestant-Christian revulsion against the sexual practices of paganism that Michelangelo's version so clearly implies'.[23] Whatever the truth of this, one factor in Rembrandt's treatment is simply that Rembrandt is feeling 'with' Ganymede.

My third example is one of Rembrandt's most extraordinary works, *Slaughtered Ox* (1655).[24] It is extraordinary in the sense that it fits none of the standard genres of the time (though, of course, the subject reaches back to the caves of Lascaux and forward to Damien Hirst) except, formally, still life. In fact it is anything but a still life – nothing could be further removed from an edible lobster. Rembrandt's ox is flayed, splayed and crucified upside down, like St Peter, on a frame.

Hélène Cixous writes, almost poetically:

> Why do we adore *The Slaughtered Ox*? Because without our knowing it or wanting it, it is our anonymous humanity. . . . We are this creature, which even turned upside down and decapitated and hung beneath the earth – when it is seen with those eyes that don't reject the below, that don't prefer the above – maintains its majesty.
>
> Behold the portrait of our mortality. The being hung there (by its shins), turned upside down, twice decapitated.
>
> What we become under the axe and the slicer.
>
> There is a butcher shop on our life's path. As children we would pass trembling before the butcher's window. Later on we want to forget death. We cut the dead one up into pieces and we call it meat.[25]

The poetics are justified because Rembrandt has painted from within the ox.

Finally there is a small drawing, *A Woman on the Gallows* (1664). This is Rembrandt's judgment on the Dutch Republic's justice system. Apparently drawn from life, it depicts a Danish girl hanging in chains on the gibbet, with an axe, the instrument of her crime, displayed beside her. It is the simplest of drawings and yet it exudes the profoundest sympathy with this poor little woman, her eyes closed in death, her narrow shoulders hunched against the rope and her tiny arms hanging limply before her. The death penalty always poses directly the question: Whose side are you on? Not between the victim of crime and the criminal, as the Right would have it, but between the state and its victim. Here Rembrandt gives his quiet but definitive answer. He draws from 'inside' the woman on the gallows.

How is all this anti-capitalist? It is simply that this degree of human solidarity cannot fail to clash with the logic and priorities of a system driven by the competitive accumulation of capital. Capitalism rests on alienated labour.[26] The alienation of labour results in the alienation of workers not only from the products of their labour, but also from themselves, from their fellows and from nature.

Rembrandt's art, his creative labour, is continually trying to challenge these alienations, to reach out across these divisions.

Any argument about the anti-capitalist implications of Rembrandt's art must deal with the question of what is possibly his most famous painting, though by no means his best, *The Night Watch*, or *The Militia Company of Captain Frans Banning Cocq* (1642), even though this is something of a diversion. This is because for a long time a myth surrounded this painting – a myth which informed by far the best known account of his life, namely Alexander Korda's 1937 film with Charles Laughton in the title role. *The Night Watch* was an example of the common genre of Dutch painting known as *schutterij*, paintings of companies of civic guards who had played an important role defending Dutch cities in the revolt against Spain, and who had also taken on a certain law-and-order policing role. The story was that members of the company paid Rembrandt one hundred guilders each for the commission, but were bitterly disappointed by the result because of the painting's darkness and failure to provide a satisfactory portrait of each guard, and that this was the start of the artist's descent into isolation and poverty. Art historians today are virtually unanimous that there is no evidence to support this tale and that there is plenty of evidence to show that Rembrandt continued to receive prestigious commissions.

However, it is not difficult to see how the legend arose, for, circumstantial and documentary evidence aside, the painting itself provides evidence that it was a radical and challenging work. The Amsterdam Rijksmuseum displays *The Night Watch* alongside other paintings of militia companies by contemporaries such as Bartholomeus van der Helst, Joachim von Sandrart and Thomas de Keyser. The difference is striking. In the latter paintings the companies are lined up and arranged in a static pose, rather like a wedding photograph, with each guard's head clearly depicted and more or less equally lit (as are the surgeons in Rembrandt's *Anatomy Lesson of Dr Nicolaes Tulp*). In *The Night Watch* the company is presented in apparently chaotic, but in fact carefully structured, dynamic movement, marching out of the darkness into the light.[27] Some figures (a rather inappropriate but brightly lit girl and a shadowy dog) have been added. Others are pushed into the background or half hidden by outstretched arms. It is clear that what Rembrandt has done is subordinate the requirements of the commission to his own purposes as an artist, to his own urge to create a complex symphony of movement and light. As his pupil Samuel van Hoogstraten put it in 1678, 'In the opinion of many he went too far, making more of the overall picture according to his individual preference than of the individual portraits he was commissioned to do.'[28]

If Rembrandt got away with *The Night Watch*, he was less fortunate with what was probably the biggest commission he ever received, the order in 1660 from the Amsterdam city fathers to paint *The Conspiracy of the Batavians* (*The Conspiracy of Claudius Civilis: The Oath*) for the new town hall. The commission was for a vast painting of great patriotic significance because the Dutch bourgeoisie viewed the rebellion of Claudius Civilis against the Romans as the forerunner of their own revolt against the Spanish, much as the English view Queen Boudicca or Alfred the Great. Unfortunately, Rembrandt's painting remained in the town hall for only a few months before it was rejected as unsatisfactory. As a result Rembrandt, desperate for money by this time, cut the huge painting down to make it saleable, and only the truncated fragment remains. Documentary evidence of the reasons for the rejection has not survived (which means there is much speculative debate), but clearly

Rembrandt's mystic eerie treatment, reminiscent in my opinion of the atmosphere in *Macbeth* and *King Lear*, was deemed inappropriate for the purpose of the invention of heroic nationalist tradition.

Rembrandt's artistic solidarity with the oppressed in Dutch society, and the clash at certain points between his art and the requirements of the Dutch bourgeoisie, raises the question of what values he counterposed to rampant Dutch capitalism. In the name of what did he rebel?[29] As we have said, it was not and could not have been in the name of a worked-out socialist programme or a revolutionary proletariat, or even a revolutionary peasantry (there was no significant peasant revolt in the United Provinces). It might possibly have been in the name of a former 'Golden Age' set far in the past, à la Rousseau, or an idealised feudalism like that of the pre-Raphaelites or William Morris[30] or Ezra Pound,[31] or a romanticised nature as in Wordsworth, Keats and even Shelley at times. But it was not any of these things. Nor do such tendencies appear to have existed to any degree in Dutch society. Rather, Rembrandt's rebellion seems to have been in the name of a profound personal humanitarianism, a deep personal tenderness and intimacy – 'the intimacy of intimacy, intimitude'[32] as Cixous calls it – one might say 'love' if the word had not been so trivialised and exploited.

This seems to fit with, or at least to be compatible with, the known facts of Rembrandt's life: with his gradual withdrawal from the social scene from the late 1640s onwards, following the death of Saskia and a dreadful relationship with Geertje Dircx,[33] into the bosom of his new 'family' with Hendrickje and Titus; with his and Hendrickje's conflict with the church authorities over their 'living in sin' (in 1654, Hendrickje was summoned four times to appear before the council of the Reformed Church – three times she did not go, but on the fourth she did and was condemned for practising 'whoredom'); and with the intensification of his retreat after his bankruptcy in 1656. It also fits, again and again, with the work. Two of his last works, which exemplify the quality I am talking about, are *The Return of the Prodigal Son* (ca. 1668) and *The Jewish Bride* (ca. 1668)

The Return of the Prodigal Son depicts the denouement of the parable, when the lost son is forgiven by his father. As Arnold Hauser has noticed, the painting dematerialises reality in a way reminiscent of Michelangelo's last work, the *Rondanini Pietà*.[34] The four standing figures are ungrounded. They float, spectre-like, in the darkness. The head of the son is barely more than a modelled outline, his body almost wasted beneath his rough clothes. The only really substantial part of the painting, the only thing that really counts, is the father's gesture of reconciliation, the diamond of his arms embracing the head and shoulders of the boy. It is the placing of the hands that is decisive, not clutching, grabbing or seizing, but open and flat, fingers slightly apart, resting lightly but firmly on the shoulder and upper back, the essence of compassion and reassurance.

The Prodigal Son reminds us how often hands, and the gestures of hands, play a central role in Rembrandt's paintings. At the beginning of this study I noted the absence of hands in the *Rokeby Venus*, and elsewhere in the representation of nude women, and pointed to the contrast in Rembrandt's *Bathsheba*. Then there is the dark silhouetted hand at the centre of *The Apostle Peter Denying Christ* (1660); the hand of the dying old man caressing the head of the child in *Jacob Blessing the Sons of Joseph* (1656); the hands of the surgeon at the head of the corpse in *The Anatomy Lesson of Doctor Deyman* (1656); the hand of the philosopher reaching out to the poet in *Aristotle Contemplating a Bust of Homer* (1653); the astonishing right hand of Abraham clasping the face of Isaac, at once violent and gentle, and the hand of the angel gripping Abraham's left wrist before he can strike at his son's throat in *The Angel Stopping Abraham from Sacrificing Isaac to God* (1635); the upturned outstretched right hand of Captain Cocq at the focal point of *The Night Watch*; the gesture of wonder and welcome in the *Danaë*; the arm of the woman crisscrossing with the arm of the cherub and her fingers resting on his cheek in Hendrickje Stoffels as *Venus* (1658); and many others. It is not a trick or trademark – there are many more works in which hands do not appear or are not particularly important – but it is a motif to which Rembrandt returns, consciously or unconsciously, again and again: the helping hand, the hand of friendship, the touch of love, the hand that is the mark of our humanity.

Now let us turn to *The Jewish Bride.*[35] It is a sublime masterpiece in which forty years of accumulated craft and experience in the laying of paint on canvas are brought to bear, not for a display of virtuosity but in order to make a visual statement about the potential for love between two human beings. The atmosphere of the painting derives in considerable part from the clothes of the couple. The technique deployed here is the equal of Holbein's in *The Ambassadors* or Bellini's in *The Doge*, but it does its best to conceal itself, and the clothes have nothing to do with marking the status of the sitters. They are there for colour. The coral red of the bride's dress combines with the dark and shining golds of the groom's tunic and cloak to create a mellow warmth that suffuses the canvas. Within this glow, it is the positioning of the hands that holds the eye and delivers the painting's emotional message. His left hand resting lightly on her left shoulder and drawing her in; his right hand crossing her right arm and alighting open-palmed on her breast in the gentlest of caresses; her left hand just grazing his knuckles in acceptance. A tenderness unsurpassed in European art and not without reason, for it is the antithesis of capitalist competition and exploitation, bourgeois marriage as prostitution, alienation and reification and the reduction of human beings to 'appendages of the machine'.[36]

CHAPTER 5

A Revolution in Paint: One Hundred Years of Picasso's *Demoiselles*

First published in International Socialism *115 (Summer 2007)*

The year 2007 marked the centenary of the painting of *Les Demoiselles d'Avignon* by Pablo Picasso. There cannot be many paintings whose anniversary would occasion an analysis in the discourse of socialist theory – an honour usually reserved for revolutions and other great events in the history of the class struggle – nevertheless, *Les Demoiselles* certainly repays serious consideration. Aside from its individual stature as one of the outstanding paintings of the twentieth century, there is its enormous importance as a turning point in the history of art and, indeed, wider cultural history, and also its powerful resonance today.

Les Demoiselles d'Avignon is an oil painting on canvas begun by Picasso in late 1906 and completed in the summer of 1907. It is eight feet tall, seven feet eight inches wide, and has hung since 1937 in the Museum of Modern Art in New York. The painting depicts five nude women, clearly prostitutes in a brothel. Of the three women on the left, the leftmost is shown side on, apparently drawing back a curtain to reveal the others, and the second and third are shown frontally, staring straight out of the canvas. The depiction of all three women, especially the head of the furthest left, is influenced by ancient Iberian (prehistoric 'Spanish') sculpture that Picasso had seen the previous year in the Louvre. The two women on the right, one standing slightly in the background between curtains, the other squatting in the foreground, have been given heads that resemble the African sculptures or masks that the artist is known to have seen in the Musée d'Ethnographie du Trocadéro. The bodies of all the women are rendered by means of flat, angular planes of colour with little shading or modelling. Jutting out at the centre of the bottom of the painting is a bowl of fruit – a melon, grapes, a pear and an apple. The painting received its title not from Picasso but from his friend André Salmon in 1916, and it is either, depending on interpretation, euphemistic or ironic for it refers to a brothel or brothels on the Carrer d'Avinyo in Barcelona, of which Picasso evidently had personal experience.

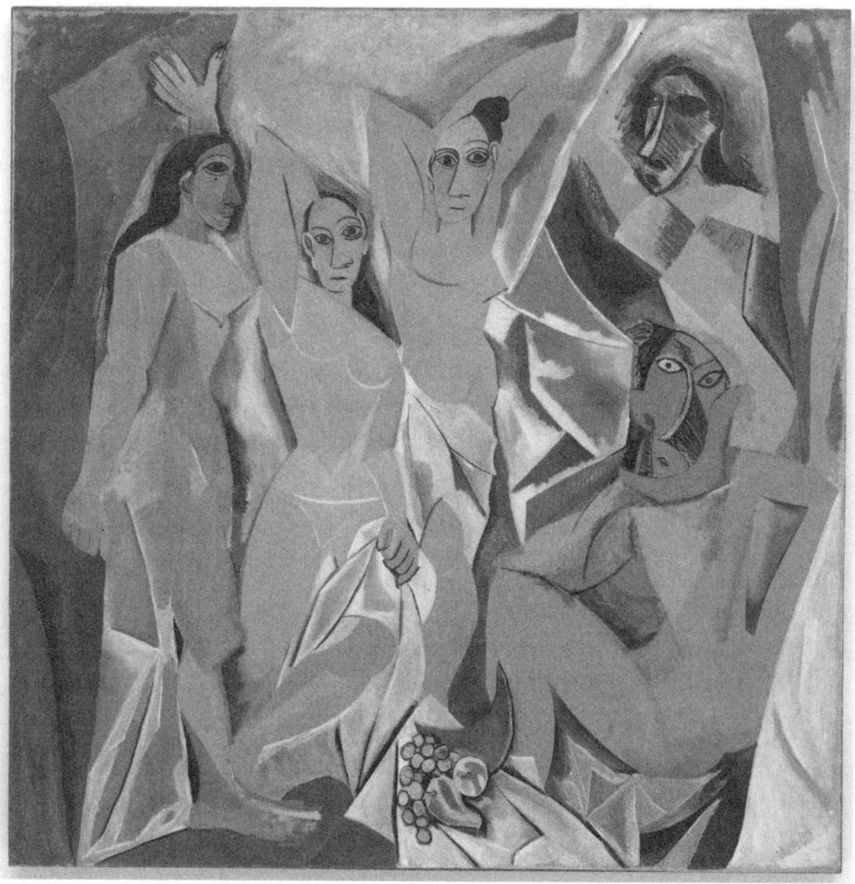

Pablo Picasso, *Les Desmoiselles d'Avignon* (1907)

So much for the basic facts. By far the most frequent comment on *Les Demoiselles*, in both journalism and art history, is that it marks 'the birth of modern art'.[1] Let us first consider the justification for, and truth of, this bold claim.

Les Demoiselles and Modern Art

The simplest, most widespread, distinction between 'traditional art' (by which is meant European art from about 1300 onwards) and 'modern art' is that the former was engaged, at a minimum (it did other, more important, things as well) in the attempt to imitate the appearance of people, objects and scenes in the real world, whereas the latter is not. Traditional art is commonly portrayed as representational, naturalistic or 'realistic',[2] whereas modern art either wilfully distorts physical appearances or, in abstract art, abandons them altogether. There are numerous problems with this crude distinction, not least the difficulty involved in regarding paintings of Madonnas, angels and Venuses as 'realistic', but there is also clearly some truth in it. At least the faces of the Madonnas, the tunics of the angels and the breasts of the Venuses looked like observable faces, tunics and breasts. And while some 'traditional' artists (Hans Holbein, John Constable, Gustave Courbet) are more mimetic (imitative) than others (Sandro Botticelli, Hieronymus Bosch, El Greco) and some 'moderns' (Paul Klee, Wassily Kandinsky) more expressionist or abstract than others (Amedeo Modigliani, Pierre Bonnard), one has only to compare a representative list of traditionals with a similar list of moderns to get the point – on the one hand, Jan van Eyck, Piero della Francesca, Titian, Rembrandt, Diego Velázquez, Thomas Gainsborough, Francisco Goya, Édouard Manet and Vincent van Gogh who, despite the immense differences between them, were all engaged in producing recognisable images of persons and things; on the other hand Georges Braque, Kandinsky, Kazimir Malevich, Piet Mondrian, Max Ernst, Joan Miró, Jackson Pollock and Mark Rothko who, despite their differences, were not.

The tipping point between the two – the clearest, most decisive assault on the past, the key breakthrough to the new – is indeed *Les Demoiselles d'Avignon*. Before *Les Demoiselles,* even Picasso's own work, his 'blue' and 'rose' periods, was clearly a continuation of the mimetic tradition, closer in many ways to Rembrandt, Goya, Manet and van Gogh than to his work of one, two or three years later. *Les Demoiselles* opens the floodgates, first to cubism and then in rapid succession to futurism, synthetic cubism, expressionism, vorticism, abstraction, suprematism, Dadaism and more besides. Within just ten years, artists were producing works, such as Malevich's *Black Square on White* and Duchamp's ready-mades, which would not previously have been regarded as art at all (and were not so regarded by the majority at the time), but which have subsequently achieved, at least within the art world, classic and iconic status. *Les Demoiselles* is a veritable revolution in paint – the art equivalent of the French Revolution, indeed of the Storming of the Bastille.

Another characteristic of traditional art, very closely bound up with its naturalism, was the high level of craft skills it involved and demanded. These skills, developed particularly in the sixteenth and seventeenth centuries, lay especially in the precise rendering of surfaces: lace, satin, velvet, sable, glass, silver, feathers, flesh tones, the folds in drapery or robes and so on.[3] This is reflected in the way people commonly talk about art – 'Look at the detail!' or, 'It makes you feel as if you can touch it' – and for many it was these skills that served as the surest guarantee of artistic quality, of the status of traditional paintings as 'real' or 'great' art. In retrospect it can be seen that the premium on these skills was waning from Claude Monet and impressionism onwards, but it was *Les Demoiselles* that was the decisive break. In 1907 it would have looked like not just a move away from the traditional skills, but a full-scale assault on them. This was the beginning of art which would provoke the outraged cry, 'My four-year-old can do better than that!'

For centuries, roughly from the Renaissance to the nineteenth century, 'beauty' was a, perhaps the, dominant concept in aesthetic theory, the value, together with the closely related 'harmonious form', to which it was held that art should aspire. Of course, there was always art which could not reasonably be described as beautiful, for example, the dark fantasies of Bosch or William Hogarth's satirical series (*Marriage à la Mode, The Rake's Progress*, etc.), but such work was generally deemed of a lower order than that of artists such as Botticelli, da Vinci and, especially, Raphael, where beauty and harmonious form were more clearly in evidence. The philosophers Edmund Burke and Immanuel Kant supplemented 'beauty' with the concept of 'the sublime' to accommodate works, such as Michelangelo's *The Last Judgment*, which, if not beautiful, were manifestly awe-inspiring. Above all, the concept of beauty ruled the genre of the female nude, where it had the added advantage of masking or providing an alibi for the issue of sexual desirability and lust. In the tradition of nude painting that stretches through Botticelli, Giorgione, Titian, Rubens, Velázquez, Goya, Ingres and Renoir, the aim of the artists was always to present their female subjects as beautiful. (Rembrandt is, I think, the only significant exception prior to the nineteenth century.) Clear inroads into this tradition were made by Manet's *Olympia*, Paul Cézanne's *Bathers* series and Henri de Toulouse-Lautrec's brothel scenes, but again it is with *Les Demoiselles* that the sharpest confrontation takes place. Picasso not only does not attempt to make the women 'beautiful' but, by the use of the African masks, positively insists on their ugliness (by the conventional standards of the day).

The enormously disturbing newness of *Les Demoiselles* is confirmed by the reaction, not of the public or the critics, but of Picasso's avant-garde artist friends when they first saw it in his studio. Both Matisse and Braque were at first repelled by it. Braque suggested that Picasso had been 'drinking turpentine and spitting fire'[4], while André Derain is alleged to have claimed that 'someday Picasso would hang himself behind his canvas'.[5]

Les Demoiselles and Theories of Modernism

There have been, of course, a number of more rounded and theoretically sophisticated accounts of the emergence of modern art than the simple distinctions discussed so far. Probably the most influential in the twentieth century, at least within the art world, is that of the American art critic Clement Greenberg. Greenberg established himself by being the principal champion of abstract expressionism and for twenty years or so (roughly the mid-1940s to the mid-1960s) was the leading art critic in America and, therefore, the world. His status in art criticism approximated to that of John Maynard Keynes in economics or F. R. Leavis in literature. Greenberg began in the late 1930s as at least a semi-Marxist in the Trotskyist-influenced milieu around *Partisan Review*, but during and after the Second World War moved, like so many, towards a mainstream or right-wing liberalism and in the process became a rigorous formalist in matters of art criticism and history, rejecting, more or less absolutely, any discussion of the content or social context of artworks.

For Greenberg, modernism was more than art and literature: it included 'almost the whole of what is truly alive in our culture',[6] and its essence lay 'in the use of the characteristic methods of a discipline to criticise the discipline itself – not in order to subvert it, but to entrench it more firmly in its area of competence'.[7] Each art form had to demonstrate in practice that the kind of experience it provided was not to be obtained from any other activity. This meant each art form systematically shedding all conventions not essential to its survival as art, and focussing with increasing intensity on its unique and defining characteristics. In the case of painting this was the making of marks on a two-dimensional surface:

> The limitations that constitute the medium of painting – the flat surface, the shape of the support, the properties of pigment – were treated by the Old Masters as negative factors that could be acknowledged only implicitly or indirectly. Modernist painting has come to regard these same limitations as positive factors that are to be acknowledged openly. Manet's paintings became the first modernist ones by virtue of the frankness with which they declared the surfaces on which they were painted. . . . It was the stressing, however, of the ineluctable flatness of the support that remained most fundamental in the processes by which pictorial art criticised and defined itself under modernism. Flatness alone was unique and exclusive to that art. . . . and so modernist painting oriented itself to flatness as it did to nothing else.[8]

Greenberg's account cannot be accepted as adequate or satisfactory. First, it treats the development of art as almost completely (and quite implausibly) autonomous from society, history and politics (except in the very last analysis of the existence of 'modern' society). Second, it operates by the sleight of hand of simply excluding from the canon of modernism all painting not participating in the project of flatness (for example, surrealism, Diego Rivera and the Mexican muralists or Francis Bacon). Nevertheless, the history of European art from about 1850 to 1950 shows that Greenberg has identified a real and important tendency. From Manet, through impressionism, Gauguin, Cézanne, cubism, Kandinsky and Mondrian, to Pollock and abstract expressionism, one can clearly see the compression of the three-dimensional picture space, which had been opened up in the fourteenth and fifteenth centuries.[9] It is like watching a stage in which the backdrop moves ever closer to the apron until it has squeezed out, in Greenberg's words, 'the kind of space that recognisable three-dimensional objects can inhabit'.[10]

There is no single painting that so clearly illustrates and exemplifies Greenberg's argument as *Les Demoiselles*: the stripping away of inessential conventions, the replacement of sculptural modelling by flat planes, the extreme compression of space between background and foreground – all these undergo a qualitative intensification in this work.

If, however, we turn to more Marxist theorisations of modern art, *Les Demoiselles* retains its pivotal role. John Berger does not fully discuss modernism as such, but he clearly regards cubism as the crucial modern movement and the revolutionary art of the twentieth century.[11] For Berger, cubism synthesises the materialism of Gustave Courbet and the dialectics of Cézanne, and is a response to the scientific and technical breakthroughs of the period (Max Planck, Albert Einstein, electricity, the Eiffel Tower, the aeroplane, etc.) and the positive economic promise of monopoly capitalism (the possibility of a world of material plenty and equality) before it was dashed by war and fascism. But for Berger it was by painting *Les Demoiselles* that 'Picasso provoked cubism. It was the spontaneous and . . . primitive insurrection out of which, for good historical reasons, the revolution of cubism developed.'[12]

Perry Anderson's account of modernism in his article "Modernity and Revolution" has a similar point of departure to Berger's but is more systematic and is applied to the culture as a whole, not just painting:

> In my view, 'modernism' can best be understood as a cultural field triangulated by three decisive coordinates. The first... was the codification of a highly formalised academicism in the visual and other arts, which itself was institutionalised within official regimes of states and society still massively pervaded, often dominated, by aristocratic or landowning classes.... The second coordinate is... the still incipient, hence essentially novel, emergence within these societies of the key technologies or inventions of the second industrial revolution: telephone, radio, automobile, aircraft and so on.... The third coordinate... was the imaginative proximity of social revolution.[13]

Les Demoiselles fits neatly into this schema. French art remained dominated by the aristocratic Academy, with its annual salons, more or less until the end of the nineteenth century, and Manet, the impressionists, and the post-impressionists (Seurat, Cézanne, Gauguin, van Gogh) were all met with derision. The automobile was developed, essentially, in the 1890s in Germany and France, and the first mass production was undertaken in the United States in 1902. The Wright brothers made the first powered flights in December 1903, and in September 1906, Alberto Santos-Dumont made a public flight in Paris. Guglielmo Marconi established the world's first radio station in 1897 on the Isle of Wight, and opened the first wireless factory in Chelmsford in 1898. Above all, the attention of Europe was captured by the 1905 Revolution in Russia. Moreover, if we examine the chronology of the landmarks of the modernist revolution in the other art forms, we find that *Les Demoiselles* almost invariably, precedes them: in music, Igor Stravinsky's *The Firebird* was composed in 1910, and *The Rite of Spring* between 1912 and 1913, while the Ballets Russes was formed in 1909 and first performed *L'Après-midi d'un Faune* in 1912; in literature, Marcel Proust's *À la Recherche du Temps Perdu* was begun in 1909, James Joyce's *Dubliners* appeared in 1914, Franz Kafka's *In the Penal Colony* in 1914 and his *Metamorphosis* in 1915.

Even from the standpoint of Georg Lukács, the principal Marxist opponent of modernism, I think it would be fair to say that *Les Demoiselles* exemplifies many of the tendencies – fragmentation, absence of perspective, abandonment of totality – which he held against modernism.

Of course, one can push this too far. From a wider perspective, such as that of Marshall Berman in his powerful work *All That Is Solid Melts into Air*, 'modernism' is a cultural response to the whole experience of 'modernity' (i.e., modern capitalism), not the product of any individual work or artist – and this is surely right. Modern art and modernism would have happened in some form regardless of whether *Les Demoiselles* had been painted. Indeed, in this wider view modernism long predates Picasso, stretching back, perhaps, to Kant and Johann Wolfgang von Goethe, or in painting to Jacques-Louis David and Goya, or Théodore Géricault and Courbet. Perhaps what we really need is the idea of two modernisms: one encompassing the progressive culture of the whole epoch inaugurated by the French and Industrial Revolutions and still continuing today; the other deriving from the specific conjuncture analysed by Anderson and Berger and lasting until the Second World War, which perhaps could be called high modernism (on the model of the High Renaissance or high Stalinism). This would have the advantage of combining Berman's broad dynamic vision with Anderson's rigour, without the latter's numbing pessimism and the door it opens to postmodernism.[14]

Nevertheless, this broad view does not negate the role played by *Les Demoiselles* at a crucial historical moment, or its exceptional influence on the tempo and form of modernism's development. Just as the knowledge that Lenin did not cause or create the Russian Revolution does not exclude the fact that his part in it was greater than that of any other single individual, so understanding the wider historical determination of modernism is perfectly compatible with recognising the exceptional role of this particular work.

The Power of Les Demoiselles

I have so far discussed the impact of *Les Demoiselles* on the development of modern art in purely formal terms, and that was indeed the nature of its influence – it produced a flood of cubist paintings of men with guitars and café tables, not a flood of paintings of prostitutes. Nevertheless, it would not and could not have had this massive formal influence if it had not been such an exceptionally powerful painting in its own right: that is, if its formal innovations had not been seen by other artists (especially Braque) to work in practice. And the moment we consider or analyse the power of *Les Demoiselles* as an individual painting, we have to deal with its subject matter, and see its formal qualities as a way of treating that subject matter. In other words we must view the painting as a totality, a particular fusion or unity of form and content.

This brings us to the simple and inescapable fact that *Les Demoiselles* is a picture of five prostitutes and is about prostitution. However, it is striking how many art historical and journalistic accounts do try to escape this fact or, at least, to avoid any serious discussion of it. *Guardian* art critic Jonathan Jones argues, 'Most of all, this is a painting about looking . . . it's misguided to see [it] as a painting "about" brothels, prostitutes or colonialism.'[15] This is evasion. Yes, it is about looking, but precisely about looking at, and being looked at by, prostitutes. Everything in the picture's composition reinforces this. Many paintings position us when we look at them – Titian's *Venus d'Urbino* makes us the courtesan/Venus's lover or patron, Manet's *A Bar at the Folies-Bergère* makes us a customer ordering a drink – but *Les Demoiselles* fixes us more definitively than any work I can think of: as the client of the brothel for whom the women are displaying themselves. The phallic bowl of fruit jutting upwards in the centre foreground becomes our phallus leading us into the brothel and towards the women. Thus the painting stages an 'in our face' confrontation with the institution of prostitution.

But if *Les Demoiselles* is 'about' prostitution, what exactly is it saying about prostitution?

There is, in the literature, a biographical story which purports to answer this question and thus to 'explain' the meaning of the painting. Picasso had a friend who died of syphilis, having been infected by an encounter with a prostitute, and, according to these accounts, *Les Demoiselles* is an expression of the fear and anger felt by Picasso as a result. But, regardless of the truth or otherwise of this story, it does not account, or accounts only very partially, for the nature and power of the finished work, which is making a more general statement.[16]

According to John Berger that general statement is

> a raging, frontal attack, not against sexual 'immorality', but against life as Picasso found it – the waste, the disease, the ugliness, and the ruthlessness of it . . . instead of criticising modern life by comparing it, as much in sorrow as in anger, with a more primitive way of life, he now uses his sense of the primitive to violate and shock the civilised. . . . He is not in the least concerned with formal problems. He is concerned with challenging civilisation. The dislocations in this picture are the result of aggression, not aesthetics.[17]

But, if the syphilis story is too narrow, Berger's 'rage against civilisation' is too broad. He is right about the element of rage in the painting, but insufficiently precise in identifying its target, again evading the issue of prostitution. Partly, I think, Berger is led astray by following the conventional view of the African heads on the women on the right as aggressive. My own view is that they are neither intrinsically frightening nor savage and that they are present in the painting for two reasons: first because in African art, art from a precapitalist society, Picasso had found an important source for a new, non-naturalistic way of representing the world; second, in terms of the content of the painting, they occur precisely as masks, as blocking mechanisms behind which the real features of the women are concealed.[18]

A number of feminist art historians have seen the rage as directed primarily against women as such, and have viewed *Les Demoiselles* as a highly misogynistic painting. One of the most forceful of these, Carol Duncan, argues that the emergence of modern art coincided with women starting to claim equality (she cites the suffragist movement) and that a great deal of modern art expressed a defensive male sexist reaction to this:

> Indeed, as women's claims to full humanity grew, the more relentlessly would art rationalise their inferior status. . . . In fact, the defence of male supremacy must be recognised as a central theme in modern art. Gauguin, Munch, Rodin, Matisse, Picasso and scores of other artists, consciously or unconsciously, identified some aspect of the sexist cause with all or part of their own artistic missions. Art celebrating sexist experience was accorded the greatest

> prestige, given the most pretentious aesthetic rationales, and identified with the highest and deepest of human aspirations. Nudes and whores – women with no identity beyond their existence as sex objects – were made to embody transcendent, 'universally' significant statements . . . the image of the whore even came to stand for woman in her purest, most concentrated form.[19]

For Duncan, *Les Demoiselles* is the epitome of this sexist trend:

> What is so remarkable about this work is the way it manifests the structural foundation underlying both the femme fatale and the new primitive woman. Picasso . . . dredged up from his psyche the terrifying and fascinating beast that gave birth to both of them. The *Desmoiselles* prismatically mirrors her many opposing faces: whore and deity, decadent and savage, tempting and repelling, awesome and obscene, looming and crouching, masked and naked, threatening and powerless. In that jungle-brothel is womankind in all her present and past metamorphoses, concealing and revealing herself before the male. . . . Picasso presents her in the form of a desecrated icon already slashed and torn to bits . . . no other work reveals more of the rock foundation of sexist anti-humanism or goes further and deeper to justify and celebrate the domination of woman by man.[20]

Duncan's comments on modern art in general have some truth in them, certainly more than is usually recognised in conventional art history. It is also true that Picasso's life, and some of his art, provides evidence of sexist attitudes. It is even the case that there is anger, misogynistic anger, in Picasso's depiction of the Avignon prostitutes. Nevertheless, I believe Duncan's judgment of *Les Demoiselles* is fundamentally mistaken, and this brings us to the heart of what the painting is about and the nature and cause of its power.

The central feature of *Les Demoiselles* is the confrontation between the artist/brothel client/viewer – at this moment they are one and the same – and the gaze of the central women (second and third from the left). Yes, he and we enter the brothel and look at the prostitutes with anger, but this look, and this anger, is returned in spades (if I may use the card-playing metaphor) in the implacable gaze of the prostitutes, which functions as both an expression of their situation and feelings, and as a mirror reflecting back his/ours. Thus *Les Demoiselles*, far from being crudely sexist or simply misogynistic, is a uniquely intense and dramatic depiction of the mutual antagonism, estrangement and alienation involved in the institution of prostitution.

Bourgeois society oscillates between two attitudes to prostitution: on the one hand, moral condemnation and legal persecution of the prostitute (largely the department of the church, the police and the courts); on the other hand, sometimes sentimental, sometimes risqué, glamorisation, largely the province of the arts. In the latter, Hollywood has played its part, but so has 'high art' (Titian's *Venus d'Urbino*, Boucher's and Ingres's *Odalisques*). In both cases what is evaded is the economic deprivation and emotional trauma which lead women into prostitution, and the sexual deprivation and emotional alienation which lead men to prostitutes.

Once this is grasped, it also becomes evident that the formal innovations, which had such an impact on the course of art, all contribute to the intensity of the dramatic confrontation that is *Les Demoiselles*. Picasso needed the radical break with traditional forms of naturalistic representation, needed the assault on conventional standards of beauty, needed the African masks, to smash and eliminate any traces of sentimentality and glamorisation. Above all Picasso needed the flattening, the extreme foreshortening of space in the painting, to thrust the women into our faces, to stage this eyeball-to-eyeball confrontation between us and them, client and prostitute, and to cut through the ingrained habit of evasion of the reality of prostitution. And it is precisely the success of *Les Demoiselles* in achieving this that makes it so genuinely shocking, not just to Braque and Matisse a hundred years ago, but to us today, when its formal qualities have long become familiar. To look at *Les Demoiselles* is still to receive the visual equivalent of a sharp slap across the face.

The issue of prostitution is still very much with us, and in all its forms, from the concentrated hatred of the Ipswich murders and the extreme exploitation and alienation of the virtual slave trade in women from eastern Europe and elsewhere, to the milder, but insidious, relegitimisation of sexism through lap dancing, lads' mags and raunch culture.

Moreover, there is more involved and more at stake here than just the critique of one particular social institution. Bourgeois society's mystification of prostitution and evasion of its realities (replicated in the art critics' evasion of the real content of *Les Demoiselles*) is habitual not just because of the hypocrisy of so many bourgeois politicians, priests and moralists, preaching 'family values' in public while privately behaving quite otherwise, but because what the commodification of sex does to the human relations between the people involved is symptomatic of what alienation and commodification (i.e., capitalism) do to human relations as a whole. Marx explained this with great clarity:

> Prostitution is only a *specific* expression of the *general* prostitution of the *labourer*, and since it is a relationship in which not the prostitute alone, but also the one who prostitutes, fall – and the latter's abomination is still greater – the capitalist, etc., also comes under this head.[21]

Of course, it is not my argument that Picasso was intellectually conscious of all of this. We do not, and cannot, know exactly what passed through his mind as he worked on *Les Demoiselles*, and paintings are rarely visual illustrations of intellectual theses. My guess would be that Picasso worked part consciously, part intuitively, and was concerned more with the representation of feelings than of thought-out ideas. But this is not really the point. What we have to work with and respond to is the painting itself, and this confronts us with the fact – surely a significant one – that the picture which revolutionised art was a hugely powerful statement of rage at the commodification of sex and life.

CHAPTER 6

State of the Art: A Review of the *Sensation* Exhibition at the Royal Academy of Arts, September–December 1997

First published in International Socialism *79 (Summer 1998)*

Thanks are due to Steve Edwards and John Roberts, who both endured lengthy arguments with me about the contents of this essay. They will not agree with it, unless I have persuaded them, but hopefully they will see in it how much I learned from the dialogue.

The British art world is cock-a-hoop. It is convinced that in what has become known as Young British Art (YBA) it has found the answer to its dreams. Young, new, energetic, dynamic, cocky, cockney, rebellious (but not too rebellious, not Marxist or communist or anything old-fashioned like that), sexy, successful, scandalous (in just the way that attracts the media and draws the crowds) and above all profitable and British – everything they ever wanted from an art movement and were afraid even to hope for. Already two books have been published specifically to celebrate 'the world of YBA': *Blimey! From Bohemian to Britpop: The London Artworld from Francis Bacon to Damien Hirst* by Matthew Collings is ironic, hip, cool, a postmodern hagiography; *Moving Targets: A User's Guide to British Art Now* by Luisa Buck is just a hagiography. Its opening paragraph sums up the tone and message of the book and also the current mood of the art world:

> More than at any other time in its history, British art is booming. For several years critics, curators and collectors from across

> the globe have been converging on the UK – especially London and Glasgow – to admire, to purchase and to select from Britain's artistic boldest and best. At home, a fully fledged mythology has grown up around the phenomenon of the Young British Artist as an uncouth entrepreneurial species that emerged fully formed from Goldsmiths' College in south London with Damien Hirst at its head to fly in the face of orthodoxy and the art establishment.[1]

Everything about this passage and about the phenomenon as a whole seems designed to make socialist hackles rise. There is the crude nationalism reminiscent of the American chauvinism that accompanied the promotion of abstract expressionism in the 1950s (including its sponsorship by the CIA).[2] There is the unabashed commercialism of the language – note 'booming', 'to admire, to purchase' and 'uncouth entrepreneurial species' – straight out of the Thatcherite 1980s, which, of course, is where a lot of YBA comes from (the Goldsmiths' year of 1988).[3] There is the conscious emphasis on media hype, played to perfection round the Myra Hindley painting (of which more later). Above all there is the looming figure of Charles Saatchi, patron of Damien Hirst, owner of by far the largest collection of YBA (at the Saatchi Gallery in St John's Wood), supplier of all the works in the *Sensation* exhibition at the Royal Academy in autumn 1997 and supposedly 'the Lorenzo de Medici of our times'. In many ways, YBA fits exactly the scenario outlined by Trotsky in "Art and Politics in Our Epoch":

> Bourgeois society showed its strength throughout long periods of history in the fact that combining repression and encouragement, boycott and flattery, it was able to control and assimilate every 'rebel' movement in art and raise it to the level of official 'recognition'. But each time this 'recognition' betokened, when all is said and done, the approach of trouble. It was then that from the left wing of the academic school or below it – i.e. from the ranks of a new generation of bohemian artists – a fresher revolt would surge up to attain in its turn, after a decent interval, the steps of the academy.[4]

The only difference is that YBAs have omitted the decent interval.

Nevertheless, socialists cannot just write a minus where the bourgeoisie writes a plus. In politics, simply inverting the judgments of the bourgeoisie soon lets one down, and in the sphere of art (as in science) it is completely hopeless. In its time the bourgeoisie has patronised Michelangelo and Rembrandt, Hogarth and David, Picasso and Pollock – all in their different ways great artists. The extremely backward Spanish monarchy managed to maintain Velázquez and Goya, and Diego Rivera was commissioned in turn by the San Francisco Pacific Stock Exchange, Edsel B. Ford (son of Henry) and John D. Rockefeller (until he insisted on including a portrait of Lenin in his proposed mural for the Rockefeller Center). In general the bourgeoisie as a class is aware of the power of art and culture and, desirous of maintaining its hegemony in this sphere as in others, 'delegates' some of its number to specialise in this area. The latter – the likes of Sir Kenneth Clark and Lord Gowrie, Peggy Guggenheim and Charles Saatchi – seek, in their own way, to promote and embrace the best art, past and present. This is not to say their taste can be trusted. In the second half of the nineteenth century, the establishment and the bourgeoisie condemned or ignored, by turn, Courbet, Manet, the impressionists, Seurat, van Gogh and Cézanne. The bourgeoisie also at times endorses the bogus (Dalí), inflates the mediocre (the pre-Raphaelites) and rewards the downright awful (Landseer). We cannot, therefore, respond to the YBA phenomenon 'on principle'. There is no alternative to confronting the actual art and judging it on its merits. In this article I attempt to do this via consideration of the art and artists represented in the Royal Academy *Sensation* exhibition.

The exhibition consisted of 110 works by forty-two different artists, and this in itself creates a problem for a review like this. It is impossible to respond to and comment meaningfully on all of them, either works or artists. At the same time there is a difficulty in responding to the show as a totality. *Sensation* was not a collaborative effort; it was a selection from a collection, and therefore one cannot simply generalise or tar everything with the same brush. The Louvre contains paintings by Raphael, Rembrandt and Louis Le Nain. They are neither similar in style nor equal in merit. Max Ernst, Joan Miró and Salvador Dalí are all known as surrealists. This does not make a judgment of one hold true for the others. Nevertheless, some kind of holistic response to the experience of *Sensation* seems both necessary and inevitable. I shall proceed by first discussing the work and artists I consider particularly significant (negatively and positively) and then by making some general comments.

Unfortunately it is necessary to begin by dealing with Marcus Harvey's *Myra*, the giant reproduction of the familiar newspaper image of Myra Hindley constructed out of children's handprints. This was the sign under which the exhibition was marketed, its logo, its shopwindow display, its loss leader. Whether or not this was the conscious intention from the outset, and whether there was actual conspiracy with the media, is hard to judge, but this was how it worked out, and very successfully too. Everyone (artist, tabloids, curator, parents of Hindley's victims, outraged old Royal Academicians, etc.) played their required parts, and the result was the record three hundred thousand–plus attendance (which at seven quid a time is a lot of filthy lucre). I say unfortunately because as art, as a painting, *Myra* doesn't amount to much. Politically it is important to reject the media's hypocrisy about this image and the absurd inflation of its power. Insofar as this particular image of Hindley possesses iconic power in our culture, it is the media's constant use of it, not Harvey, that created it. When the *Mirror* denounced the painting as a 'disgrace', it plastered it all over its front page, thus projecting it into two million homes. In other words, the fuss is not about the image itself but about making it into 'art', or calling it 'art'. Does this mean paintings of monstrous people cannot be art or morally speaking ought not to be art?[5] Where does that leave Holbein's Henry VIII portraits or John Heartfield's photomontages of Hitler and Goering? However, defending the 'right' of the Academy to show *Myra* is not the same as proclaiming its great artistic merits. Technically there is nothing especially original, interesting or excellent about its conception or execution. Insofar as it makes a point, it is that the image of Myra Hindley is made out of the bodies of murdered children – this is the function of constructing the image from children's handprints. But we know this already, and the painting does not make the point with any particular power.

What really gives the game away, as far as Marcus Harvey is concerned, is his other work in the show: *Proud of His Wife* and *Dudley,*

Like What You See? Then Call Me, two crudely sexist nudes in which art imitates pornography. Of course, it is 'knowing' and 'ironic', so that's supposed to make it alright. It doesn't. The catalogue tells us that these paintings 'simultaneously contain and exceed their salacious imagery'.[6] They don't. From John Berger's *Ways of Seeing* onwards, Marxist and feminist critics of the representation of the female nude by the likes of Titian, Velázquez and Ingres rejected the defence that these were 'great artists' and 'wonderful handlers of paint'. Titian and co. were indeed great artists and superb handlers of paint, but this did not change the fact that their representations of women were sexist or that, because they were sexist, they were inferior as art to those exceptional works such as Rembrandt's *Bathsheba* that managed to rise above the 'women as sex objects' tradition. The catalogue tries to justify Harvey in terms of his 'vibrant splashy brushstrokes' and 'expressionistic fervour'. But is Harvey's handling of paint better than Titian's or Velázquez's? I think not.

However, when it comes to being offensive, and I mean genuinely offensive to human values, not shocking to the bourgeois, Harvey's 'Readers' Wives' cannot hold a candle to Jake and Dinos Chapman. The Chapman brothers' *Great Deeds against the Dead* is a life-size fibreglass reconstruction of an etching of the same name by Goya from the series known as *The Disasters of War*. These etchings depict scenes of appalling brutality from the revolt of the Spanish peasantry against the Napoleonic army of occupation. They show piles of dead bodies, people being garrotted, mutilated and hacked to bits. *Great Deeds against the Dead* presents us with two figures tied to the front joint and back of a tree trunk and castrated, and a third figure hanging upside down over a branch of the tree, castrated, arms cut off and decapitated – the amputated arms also hang from the branch and the severed head is impaled on a smaller branch.

My objection to the Chapmans' piece, and I object to it vehemently, is not based on the subject matter it depicts. That is identical to the subject matter depicted by Goya, and the Goya etchings are among the greatest works in the history of art: it is impossible to see them without being physically stunned by their utterly authentic presentation of the horror of war and, at the same time, moved by their profound humanity.

Nearly two hundred years on they retain – and thank God they do – all their power to shock, but they contain (the word is appropriate) not an ounce of sensationalism. In contrast, the Chapman brothers have produced a piece of plastic kitsch in which the torture is drained of its terror and the art drained of its humanity. They have indeed committed 'great deeds against the dead'.

With *Zygotic Acceleration, Biogenetic, De-Sublimated Libidinal Model (Enlarged × 1000)*, also by the Chapmans, it is not the dead but the living we have to worry about. Once again we have fibreglass mannequin-type figures, this time children, about a dozen in all, melded together into an outward-facing ring. Lacking sexual organs in the genital area, some of their noses are transformed into penises, some of their mouths into vaginas and anuses. The image as a whole is blatantly paedophiliac. This raises the question of whether the charge that a work of art is paedophiliac is in itself enough to condemn it. No doubt this would produce vigorous debate, but let me put the question a slightly different way so as not to stray too far from this particular work. How might those wishing to defend *Zygotic Acceleration* respond to the charge that it is paedophiliac?

They might ask what's wrong with paedophilia. To my knowledge, no one has said this openly, but if they did, that would be a different debate. I intend to assume here that the sexual use of prepubertal children by adults is seriously damaging to children and that we condemn it. They might say that this is only an image, not the reality. This is true and we must remember it (I am not calling for the Chapman brothers to be prosecuted for child abuse), but the accusation is that this image appeals to and encourages paedophile tastes just as other images might appeal to and encourage racism or violence against women.

They might say that the charge is false, and that *Zygotic Acceleration* is not paedophiliac. This defence is not convincing. The mannequins are plainly children. The absence of breasts and normal genitalia, the 'innocent' expressions on their faces, their haircuts and the oversized trainers on their feet all reinforce this. Yet the transformation of their noses into penises and their mouths into anuses and vaginas immediately sexualises them; in particular, the rendering of the mouths as open orifices and the fact that one figure is bent over at the waist while another is upside down so that its anus/mouth and penis/nose are at genital level all suggests sexual access.

Then there would be what might be called the 'postmodern' defence, that the work is so obviously paedophiliac that it must be ironic. Along these lines it could be argued that the trainers signify commodification and therefore that *Zygotic Acceleration* critiques the commodification of paedophiliac images. Clearly I am no expert on the conscious and unconscious motivations of the Chapmans, but it seems probable that something like this was their intention. Unfortunately, there is no necessary correspondence between intention and outcome in art. I am by no means convinced that it is even possible to play ironically with titillating paedophiliac visual material, and in this particular case one is forced to conclude that, in a work which itself was and is bound to be commodified, the paedophiliac element of the mannequins overwhelms the commodity critique of the trainers.[7] Irony is always risky (Johnny Speight intended Alf Garnett's racism to be taken ironically, but Alf became the racists' hero), and here, if irony was the intention, the work has been captured by that which it tries to ironise.

The curators and producers of the catalogue have been particularly dishonest on this question. On the one hand, the catalogue makes no reference to this work's paedophiliac tendency – it fails even to acknowledge the existence of the accusation – covering up the issue in language that is simultaneously pretentious and disingenuous, speaking of 'genderless, self-reproducing manifestations of excess libidinal energy gone awry'.[8] On the other hand, *Zygotic Acceleration* was placed in a room for over-eighteens only. Given this was an exhibition with *Great Deeds against the Dead*, *Myra* and the 'Readers' Wives' paintings on open view, there can only have been one reason for this restriction: an unacknowledged recognition that the work is paedophiliac or likely to be perceived as such.

Finally, the paedophilia might be acknowledged and admitted as a problem, but the work is still defended on the grounds of mitigating circumstances: either that it offered important insights into the nature of paedophilia or that paedophilia was only one element in an otherwise-valuable work,[9] or that despite its content, it was especially skilful or well made.[10] But none of these arguments work for *Zygotic Acceleration*. As for being well made, one has only to look at Ron Mueck's *Dead Dad* (also in *Sensation*) to see what can be done with these kind of materials and how shoddy the Chapmans' piece is. Nor does it offer any special insight into paedophilia (other than possibly the aforementioned point that paedophilia can be commodified) or into anything besides paedophilia. It simply is paedophiliac, and that makes it into something quite rare – a thoroughly meretricious work of art.

But if the Chapman brothers plumb the depths, there is also a substantial amount of serious, high-quality, perhaps even major art in *Sensation*: notably the work of Damien Hirst and Rachel Whiteread. With eight pieces on show, Damien Hirst is the best-represented artist in *Sensation*, and as he is the central figure in the YBA movement, this is fitting. Of the eight, two are paintings and six are the three-dimensional 'sculptures' or 'installations' for which he has become famous. The paintings are, in my opinion, not of much consequence: *Argininosuccinic Acid* is a large multicoloured dot painting which is pretty but offers little beyond what has been achieved in much twentieth-century geometric abstraction; *beautiful, kiss my fucking ass painting* is a circular canvas on which bright primary colours have been spun, but it doesn't even manage to be pretty. The 3-D pieces are a different kettle of fish – at the very least they are an original and major provocation.

Much of the provocation and much of the 'scandal' attaching to Hirst derives from the materials he uses: the bodies of dead animals. In modern art there is a history to this question of materials. For about five hundred years, virtually all art was made from the same limited range of materials: tempera, oil paints, watercolours, bronze, marble and so on. Explicitly or implicitly, these materials came to be regarded as inherently artistic and other materials as inherently nonartistic (just as certain subjects were regarded as fit for art and other subjects as unfit). The first breach in this convention was made by Picasso in his 'synthetic cubist' phase in 1912, when he introduced pieces of oilcloth, newsprint and wallpaper into his paintings. Picasso took the process further in his transformative sculptures, like the bull's head made of handlebars and a bicycle seat and the monkey made of toy cars. So did Duchamp, with his bottle rack and urinal 'readymades' and his complex *Large Glass* 'sculpture'. Later came sculptors who used iron, steel, aluminium, plaster, bricks, fluorescent lights and so on, and Rauschenberg, who combined painting with screen printing, photography and objects found in the streets, including a motor tyre and stuffed goat. However, even against this 'anything goes' background, Hirst's use of a large shark and cut-up cows was a dramatic innovation.

In general in art, formal innovations occur not just for their own sake but because the artist has something new to say which requires the formal innovation for it to be said. Hirst's use of real dead animals is an example of this. Its purpose, I think, is to force a face-to-face confrontation with the brute fact of death on a blasé modern audience for whom images of death are superabundant while its reality becomes ever more removed and hidden. Short of exhibiting an actual human corpse, this was about as far as Hirst could go.

In order to progress a little further in explaining how Hirst's art works, I want to employ the concept of the 'objective correlative', developed by T. S. Eliot: 'The only way of expressing emotion in the form of art is by finding an "objective correlative"; in other words, a set of objects, a situation, a chain of events which shall be the formula of that particular emotion; such that when the external facts, which must terminate in sensory experience, are given, the emotion is immediately evoked.'[11] This seems to me exactly what Hirst is doing: constructing an object (using, as we have noted, unusual and original materials) which will be the objective correlative of certain thoughts and emotions, of certain 'felt ideas'. Thus the huge shark piece works as the 'objective correlative' of death in at least four ways: (1) it is an actual dead shark; (2) the shark is a powerful cultural signifier of the fear and threat of death; (3) the curvature in the glass of the tank containing the shark reinforces point two by making the shark appear to move threateningly in the direction of the viewer; and (4) the title of the work, *The Physical Impossibility of Death in the Mind of Someone Living*, works in tension with the piece itself and with the taboo on 'death' in our culture. Thus the one object serves as an objective correlative for the fact, fear, threat and taboo of death.

In *A Thousand Years*, with its cow's head, breeding maggots, flies and Insect-O-Cutor, we have a work that is even more transgressive in its materials – not only dead flesh but living creatures that are killed before one's eyes – and which incorporates a new element, smell (or rather stench). Here we have represented not just death but a whole life–death cycle, a mini-ecosystem complete with breeding, feeding and human intervention. If it is a spectacle which evokes disgust and nausea, then that too is part of its statement. It asks us to examine our responses. *Away from the Flock* – a white lamb with black face and feet suspended in a white steel and glass tank – serves as objective correlative for rather different ideas and emotions. The work itself interacts with its title (titles usually play an important role with Hirst) to represent and evoke separation, isolation, loneliness and abandonment, especially as these might pertain to a child. As such it generates an acute pathos. *Isolated Elements Swimming in the Same Direction for the Purpose of Understanding* works with a related theme but to different emotional effect. It consists of a large glass cabinet containing six shelves, and on each shelf is placed a row of six or seven Perspex cases, each containing a suspended fish, all 'swimming' head to tail. We are presented here with an embodiment of individuals as part of a conformist collective yet all isolated and hermetically sealed from one another (a 'series', not a 'fixed group', in the old language of Sartre). Of course it might be objected, à la Lukács, that this is a profoundly false view of life. In the final analysis I would agree, but it is also the case that this is an important element of human experience in this alienated society and that here Hirst has succeeded in giving powerful visual expression to this experience. The construction, it should be said, is very beautifully composed in terms of its ordering of forms and colours, possessing some of the visual qualities of a Mondrian or Klee. Emotionally, it induces not pathos or sympathy but an almost terrifying chill.

Mother and Child Divided was not in this show, but I want to comment on it here (in preference to the cut-up cow and pig works in *Sensation*) because I think it is Hirst's most important work to date and because it brings together a number of the themes from the other works. It consists of a bisected cow and a bisected calf. Each half of the cow is placed in its own glass tank, and the tanks are adjacent to one another but with enough space to walk between the tanks and observe close up the insides of the cow. The same is done with the halves of the calf, but the two calf halves are placed several yards away from the cow. Of all Hirst's pieces this is the one that seems to have made the biggest impact on the public consciousness, and this in itself testifies to the power of its conception.[12] However, what is most impressive about it is the way in which it functions as objective correlative for a range of different, almost conflicting, ideas and emotions. First there is the confrontation with death and dead flesh. Then there is the 'shock' of the violence of the bisection (shock like the shock of Goya, not the Chapmans), and disgust and distaste at the exposure of the innards. But this works in tension with the knowledge that this is how we treat animals and this is what we eat as food. One does not need to be an animal rights supporter or vegetarian to feel the force of this, just as one does not need to be a pacifist to respond to Wilfred Owen: Hirst is merely insisting we face facts. Finally, the title (again) and the placing of the cow/mother and calf/child evokes the pathos, despair and separation anxiety of *Away from the Flock* and *Isolated Elements Swimming. Mother and Child Divided* has the integration of thought and feeling, and the combination of complexity with visual and emotional power, that is characteristic of major art.

Two final comments on Hirst. First, significant art, no matter how 'new' or 'original', always turns out to be the next step in an ongoing tradition. Nevertheless, Hirst, on examination, is seen to be the point of confluence of a remarkable number of artistic streams. Most immediately there is the influence of Francis Bacon in the themes of framed and caged flesh (and also a distant echo of Rembrandt's great painting of a beef carcass, *Slaughtered Ox*). In the use of readymade materials, in the making of art out of apparent anti-art moves, in the mix of playfulness and high seriousness, he is clearly the heir of Marcel Duchamp. The use of the glass case also looks back to Duchamp (*The Bride Stripped Bare by Her Bachelors, Even*, aka *The Large Glass*) and the vitrines of Joseph Beuys. The white steel boxes expand the form pioneered by Sol LeWitt and the minimalists in the 1960s.[13] And in the self-conscious deployment of hype, there is the unmistakable legacy of Warhol.

Second, it is an art cliché that reproductions cannot compare with the original works. Often there is an element of myth involved here, for the extent to which this is true varies greatly from artist to artist and work to work. In fact, you can get a better idea of the ceiling of the Sistine Chapel from good reproductions than you can from the floor of the chapel. Gauguin, Miró and Mondrian reproduce excellently: van Gogh (because of the texture of the paint) and Pollock (because of the texture and the importance of the size) much less well. Indeed with most paintings and some sculpture, you get 'a pretty good idea' from quality modern reproductions. This is not the case with much of Hirst's work. The curvature in the glass in the shark piece and its visual effects do not appear in photographs. The same is true of the flying and dying flies in *A Thousand Years*, not to speak of the smell, and you have actually to walk through the bisected cow and calf in *Mother and Child Divided* to experience its full effect. In short, Hirst demands to be seen firsthand. Whether this is a good or bad thing is a debate for another occasion, but it is a fact which must be taken into account in discussing his merits.

The same applies to Rachel Whiteread, who makes casts in plaster and other materials of the insides and underneaths of things. Indeed, it applies to her with particular poignancy, for of her two most important works, *House* and the Judenplatz Holocaust Memorial in Vienna (aka the Nameless Library), the former was destroyed and the latter never built.[14] Whiteread had five works in *Sensation*: casts of the underspaces of one hundred chairs and stools, of a kitchen sink, of two baths and of the inside of a Victorian room.

Before discussing these, let us reflect a moment on Whiteread's distinctive method – the casting of the negative space of an object – and consider its slightly uncanny nature. It is tempting to say that to make a cast of the inside or underneath of something is to make the invisible visible – before you couldn't see it, now you can. Except that isn't quite right. You might as well say that before you could see the space and now you cannot because it has been filled up, obliterated – the visible has been made invisible. The 'things' whose negative spaces Whiteread casts are (so far at least) domestic, familiar. So perhaps she makes the familiar unfamiliar, but perhaps one can become familiar with a tangible object in a way one cannot become familiar with a space. So the intangible is rendered tangible? Yes, except that in the gallery they won't let you touch it. Christo, the Bulgarian artist famous for wrapping the Reichstag and the Pont Neuf, has argued that wrapping a building blots out the decorative details and brings out its underlying structure. Does making a cast do the same thing? Nearly, but not quite, since it is the structure in reverse. Can we compare the cast to a fossil? Yes, and it bears those associations, and yet an internal cast is an inverted fossil. So what is Whiteread's art – just a play on words, a clever but soluble conundrum or a real enigma? The answer depends, I think, on how her technique is realised in specific works.

Untitled (One Hundred Spaces) consists of a hundred resin castings, in various colours, of the spaces beneath different-sized chairs and stools. It is visually attractive, arguably beautiful (in fact it is rather more beautiful in the catalogue photograph, where it is placed in a pure ice-blue gallery space, than it was in the cluttered Academy), but in the end rather inconsequential. The 'underneaths of chairs' simply do not carry enough associations or meanings with sufficient emotional charge to give the work any real point or power. *Untitled (Square Sink)* works better in this respect – it is an object of genuine curiosity, at once highly modern and suggestive of the past, both recent and distant. Nevertheless, it is still a relatively minor piece. The two bath pieces are on a higher level. *Untitled (Bath)* in white plaster with a glass top manages, almost effortlessly, to condense a multitude of 'bath associations': the enamel bath in the cold bathroom that once marked the English petty bourgeoisie (in contrast to the tin bath of the working class), signifier of narrow respectability, genteel impoverishment and austere aspiration; but also the sinister bath, the bath as site of murder, the bath in the *Chamber of Horrors*; and finally, the white plaster suggests stone, and the stone suggests sarcophagus. *Untitled (Orange Bath)* is remarkable in a different way. Made of rubber and polystyrene, it is the nature of the material itself that comes to the fore. To the viewer it resembles a giant rubber eraser which might be bent or broken in two, or scratched with the fingernails, or have its corners worn down through use. It is enormously intriguing, and the attendants have to be constantly on the alert to inhibit the probing fingers of visitors.

However, it is in the large *Ghost*, the cast of the inside of a room, that Whiteread's method really bears fruit. *Ghost* is not like the Hirst pieces, where one can attribute fairly precise feelings and ideas to particular aspects of the works: it is an altogether more mysterious object. Nevertheless, it has extraordinary presence. In the Academy its looming bulk made me feel pressed up against the gallery walls, or perhaps it was pressed against the walls of the room that are no longer there – a kind of claustrophobia in reverse. In a way the title – *Ghost* – sums up the work. It is the trace of what has departed, the presence of an absence, the materialisation of memory. Indeed it is haunting, despite the all-too-obvious pun. But what is remarkable – the measure of Whiteread's achievement – is that one can talk in these terms, the terms of ghostliness, about a one-thousand-cubic-foot, apparently solid, white cube which also manages to look as if it were made of concrete.

The success of *Ghost* is what makes me so regret not having seen the original *House* in Grove Road, Bow, before it was demolished in 1994.[15] More or less everything I have said about the casting technique in general and about *Ghost* would probably have applied to *House*, but my guess is that the poignancy of the work would have been greatly increased by its positioning alone in an otherwise-bulldozed street in a traditional working-class area. Even more regrettable is the nonconstruction of the proposed Holocaust Memorial in Judenplatz, Vienna.[16] Tremendous aesthetic/political problems attend any attempt to memorialise the Holocaust. How can the work be adequate to that which it is meant to commemorate, and if it is not, how does it avoid being an insult? Clearly the Holocaust cannot be visually depicted or described as a totality – in naturalistic mode all that could be achieved would be the illustration of an instance, and is that good enough? If it is shocking, it runs the risk of being insufficiently solemn, if it is solemn, of being too undemanding. It is just possible, I think, that Whiteread would have overcome these problems. Her proposal was for a huge concrete cast of the inside of a library. In one way, therefore, it would have been a place of quiet dignity, redolent of study and reflection, of the preservation of civilised values in the time of barbarism and of the recording of history. Yet, following *Ghost*, it might also have had the same effect of filling that Viennese square to bursting, of pressing itself insistently on every visitor and every passerby so that they could not have avoided the reminder and the challenge that it constituted. Which was just what was needed in Judenplatz in Vienna.

I have now discussed the worst and the best of *Sensation*, and should make it clear that I think Hirst and Whiteread are not just the best of this show but probably the major artists of this generation. Nevertheless, the exhibition contains a number of other works I want to mention. There are two outstanding individual pieces: Mat Collishaw's *Bullet Hole* – a huge close-up of a head wound mounted on fifteen light boxes which is genuinely painful to look at, as it should be – and Marc Quinn's *Self* – a frozen Perspex cast of his head filled with his own blood, which achieves an intense lyrical beauty. But I suspect that both of them may be one-offs. There are three women artists – Jenny Saville, Sarah Lucas and Tracey Emin – all of whom make an immediate 'sensational' impact.[17] It is easy to see the appeal of Saville's huge nudes, but they are painted in the style of Lucian Freud, only not as well, and the 'fat is a feminist issue'-type points they make are by now rather obvious and well worn. With mass media that preach puritanism and practise prurience, Lucas's up-front sexual pieces are bound to cause a minor stir. Some of her sexual symbolism (the cucumber, oranges, bucket and melons of *Au Natural*) is too unimaginative to take very seriously, but *Two Fried Eggs and a Kebab* (which neatly combines references to street slang and Magritte) is a witty and pointed challenge to sexist putdowns. Also there is *Sod You Gits*, made of large, blown-up photocopies from the *Sunday Sport*, which both exposes and somehow copes with the assault of alienated tabloid culture.[18] Tracey Emin's *Everyone I Have Ever Slept With, 1963–95*, in which the names of her bedmates are stitched to the inside of a tent, is based on a powerful idea, both sad and grimly funny, but it lacks visual impact. Emin's vulnerability is so evident that where her future is concerned, one hopes for the best but fears the worst. In a different league is Palestinian exile Mona Hatoum, who may well prove to be the third major figure alongside Hirst and Whiteread. Unfortunately, Hatoum has only one piece here, *Deep Throat*, showing film of her throat in the middle of a plate at a place set on a table, and this is one of her weakest, least evocative works.[19]

Finally, there are the photographs of Richard Billingham. These depict members of Billingham's family – principally his parents – with apparently alarming candour, in their daily life of drunkenness, squalor and TV dinners. The point about this work, and the reason for leaving it until last, is the way it forces one to choose: for or against. I don't mean deciding whether it is good, bad or indifferent, or whether one likes it, or even whether it is socially progressive. I mean one has to make a fundamental decision as to whether or not it is in good faith. In this case that means trying to decide on the nature of the relationship between the work and the subjects it depicts. Is it, fundamentally, a work of solidarity and sympathy, or a work of exposure and exploitation? I repeat, this is a decision about the work, not the artist. The artist's motives are doubtless relevant, but not decisive; in the end, the choice must be made on the evidence of one's eyes, not the evidence of history or gossip. Personally, in this instance, I have decided against. I think Billingham has humiliated his parents by holding up working-class life as an exhibit for the bourgeois gaze, much as the inmates of Bedlam were exhibited to bourgeois visitors in the eighteenth century.[20] Could I be wrong and doing Billingham an injustice? Certainly I could – the dividing line is a fine one – but what I want to stress is that the work forces me to make the decision, at least implicitly, and in this it is representative of the *Sensation* exhibition as a whole. One has to make very much the same decision about the Chapman brothers' work, about Harvey's 'Readers' Wives', about Hirst's bisected animals and putrefying cow's head, about Collishaw's bullet wound and Mueck's dead dad.

It could be objected that all serious art confronts one with choices and judgments. This is probably true, but it is not usually this particular kind of choice. Faced with Seurat's *Bathers* in 1884, the choice was: Is it great art, or is it irredeemably vulgar and commonplace? With Salvador Dalí it is: Are these really profound images from the human subconscious, or are they artificial and fabricated? With Carl Andre's *Equivalent VIII* (the infamous 'bricks') it is: Can something so minimal be art? Can it be meaningful and can it be beautiful? With *Guernica* in 1937, a number of questions arose: Does it work as a painting? Is it moving? In what way is it moving? Which side am I on in Spain? Does it help the anti-fascist cause? *But not*: Is the painting in solidarity with those on the receiving end of the bombing, or is it relishing and exploiting their suffering? Yet that is precisely the question posed by Billingham's work, and the dominant question posed by the exhibition as a whole.

Why does this question arise in relation to this body of art more insistently than is generally the case in the history of art? Because the underlying theme of all the more striking work here, its common denominator, is alienation – the alienated individual in an alienated society.[21] This is the other side of the coin of the Thatcherite entrepreneurialism of the 1980s. It is smack and crack on estates in Hackney (where many of the YBAs have lived and had studios). It is poverty, the dole and a sense of collective powerlessness in the face of 'a power which has become more and more enormous and, in the last instance, turns out to be the world market'.[22] It is personal rebellion in the absence of any felt connection to a wider force for social change.

In this situation, art can go different ways. Hypothetically, it could retreat into formalism and decoration (what Clement Greenberg in 'Avant-Garde and Kitsch' called 'Alexandrianism'), but the history of art in the twentieth century has more or less closed off that option.[23] It can embrace the alienation, wallow in it, internalise it and as a result produce art that is itself alienated in the extreme, alienated to the point of cruelty and collusion in cruelty – with a repudiation of all ties of human solidarity. Or, even in its alienation and isolation, it can battle through by exploring the depths of its condition 'in the place of excrement',[24] with intelligence and without surrender to produce work that in its own way is positive and life enhancing. Hence the polarisation in '*Sensation*'. The first option produces work that is the stuff of Lukács' worst nightmares. The second produces work that can stand in the tradition of Kafka and Ginsberg, Goya and Picasso, Duchamp and Brâncuși.

This, then, is the moment of *Sensation.* Soon it will pass (life has already moved on), but not before it has left its mark on our culture and on the history of art, for both better and worse.[25]

CHAPTER 7

The Emin Phenomenon or the Phenomenal Emin

This is the complete version of an article that first appeared in edited form as 'Emin Matters' in International Socialism *106 (Spring 2005).*

Tracey Emin is a new phenomenon and consequently, like many new phenomena in the past, is met with widespread incomprehension, misunderstanding and vilification. When I read much of the press coverage she receives, including from some 'respectable' critics, I am reminded of the reaction, documented so tellingly by T. J. Clark, to Manet's *Olympia* when it first appeared in the Salon in 1865. Then the critics, faced with a painting that contested the prevailing conceptions of art, women, sex and class, were not even able to recognise or articulate the nature of the challenge offered, and therefore responded with misplaced sarcasm and invective. Something very similar occurs with Emin, who as it happens – and I do not think this is coincidence – deals with just the same issues today. At the same time, there is very little serious or academic discussion of Emin's work, which is rather remarkable given the vast recent academic discourses on all things 'artistic' and 'cultural'. This essay is an attempt to redress the balance and to argue, on the basis of her work, that Emin is a serious and important artist.

First, however, I want to discuss the nature of Emin's fame, which is one of the things about her which is new. Tracy Emin is currently the most famous contemporary artist in Britain, and a woman. I don't think this has ever happened before. Obviously there have been famous women artists in the past – Barbara Hepworth, Frida Kahlo and so on – but they have not been the leading artists of the day. Hepworth was overshadowed by Moore and Bacon, Kahlo by Rivera, not to mention Picasso. Again, this is not by chance. When the YBAs – Young British Artists – broke into the mainstream with the Sensation show in 1997, eighteen out of the forty-two artists exhibited were women – still a minority, but a far larger minority than would have been the case in an impressionist, surrealist, abstract expressionist or pop art show, or any previous art movement that I can think of. Moreover, of that minority, not only Emin but also Rachel Whiteread, Sarah Lucas, Jenny Saville, Fiona Rae, Gillian Wearing and Sam Taylor-Wood have emerged as major figures in the art world. Clearly this reflects underlying changes in the social position of women. Equally clearly, however, there is an element of barely concealed misogynistic backlash in some of the responses to Emin.

Also new and different is the precise nature of Emin's fame: she is a 'celebrity'. In a sense many artists have been celebrities before – Michelangelo, Titian, Rubens and especially Picasso were all celebrities of a kind (far bigger celebrities than Emin), but in their case it meant being lionised, almost worshipped, in 'cultural' circles. Emin is a celebrity in today's 'celebrity culture', which is a mass media popular culture; it means she appears on *Have I Got News For You?*, *Desert Island Discs* and *Richard and Judy*. This is a world in which there is absolutely no guarantee of deference or even respect. On the contrary, this kind of celebrity, although it pays very well, actually opens Emin up to exposure and derision. The contrast is well illustrated by an anecdote about Francis Bacon. After one of his rather hazardous sexual escapades in the sixties, Bacon found himself under arrest (this was before the legalisation of homosexuality). The consequence was not being plastered all over the tabloids but a phone call from Lord (Arnold) Goodman, the prime minister's legal fixer, to the metropolitan police commissioner explaining that it would not be a good idea for 'Britain's greatest living painter' to appear in humiliating circumstances at Bow Street Magistrates' Court. He was swiftly released. Obviously Emin enjoys no such protection.

But why, out of all the Young British Artists available, has Emin in particular been selected by the media for celebrity status? One reason, of course, is that she is sexually candid and the media is obsessed with all things sexual. Another reason, however, is that the media has picked up the fact that, with a layer of people, Emin is genuinely popular – that is, she has a fan base – and therefore her presence on a quiz or chat show is likely to boost its audience.

The very use of the term 'fan base', while appropriate, immediately distinguishes Emin's fame from that of Henry Moore or Jackson Pollock or even Damien Hirst, but it is not intended pejoratively. It indicates that Emin's art has reached people not normally touched by 'fine art' and that they have responded intensely. Who are these people, and what is the nature of their response? Evidence on this can only be anecdotal and impressionistic. My evidence, for what it's worth, is based on observing the public at the 1999 Turner Prize show at the Tate Britain and talking to people – mainly, but not only, students at the School of Art, Design and Media where I taught. The Turner Prize show was significant because there were four artists represented, but something like 70 to 80 per cent of the public were concentrated in Emin's space; many of them were young women, students on school or college trips, and they were poring intently over Emin's work, examining it avidly and in detail. It was quite different from the way either tourists or art aficionados relate to Old Masters in the National Gallery. In fact, I don't think I have seen any group of gallery visitors so engaged with works of art. Subsequent conversations have broadly confirmed this picture. Emin's fans are predominantly, though certainly not exclusively, younger women, part of the recently found audience for contemporary art but not art world insiders, and they hold their position on the basis of Emin's work, not because of media hype, which has largely been hostile.

There is nothing mysterious or accidental here. Such people relate to Emin because Emin's work relates, like that of no other artist I can think of, to their experience.

As virtually every other commentator on Emin begins by observing, most of her work is autobiographical. Its main subject matter is her traumas and triumphs, sufferings and joys of growing up in Margate, maturing in London and elsewhere and so becoming the person she is today. As a result, Emin's work is often criticised for being 'self-centred', 'narcissistic'. In my opinion, this criticism completely misses the point, the point so eagerly seized on by her 'fans', namely that the experiences represented in Emin's art are not just personal experiences, but are common to a wide layer of young women growing up in this time, in this society. Normally these experiences remain private, confided perhaps to 'best friends' but otherwise hidden from public view and therefore in a sense shameful. By making these experiences into art (which is different from just exposing or 'confessing' them), Emin actually engages in a process of 'democratic sharing' with her audience. It is particularly democratic because the work is not didactic and does not preach. It does not seek to impose or determine a specific response. It simply says, 'This is what happened to me; this is how I felt about it'. And perhaps, 'This is how I dealt with it'. If it strikes a chord, as it evidently often does, then so be it.

Emin's first work to make a public impact, her tent, or *Everyone I Ever Slept With, 1963–95*, shown in the *Sensation* exhibition of the Royal Academy in 1997, is a good example of this. The smallish tent sits on the gallery floor. On the inside Emin has sewn the names of her bedmates of the previous thirty years. To see or experience the work, the viewer has to crawl into the tent. Thus Emin has created a 'private' space, a den with private information about her life which the public is invited to share. The fact, which she has made a point of calling attention to, that the names included not just lovers but also others she has shared 'the intimacy of sleep' with (such as her twin brothers and aborted foetuses) is important. It does not negate the sexual interpretation of the title, which in our culture is the obvious first reading, but it modifies it, ensuring that the sexual is not separated from the emotional. What we are offered to share is not gossip or titillation but feelings, including painful feelings.

Emin's most famous work, *My Bed*, is actually a complex piece which has appeared in different forms in different places, for example with and without a noose hanging over the bed, and which I cannot explore fully here, but essentially it works on the same principle. According to the sexist stereotype, women are the homemakers and responsible for clearing up. A messed-up house shames a woman, makes her a 'slut', much more than it does a man. The bedroom, and above all the bed itself, represents a place of privacy, intimacy and sex, pain and illness. The stained sheets are a visible trace of all this and thus taboo. 'You don't wash your dirty linen in public.' *My Bed* takes all this as its starting point and confronts it, knowing that for some of us all the time, and many of us some of the time, it is a lie. It is a spectacular coming-out. And out there thousands, perhaps millions of people say, openly or privately, 'Yes! I've been there, I know what that's about!' That is the mechanism and that is why *My Bed* is one of those few works of contemporary art that captures people's imagination and stays in the public memory.

In this context it is well worth dealing with the prevalent notion that Emin is lacking in technical artistic skills. For example, much of the media coverage of *My Bed* seemed based on the assumption that she had simply transplanted her actual bed or bedroom into the Tate. This, as a moment's thought would have made clear, was nonsense. *My Bed*, which had already appeared in Tokyo, was a consciously constructed work, as much a made work of art as van Gogh's painting of his bedroom. Insofar as it was a sufficiently convincing representation of a disordered bedroom to persuade journalists that it was the real thing, this is testimony to Emin's skill, and actually it was visually very powerful.

In fact, Emin is a skilled practitioner in a range of media, but it is her drawing, as manifested in her many monoprints, that I particularly want to focus on. In my opinion Emin's drawing is superb. This, of course, is a value judgment which is difficult to justify or even convey in words. I would make two points: First, that Emin is able, with great economy, to achieve very accurate and telling representations. For example, we know from a number of photographs what Emin's legs look like; they have a peculiar athletic rangy quality. Her drawings capture this quality exactly. Compare the photograph *I've Got It All* with the monoprints *I See It Thoe* and *Walking Drunk in High Shoes*. Second, that her line combines strength and vulnerability, confidence and pain in exactly the right proportions for her subject matter, and matching visual form to intellectual/emotional content is precisely the key skill of the visual artist.

To bring out further the significance of Emin's art, I shall examine in turn three of its themes – class, sex and art – which are more or less omnipresent and which taken together make for its distinctiveness and power.

Class

Perhaps the most immediately striking and unusual thing about both Emin's persona and her work is the way in which she positions herself as a working-class artist. The whole question of class and art is so highly charged that I must straight away take care to explain precisely what I mean, and what I don't mean, by this statement.

Clearly Emin is not currently working-class in any shape or form. She is probably a millionaire, certainly rich, and she functions, as all successful visual artists do, as boss of her own small business. Nor am I referring to her class background, which is complex. Up to the age of seven, her mother had a largeish hotel in Margate, but then, when she broke up with Emin's father, bankruptcy and poverty ensued and Emin's youth, whether or not strictly proletarian, was plebeian. As we know, this had a major influence on her art, but that is still not what I mean here. Nor is she an artist who sees or presents herself as associated with, or representative of, the working-class movement (like Käthe Kollwitz, John Heartfield or Diego Rivera, to give classic examples). What she *does* do, however, is present herself as culturally working class. This is evident in the whole way in which she conducts herself: in her accent, of course, but more importantly in what she says and how she says it. She makes no attempt to engage in 'intellectual artspeak' but sticks to unaffected everyday language. (Unlike, for example, Jake Chapman of the Chapman brothers, who is highly accomplished at theoretical discourse.) This was an element of her drunken walkout from the Channel 4 art discussion programme with David Sylvester, Waldemar Januszczak et al. – 'I'd rather be with my mum and my friends' – and plays a part in her willingness to participate in popular cultural shows. This is highly unusual in the art world, the ethos of which is very upper class. There has always, of course, been a smattering of working-class artists rising through the art schools, but normally they adopt the dominant cultural style.

The most obvious parallel to Emin in this is Damien Hirst, especially the young Hirst, but there is a difference: in Hirst the working-class attitude does not carry over into the work itself, while with Emin it does. The language used in her many appliquéd quilts/blankets, her films and her monoprint drawings is the language of the street, including the swear words, the grammatical errors and the misspellings. The question of the spelling mistakes is interesting here. Emin denies either that she has dyslexia or that they are deliberate; she insists that she simply makes mistakes but doesn't care. But I am convinced that Emin is being a little disingenuous here. First, the spelling mistakes and letters wrong-way-round reference the work of Jean-Michel Basquiat, originally a New York graffiti artist, and (as they do in Basquiat) carry connotations of writing on street and toilet walls. Secondly, they occur in the appliquéd (sewn) works where mistakes seem unlikely, especially in the blanket called *Pysco Slut*, where 'Pysco' is much wittier and more to the point than 'Psycho'. But, above all, the experiences her art deals with are, by and large, the experiences of working-class girls.

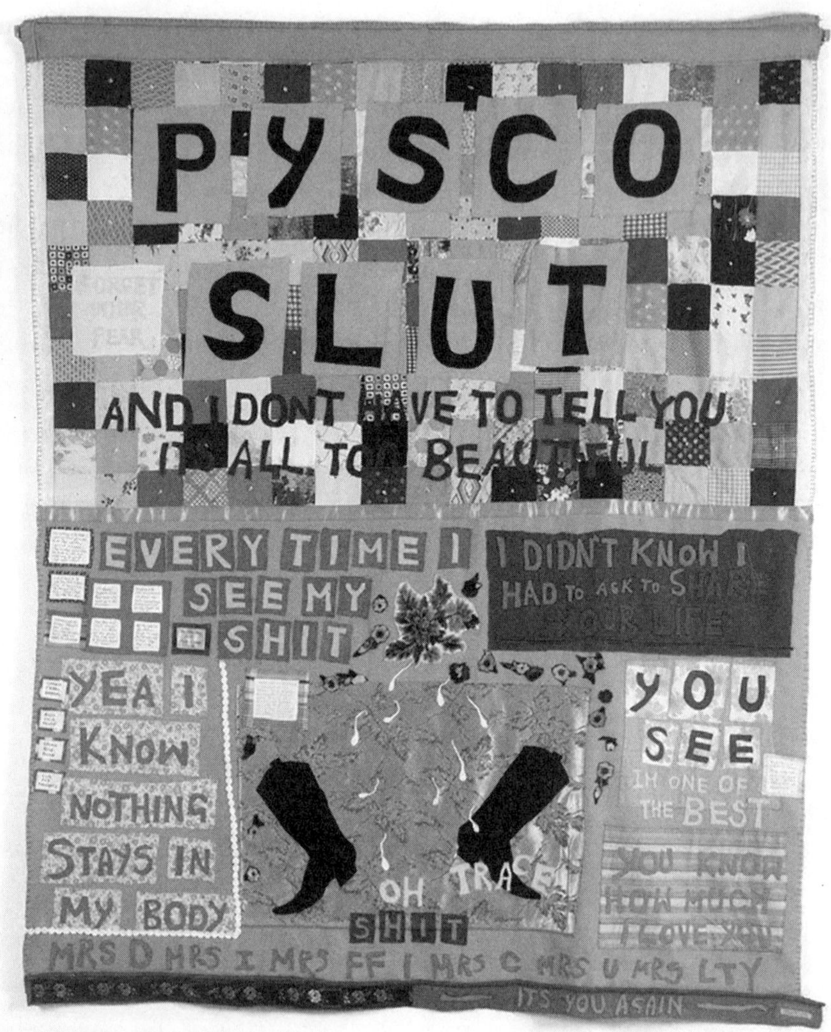

Tracey Emin, *Pysco Slut* (1999)

This is the case with the short film *Why I Never Became a Dancer*, in my opinion one of her most important and powerful works. The film tells of Emin's aspiration to be a dancer and her participation in a dance competition in Margate, the prize for which meant going to London. Just as she feels things are going well, she finds herself surrounded by a circle of local lads (many of whom she has had sex with). At first she thinks they are clapping her, and then she realises that in fact they are chanting in unison 'Slag, slag, slag', and she runs from the ballroom in dismay. The film ends with her dancing, alone and just for herself, and saying to the camera, 'Shane, Eddie, Tony, Doug, Richard... this one's for you.' It also applies to her recent film *Top Spot*, on teenage suicide, about which Amy Lane, in *Socialist Review,* wrote: 'There is nothing contained in *Top Spot* that does not reflect the reality of Britain's working class estates.... [It] is a painfully accurate portrayal of modern adolescent experience.'[1]

Just as there is an element of misogyny in the media and critical hostility to Emin, so also there is an element of class prejudice. In particular I think middle-class critics often miss the point of her work because the kind of experiences she deals with are not their experiences and not part of the world they inhabit. The recognition factor which is key for Emin's 'fans' and for what I have called the process of 'democratic sharing' is missing.

Emin's consciousness of, and concern for, this relationship with her audience was evident in her fury at *Top Spot* being given an eighteen-plus certificate by the censors, and her consequent withdrawal of the film that would thus be prevented from reaching the very people it was intended for.

The discussion of class obviously raises the question of Emin's politics. It is often said of her that she is not political. If this were true, I would not find it a problem for, as Leon Trotsky always insisted, art cannot simply be judged on its politics. As it happens, it is not true. I have already noted that Emin does not see herself or function as an artistic representative of a working-class political movement – given that her formative years were the eighties, this is not surprising – but she does have a political consciousness and outlook, and this is clear from many of her public statements and appearances. Broadly speaking she is on the left. She did work for Ken Livingstone's mayoral campaign. She is anti-racist, anti-homophobic and anti-war. My colleague Milly Thompson, formerly of the BANK collective, who knows the London art scene, says that in that world Emin is known as 'a committed socialist'. Moreover, some of her recent work from 2004, exhibited in New Zealand, does deal explicitly with questions of war and peace.

Of course, against this can be set the fact that Emin has now made a lot of money, doubtless has a very comfortable lifestyle, wears Vivian Westwood clothes, mixes from time to time with various unsavoury rich bastards like Charles Saatchi and is evidently very pleased with this state of affairs. All of which provides good grounds for complaint from young, angry, impoverished artists.

I set this down for the record, but I do not believe that either her leftish views or her affluent lifestyle constitute major grounds for the evaluation of her art.

Sex

That sex should be a major theme in Emin's work is hardly surprising. Sex has been a central theme in European art from the Renaissance to Picasso and beyond (not to speak of ancient Greece and Rome, Japan and so on). But it should be said at the outset that there is no element of eroticism or titillation here, unlike in Botticelli, Titian, Bronzino, Boucher, Ingres, Renoir, Rodin, Klimt and so on. Nor is it sexual fantasy or dreams, as we might find in surrealism. Nor is it the sex of the brothel featured so heavily in late nineteenth- and early twentieth-century French art. It is real, everyday sex – as experienced by her, of course, but also by millions of other people. This, in itself, is remarkable. It seems strange to say it, but I do not think there is a precedent for it in the whole of European visual art .

The history of art develops dialectically, with each new generation or movement or individual artist usually defining themselves in opposition to the immediately preceding dominant trend. Part of this process is the discovery of new material, both physically and in terms of subject matter; to make art out of material which was often previously thought of as 'unartistic' (or vulgar, prosaic, mundane, ugly, etc.). This is one of the reasons why new art so often meets with the reaction that it is 'not art'. Thus, following the call of Baudelaire, mid-eighteenth-century French art painted 'the heroism of modern life' as opposed to the heroes of classical mythology; thus the post-impressionists restored form where the impressionists had neglected it, and the futurists and constructivists aestheticised the machine and technology previously anathema to classicists and romantics alike. Thus pop art turned to the imagery of mass popular culture dismissed as kitsch by Clement Greenberg and the abstract expressionists. Picasso spoke once of the difficulty of finding new subject matter and cited van Gogh's *A Pair of Boots* as an outstanding example. But find a new subject is what Tracey Emin has done.

A key feature of Emin's treatment of sex is her disclosure, in *Everyone I Ever Slept With 1963–95*, *Why I Never Became a Dancer* and her written piece *Masculinity*, of an early teenage phase of promiscuity in Margate. In the voiceover on *Dancer*, she describes it as follows:

> And then there was sex. It was something you could just do, and it was for free. Sex was something simple. You could got to a pub, you'd walk home, have fish and chips, then sex... on a beach, down an alley, a green, a park, even a hotel. It didn't matter that I was young, thirteen or fourteen. It didn't matter that they were men... 19, 20, 25, 26. It never crossed my mind to ask them what the attraction was. I knew... sex was what it was... by the time I was fifteen I had stopped shagging.

I suspect that even if it is not a majority experience, such a phase among working-class girls is quite common, driven by a complex mixture of low self-esteem, the search for love, affection, intimacy, pleasure, excitement, desire to grow up, ambivalent yearnings for a baby and so on. Usually the experience remains hidden; hidden at the time for obvious reasons, from parents, or school and the authorities – though shared perhaps with a best friend; hidden, or at least not talked about, later when adult respectability has been achieved. It therefore remains largely unrecorded and unrepresented. Films and novels have occasionally visited the territory, but not, until now, the elevated world of fine art.

Emin's treatment of this experience appears simple – a plain rendering of the facts – but it is in fact quite complex and nuanced. In *Dancer,* she defends herself against the charge of being a 'slag' and records her conviction at the time that she was 'better than all those boys'. But in *Masculinity* she writes that she 'developed the ridiculous habit of sleeping with men much older than me.' In her interview with Melvyn Bragg for *The South Bank Show*, she says she must accept some responsibility because she 'egged the men on, followed them, flirted' but also that in their twenties these men should have known better than to sleep with a fourteen-year-old. However, in the same interview, she also claims for her promiscuous phase that it was very 'educational'.

This 'ambivalence' towards her sexual experiences runs throughout her work.

Jennifer Doyle, in her essay 'The Effect of Intimacy', calls this 'Tracey Emin's bad-sex aesthetics'.[2] I think this term is wrong. Emin records many bad sexual experiences in her art, but she does not 'aestheticise' them. They are not presented as anything other than bad experiences with all their negative emotional effects. She deals with childhood abuse, humiliation, abandonment, rape and abortion in the way these things actually happen to women (never as her own or another's fantasy material) and with the severe emotional trauma and pain they caused. There is no romanticisation of abjection (though perhaps the appliquéd *Love Poem* is a partial exception to this).

However, this central theme is held in tension with two others. The first is that her experiences, though often bad, have not proved insuperable. Yes, they were deeply painful, but they were not, including the rape, 'unspeakable' or the worst thing imaginable. She does not, I think, revel in her suffering, but in her ability to have overcome it. *Why I Never Became a Dancer* ends with a seagull soaring up and away from the shores of Margate. The second is the retention, despite the traumas of the past, of an open affirmative attitude to sex and sexuality, that is, to good sex:

> You don't fuck me over
> You gently lift me out of bed
> Lay me on the floor
> And make love to me.

Holding these three elements, each of them a humane and progressive response, in tension with each other but without allowing any of them to be compromised, is a very considerable artistic and emotional achievement.

Emin does not present herself as a feminist artist and is not generally thought of as one. The previous generation of feminist artists and critics tended to view Emin and other so-called 'bad girls' with disdain as frivolous betrayers of the feminist/art/theory cause. But, in fact, in dealing with sex Emin deals also with sexism. *Why I Never Became a Dancer* confronts the – very crude – sexism rampant among certain kinds of teenage boys and young men. *My Bed* challenges the sexist attitude that makes a disordered bedroom much more shameful for a woman than a man. Indeed, there is a sense in which the totality of her art practice and persona challenge the double standards about sex. The question of class interacts with the question of sexism here. Emin is not seen as a 'feminist' artist because feminism, and especially feminism in the art world, has been a largely middle-class phenomenon, focussing mainly on the issues that concern middle-class and professional women; how women are represented in the media, how gender affects promotion chances and so on. The issues Emin deals with – how teenage girls get 'slagged off' and 'broken into' – are not recognised as feminist, because they come from a different world. But the fact is that Emin tackles feminism at the sharp end. Although, as we shall see, she has also produced work about sexism in the art world.

Art

I Need Art Like I Need God is the title and content of one of Emin's pieces in neon lighting, and 'art', in particular Emin's relationship to art, is a central theme in her work. In interviews she strongly defends her own artistic integrity and the general integrity of contemporary art, and consistently proclaims her faith in 'art'. When some of her work, along with much other contemporary art, was destroyed in a warehouse fire, her first public response was measured, putting the event in perspective of the real disasters that occur in the world, but she was hurt and angered by the mockery of sections of the press and public. This should not be surprising, for it is through art that Emin dealt with many of her personal problems and completely transformed her life. She celebrates this – she thought of calling her last solo show at White Cube *Upgrade*.

One of the ways 'art' features in Emin's work is through her references to other artists. Of course, many artists do this – Picasso reworks themes from Velázquez and Delacroix, Manet's *Olympia* echoes the pose of Titian's *Venus d'Urbino*, Warhol takes one of his images of Christ from da Vinci's *The Last Supper* and so on – but Emin's range of reference is broad and impressive (which gives the lie to another of the myths and misconceptions about her, prevalent in the media, that she is some kind of 'primitive' or 'naif'). Most obviously she is indebted to her hero Edvard Munch, and to Egon Schiele; the use of language in both the monoprints and the blankets nods to Basquiat; the neon lighting pieces are influenced by Dan Flavin and Bruce Nauman; *My Bed* recalls Rauschenberg's *Bed* and, more subtly, the bed of Manet's Olympia; *The Helter Skelter* construction references the Tatlin Tower; the blanketry work in general builds on the use of sewing and textiles by feminist artists of the seventies and eighties.

Of course, if quoting other artists was the main point of these works, it would make them banal, but with Emin's pieces this is not the case. Her principal tribute to Munch is *Homage to Edvard Munch and All My Dead Children* and is accompanied by her verbal scream (for her aborted children), which is truly disturbing and terrible. Her drawings may owe something to Schiele but are in no way imitations or similar in content. In the case of the blanket work, Emin has transformed the genre, freeing it of its craft and genteel associations, and making it into a vibrant dramatic new form in its own right.

One of Emin's most important works, while remaining partly autobiographical, is also a powerful comment on the role of women in art. This was a performance piece originally entitled *Exorcism of the Last Painting I Ever Made*, enacted in the Gallery Andreas Brändström in Stockholm in 1996. Emin spent three weeks living naked in an enclosed studio space, visible to the public during gallery opening hours through fish-eye lenses in the walls. At first she was just there being observed, then gradually she started to paint. The performance was recorded, and we can see it in a photo series called *The Life Model Goes Mad*.

The piece has many meanings, but among them is the fact that traditionally, say one hundred years ago, at the birth of modernism with

Picasso and Matisse in Paris, or even fifty or thirty years ago, the principal role of women in art was as models (and the line between model, lover and prostitute was often blurred). As the Guerrilla Girls put it in their famous poster *Do Women Have to Be Naked to Get into the Met. Museum?*, 'less than 5% of the artists in the Modern Art sections are female, but 85% of the nudes are female'. If Emin had been around in 1900 or 1950, the combination of her class and gender would almost certainly have made her a model and not an artist. Indeed, Emin actually was a life model for a while at the start of her career. Recently things have begun to change, and Emin is part of that change. *The Life Model Goes Mad* (the 'goes mad' is a reference to her earlier blanket piece – and self-adopted slogan – *Mad Tracey from Margate*) enacts the process; the object becomes subject, the passive becomes active, the life model turns into an artist. As usual in Emin, the piece is both autobiographical and socially representative at the same time.

Conclusion

'Remember the golden rule. . . . Those who have the gold make the rules.'

As we know from Marx, in class-divided societies the ruling class invariably dominates the culture (though seldom completely). However, the domination in the field of visual art, especially painting and sculpture, has been more complete, more extreme than in other art forms. This is because, whereas the poet or novelist needs only pen and paper, visual art must be embodied in materials (which are very expensive), stored and exhibited, either in museums and galleries or in public places (which of course are never controlled by the public). And because in the capitalist epoch the art market has focussed on the buying and selling of 'unique' and 'original' works, in contrast to music and literature which centre on either the large-scale selling of mechanical reproductions – books, records, CDs and so on – or live performances to collective audiences. As a result, from Tutankhamun to Lorenzo de' Medici and Henry VIII to Rockefeller and Saatchi, visual art has been dominated by the very rich and very powerful. This in turn has meant that the exclusion and marginalisation of working-class people, women and black people has been even more marked in visual art than in other art forms. There is no female painter whose standing in the canon compares with Jane Austen or George Eliot. There is, to my knowledge, not a single painting by a black artist in the National Gallery, and until very recently, there were none in the Tate either. In this context, the existence and work of Tracey Emin is both an example of the limited change that has occurred and a challenge to the present and the future.

Marx also tells us that art, like religion, philosophy and politics, is part of the superstructure of society, which arises from and is conditioned by the economic base. I would add that the economic base (i.e., the forces and relations of production) give rise to and shape a developing ensemble of social relations which range from how people dress (with all its connotations) to family and sexual relations, to how people look at a king or a beggar and how a king or a beggar looks at the people, to how we experience the sea, the countryside and the city. What major art does is express and comment upon these changing social relations in a visually powerful way. Giotto and Michelangelo, Holbein and Bruegel, Hals and Rembrandt, Hogarth, Constable and Joseph Wright of Derby, David and Goya, Courbet and Manet, Picasso, Léger, Malevich, Rodchenko, Ernst, Bacon and Warhol all do this in their different ways. And so does Emin.

The changing social relations that Emin addresses are those shaping the relative positions in society of women and men, especially young working-class women and men. The changes in this sphere in the course of my lifetime (i.e., the last half century or so), have been spectacular: the huge rise in the number of women (especially married women) in paid labour; the Equal Pay Act; the Sex Discrimination Act; the pill; legalised abortion; freer divorce and lip service to equality all over the place. In other ways they remain strictly limited: no fundamental change in the division of labour in the home, no equal pay in reality, women still hugely underrepresented in top jobs, sexist images all over the media. Of course, the change has not been evenly spread across society. In my judgment the least has been at the very top, among those who own the wealth, run industry and finance and control the state. There, bourgeois male power remains firmly entrenched. The biggest change has been among the professional middle classes – academics, intellectuals, media people and the like, where the success of girls in education and higher education has had its effect and equal-opportunities policies abound. Many working-class women have also benefitted from the changes, from the shift in general attitudes and the increased educational and job opportunities. But for the majority, especially in the manual as opposed to white-collar working class, where money for child care is scarce or nonexistent and the struggle for survival dominates, the change has been minimal. Some working-class men, in the main the politically more progressive, have changed their attitudes, but many have not, and the old sexism remains rampant. The problems are particularly acute among teenagers and young men anxious to establish their virility, and this is what working-class girls and young women have to cope with.

These are the contradictions which Emin has lived and which her art expresses and responds to with clarity and passion. Politically, there is an obvious problem in that, while Emin's work, for all its dealing with trauma, ultimately carries a message of hope, it is hope for an individual – not a collective or social – solution, and this can only be possible for a small minority. Unfortunately we don't get our art to political order, and given the historical period of Emin's artistic formation, the eighties and early nineties, it is hardly surprising that collective working-class emancipation through political action was not high on her agenda. What matters more than the correct politics is whether the problems addressed are real, whether the art has integrity and whether it is visually imaginative and powerful. Emin's work succeeds on all these counts, with the extra factor that it really speaks to people, and people beyond the normal range of 'art lovers', in a way that is achieved by no other contemporary artist.

AFTERNOTE: It should be noted that Tracey Emin's political response to her success, wealth and celebrity led her to become a Tory. This would appear to be a very crude example of Marx's proposition that 'social being determines social consciousness', cruder than is usual among rich artists, who normally retain at least a veneer of radicalism. This evolution does not, I believe, invalidate her earlier work or my evaluation of it. Unfortunately life, and the history of art, is full of such developments and contradictions. However, it is worth saying that much of her more recent work, her ink drawings and bronze sculptures – though it lacks the 'punch' of her early pieces – remains, I think, of high quality.

CHAPTER 8

The Liberty of Appearing: The Photographs of Yasser Alwan

This essay was written for The Liberty of Appearing: Photographs of Egyptian Working People, *the catalogue for Yasser Alwan's travelling exhibition of photographs which was shown at Foyles Bookshop Charing Cross Road, London, 7–20 November 2008, and then at the Eldon Gallery of Portsmouth University from 2 November to 5 December 2008. The beautiful catalogue, which contained over fifty of Alwan's photographs, was designed and published by Richard Peacock.*

Yasser Alwan was born in Nigeria to Iraqi parents and grew up mainly in the United States before moving permanently to Cairo in 1994. I got to know Yasser and his work in the course of several visits to Egypt, for political purposes, in the mid-noughts. It is a source of pride for me that the prediction at the end of the essay that the people in Alwan's photographs 'may be about to take "the liberty of appearing" on the centre of the world stage' came true in the Egyptian Revolution of 2011. It is equally a source of great sadness that in 2013 this great revolution was defeated and suppressed by the hideous regime of General Abdel Fattah el-Sisi.

Yasser Alwan's photographs express a profound humanitarian egalitarianism that is rare in the long history of art as a whole and almost unique in the relatively short history of photography. 'Photographs of Egyptian working people' – already this bare factual description raises a multitude of issues and announces an artistic and political stance.

We live in a culture – and by this I mean the total culture of global capitalism and the total historical culture of Western and non-Western civilisations – in which working people (peasants, agricultural labourers, slaves, artisans, manual and nonmanual proletarians) are massively underrepresented. For the last five thousand years, working people have been the immense majority of humanity, but in the world's poetry, drama, novels, film, TV and visual art – music and dance may be a partial exception – their presence is marginal.

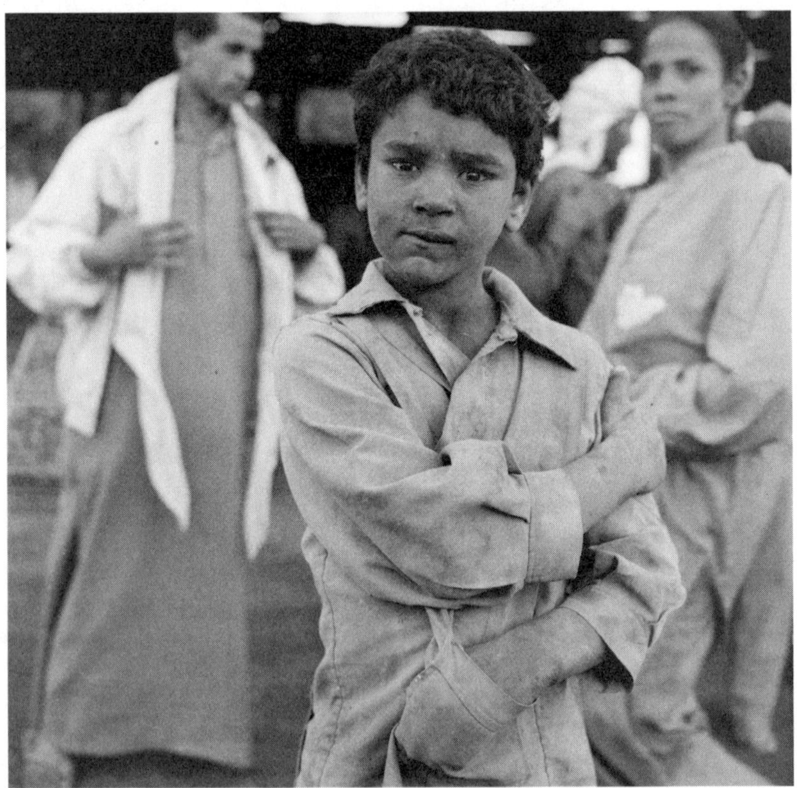

Yasser Alwan, *Boy from the Tannery* from *The Liberty of Appearing* (2008)

From Homer to Hollywood, working people are the extras, the walk-on parts. For every painting of peasant life by Bruegel, for every etching of a beggar by Rembrandt, there are a hundred, maybe a thousand portraits of emperors, kings, queens, aristocrats and bourgeois. This is not prejudice but a simple reflection of reality. In class-divided societies, that is to say, *every* society after the transition from foraging to agriculture, the upper classes are few but important and the working classes, the common people, are many but unimportant. Against this background, any artist who, like Yasser Alwan, turns this hierarchy upside down and places working people centre stage, is making a political statement.

Add the designation 'Egyptian' to the class category and the magnitude of the underrepresentation increases manyfold. This is something that applies not just to Egypt, though Egypt has its particularities in this narrative, but to all 'non-Western' societies and cultures. The Eurocentric view of history, developed alongside racism as an ideological accompaniment to material conquest, credits Mesopotamia (Iraq) and Egypt with the birth of civilisation and then moves swiftly to ancient Greece and Rome, from which point the non-European world simply disappears, except exclusively as an object of European discovery and military engagement. The result is a profound ignorance. The *only* figures from Egyptian history between Cleopatra and Nasser known to the Western public are Salah ad-Din (Saladin) from the Crusades and, perhaps to a few, Mohammed Ali. Ask a British university class (I have tried this often) to name three non-Western artists, three non-Western scientists, three poets, three philosophers, and you are setting a test which the large majority are destined to fail – the odd 'Frida Kahlo' and 'Confucius', and the rest is blank. Results would not be much better among the faculty.

Of course, it is a question of the nature of the representation as much as its quantity. Racial, gender, orientalist and colonial stereotyping have all been substantially explored in academic and cultural circles in recent decades, but class has received less attention. However, we should remember that while Shakespeare gives us Othello, Shylock and Cleopatra (each, incidentally, an achievement of genius), his 'common people' are rendered in prose and offer only comic interludes, albeit pointed ones. And what John Berger wrote about Dutch genre painting (that of 'low life') of the seventeenth century applies to many subsequent representations of working people: 'The purpose of the 'genre' picture was to prove – either positively or negatively – that virtue in this world was rewarded by social and financial success. Thus, those who could afford to buy these pictures . . . had their own virtue confirmed. Such pictures were particularly popular with the newly arrived bourgeoisie.'[1]

Even artists and writers avowedly sympathetic to working people have often produced representations of them that were highly problematic. Thus George Orwell, who broke with his middle-class public school background to the extent of living (for a time) with the poor and down and out, and fighting with the POUM in the Spanish Civil War, and who wrote in *1984* that '[i]f there is hope ... it lies in the proles', nevertheless depicted those proles as narrow, animalistic creatures more or less incapable of consciousness and higher feelings, while in *Animal Farm* they were represented by the cart horse Boxer, who was congenitally stupid. Even Brecht never produced a play foregrounding working-class characters. (I say this not to criticise Brecht – possibly the greatest playwright of the century – but to show the difficulty of the task.)

This, then, is the general context in which Yasser Alwan's photographs of Egyptian working people demand 'the liberty of appearing'. But, of course, Alwan's work also exists in the specific context of the history of photography, which to some extent constitutes a special case. On the one hand, the relative cheapness and availability of its means of production (the camera) and the ease of mechanical reproduction of its output give photography a democratic character absent from its adjacent art forms, painting and film. As a result, there is a substantial tradition of the sympathetic photography of working people running from early photographers, such as John Thompson, through the Americans Lewis Hine, Walker Evans and Dorothea Lange, the German August Sander, Brassaï and Henri Cartier-Bresson in France, to the contemporary Brazilian Sebastião Salgado, and in which Alwan consciously stands.

On the other hand, there is in photography – due to its mechanical and instant character – a potential for domination, coldness and cruelty not present, or not present to the same degree, in painting or drawing. This is manifested in its language – the photographer 'captures', 'shoots' and 'snaps' her subject–in its role in social control (mug shots, ID, passports, etc.) and as handmaiden of imperialism and colonialism (lucidly analysed and illustrated by Alwan himself in his superb study of the photographs of Lehnert and Landrock, *Imagining Egypt* (Cairo: Orient Art Publishing, 2007) and in the paparazzi phenomenon. In the world of art photography, it has given rise to the elements of the freak show, objectification, mockery and exploitation, found in varying degrees in the work of Diane Arbus, Joel-Peter Witkin, Robert Mapplethorpe and Martin Parr – a tendency to which Alwan is consciously opposed.

One way of grasping the stature of Alwan's work is by means of comparison with some of his photographic forebears.

Lewis Hine photographed child labour in the United States at the beginning of the last century in order to expose it and promote social reform. He photographed workers building the Empire State, suspended in the sky above Manhattan, to demonstrate the extraordinary skill and courage of working people in their daily lives. Alwan is also opposed to child labour, supports social reform and is aware of workers' amazing feats in their work, but this is not the driving force of his photography.

The driving force of Brassaï's photography is the evocation of an atmosphere – the atmosphere of nighttime Paris in the thirties, of Montmartre and Montparnasse. There are some photos of working men at Les Halles, but they are subordinate to the prostitutes, carnival performers, lovers and petty gangsters of bohemia, and the individuals in the pictures are subordinate to the overall ambience.

Cartier-Bresson is certainly interested in ordinary people, but what governs his photography is capturing the 'decisive moment' when those ordinary people can be configured in a brilliant composition. Sander, who has been a big influence on Alwan, set out to document the German people of the twenties by 'type' according to a systematic classification, rather as in Engels's classic prescription for realism, 'the truthful reproduction of typical characters under typical circumstances'. At first sight it might appear that Alwan is trying to do something similar for Egypt, but any attempt at system is subverted by his interest in the particular subject, as a person, and this gives his work a human warmth lacking in Sander.

In fact, there are echoes of all these photographers in Alwan, but his work is distinguished from all of theirs by its greater engagement with, and representation of, the personalities of his subjects.

Take, for example, the photographs of the woman trader at Umm Reda, Waily, and the incense man at Dar al-Salaam. Both are obviously poor – everyone at that level of society in Egypt is poor – but neither is photographed to *represent* poverty; nor are they there for their *typicality*. Rather it is their individuality, their respective specific spirit, that has drawn Alwan, and that Alwan has communicated in his superb photographs.

Alwan is interested in individual people. It sounds like a cliché, and a bourgeois cliché at that, but the moment you insert class into the statement – individual *working* people – it becomes artistically and politically highly charged. An intellectual who, in life, is genuinely interested, as an equal, in *specific* working-class people is a rarity, and one who is interested in them artistically is even rarer. The notion that working people are simple, that they have simple ideas and emotions, compared to the complexity of the middle classes, is a prejudice with five millennia of class society behind it. Breaking with it as Alwan has done, not just in theory but organically, as an artist has to do if the break is to be realised in their work, speaks of an art and a politics far more radical than that of social reform, the New Deal or the Popular Front.

Two political points need clarification here. The first concerns the suffering of working people. In the world today, working people suffer relentlessly, unforgivably and on an unimaginable scale, but those for whom, in the words of Marx, 'the proletariat exists only as the most suffering class', miss the main point, which is the capacity of working people to resist, to end their suffering and to emancipate themselves and humanity.

The second concerns the relation between the individual and the collective. It is often assumed that an emphasis on the individual is bourgeois and right wing, while stressing collective interests and collective struggle is proletarian and left wing. There is an important element of truth in this, in that the working class must struggle collectively to defend its interests and change society, but it can easily be overstated and becomes damaging if it is understood as opposition to individual development and freedom. This was not Marx's view. For Marx there was always a dialectical interaction between the individual and the social:

> [T]he communists do not put egoism against self-sacrifice or self-sacrifice against egoism.... they are very well aware that

> egoism just as much as self-sacrifice *is* in definite circumstances a necessary form of the self assertion of individuals. Hence the communists by no means want . . . to do away with the 'private individual' for the sake of the 'general' self-sacrificing man.[2]

Elsewhere, he writes, 'What is to be avoided above all is the re-establishing of "Society" as an abstraction vis-à-vis the individual. The individual *is the social being*.'[3] And, 'In place of the old bourgeois society . . . we shall have an association in which *the free development of each* is the condition of the free development of all.'[4]

How do these theoretical points translate into the language of photography, and how do they relate to Alwan's photographs in particular? The capacity of workers for resistance and self-emancipation can, of course, be shown in photographs of strikes, picket lines, demonstrations and so on. Such photographs are absolutely necessary, just as leaflets, banners and posters are necessary, but they are also artistically limited. (Artistically, the best demo photos I have seen are by Tina Modotti, but they tend to sacrifice the demonstrators and their aims to the achievement of a brilliant, almost abstract, composition.) Another possibility is to produce idealised images of well-toned workers gazing determinedly into the future. This was the Stalinist way, and it was politically and artistically false. Yasser Alwan's way is to show that working people, despite poverty and toil, remain complex and dignified human beings, damaged but not utterly defeated, with their own take on life and the world.

Consider, for example, the photos taken in the tanneries, which show men and boys working in hellish conditions, ones that probably condemn them to early graves. And while this is an essential part of their story, it is not the whole story. The key photographs in the series – the boy looking out from beneath the hides on his head, and the seated young man squarely facing the camera with a cigarette in his fingers – say more than this. In the eyes of the boy, almost welling up with tears, we see *both* pain at the almost unendurable weight (physical and metaphorical) pressing on his shoulders *and* determination to carry on, with just a glint of hope for the future. A similar contradiction beats in the breast of the seated young man as he bites his lip and looks quizzically at the camera, trying to make sense of his oppressive world.

Then there are the pictures of the limestone quarry diggers at Helwan, south of Cairo – I have been to Helwan, and it is an aptly named place. The long shot gives us the overall scene and the sense of the searing heat of the desert. The close-ups show us the specifics of their work; they are bent double, wielding their axes with pinpoint accuracy, releasing precisely cut blocks of great weight to be shouldered and shifted by hand. Then, suddenly, there is the picture of the single digger with the white turban, poised with his pickaxe ready to strike. Of course, it is a work picture. He is about to smite the limestone, not the international bourgeoisie, and yet . . . ! It is an astonishing photograph.

It might seem that the photographs taken at the Gezira races don't fit this argument. Not so. Throughout the world the poor gamble – even though gambling increases their poverty. The rich gamble too, but in a different way and for different reasons, to show off, to display their wealth or their masculinity, to inject risk into their risk-free lives. The poor, especially the older poor, gamble for the right to dream. For the price of a lottery ticket, they buy the right to a secret fantasy life for a day or a week. For the price of a few betting slips, they purchase hours of intense engagement with life, hours when they can pit their wits against the system and 'win', get something for nothing, get paid without working! Of course, they don't usually win, but sometimes they do. And where else in poor people's lives do they ever win? Where else can they take on the man and not be instantly crushed? The gambler is not a man resisting politically, but he is a man resisting in his own way, refusing to give in completely; and he is a person, not just a type. He is the white-haired man, about to put a cigarette to his lips (what a great photograph this is) who, at least outwardly, has kept his dignity, even a little of his authority, and certainly his manners. He is the wiry old man with a strange peaked cap and a sheet of paper in his hands (a list of runners, a form guide?). What has he been in life? Where did the hat come from, and what does it signify? The hopes of the man in the white jellabiya who screws up his eyes to gaze at the results board may be reduced to the outcome of the 3:30, but they are hopes nonetheless.

Everyone who appears in an Alwan photograph is shown in a social context that constrains and shapes them but does not totally define them. Each is a person and personality in his or her own right, making their life, albeit in circumstances not of their own choosing. This is what I mean by the 'profound humanitarian egalitarianism' of this work.

The Liberty of Appearing, the title of this exhibition, is a double reference. It is taken from a sentence in Thomas Paine's *Rights of Man*: 'But such is the irresistible nature of truth that all it asks, all it wants, is the liberty of appearing.' But this quotation also appears in *The Family of Man*, the book of Edward Steichen's famous photography exhibition from 1955. Both references are appropriate for these photographs, but the phrase also points in a third direction.

At the beginning of this essay, I spoke of the cultural invisibility of working people, especially those in the poorer parts of the world. In recent years, however, the working people of Egypt have been making themselves steadily more visible. Paradoxically, working people make themselves most visible when, together, they stop working, that is to say, when they go on strike. This Egyptian workers have been doing with increasing frequency. Early in 2008, food riots caused by rising prices were followed by a wave of strikes emanating from the Mahalla textile factory, the largest workplace in the region. In political circles the name Mahalla has since become symbolic of working-class struggle internationally.

The objective political importance of Egyptian workers is also becoming ever clearer. This is the largest and potentially most powerful working class in the whole region between Europe and India, that is, in the central battleground for control of energy supplies and the front line between imperialism and anti-imperialism. It holds the key to the defeat of the brutal Mubarak regime and hence to the overthrow of the other pro-US dictatorships in the area, which in turn would open the door to the defeat of Zionist Israel, in a way that is beyond the power of the Palestinians acting alone.

There is a photographic/artistic reference point here as well as a political one. The photographer whose work might seem to precede, and even preempt, Alwan's is Sebastião Salgado. But there is a fundamental difference. Salgado's photographs of the Serra Palada gold mine in Brazil are brilliant, but his study of workers as a whole, *Workers: An Archaeology of the Industrial Age*, is premised on the mistaken (though widely held) notion that the working class is in the process of disappearing. This affects the photography. Salgado, deliberately I think, gives his pictures a grainy, elegiac quality as he commemorates this dying breed and so engages in a kind of romantic mythmaking. There is none of this in Alwan, whose working people are insistently present in the here and now, and have no need of idealisation.

And, in fact, the world working class is here today – in Korea and China, Indonesia and India, the Middle East and South America, in larger numbers than ever before in history. Concentrated in great cities like São Paolo, Mumbai, Canton and Mexico City, it possesses awesome potential power. Cairo is one of the greatest of these cities, and the Egyptian working class is a key contingent in this international army.

Yasser Alwan's photographs do not give us the demos, strikes and uprisings, but they give us the people in all their human contradictions. It is highly appropriate that this exhibition should appear at a time when these people may be about to take 'the liberty of appearing' on the centre of the world stage. There is a chance, only a chance, but a real chance nonetheless, that the young brick and shingle maker, who shoulders a bucket the size of his torso and whose face is obscured by his own arm, will grow up to make history.

CHAPTER 9

Shorter Reviews

Jackson Pollock

First published in Socialist Review *229 (April 1999)*

Every reader with an interest in art should try and visit the Jackson Pollock retrospective at the Tate Gallery in London. Here is a unique chance to see the work of one of the century's most influential and controversial artists. Pollock, for reasons of scale, texture and colour, demands to be seen in the original, and most of the time there are only one or two works on view in Britain. In this show there is work from throughout Pollock's career, including about a dozen of the great drip paintings on which his reputation and notoriety primarily rest.

None of us judges or even 'sees' without preconceptions, and in the case of Pollock there are at least five 'interpretations' in sufficient circulation to condition our initial responses. The first, and predominant, interpretation seized on the 'drip and flick' method of applying paint to suggest Pollock's work was just a random mess, an absurd tangle of lines and splodges. 'This is not art – it's a joke in bad taste', as a *Reynold's News* headline put it in 1959. Doubtless this is a view that still plays well in the columns of the *Sun*, but it is comprehensively refuted by any serious scrutiny of the paintings. A few minutes spent looking, in turn, at *Summertime*, *Lavender Mist* and *Blue Poles* demonstrates that Pollock achieved strikingly different aesthetic effects in different works and that this was a highly controlled process.

The second, more favourable, interpretation was a kind of inversion of the first. It too focussed on the drip method, which it called 'action painting' and celebrated as a wild romantic outpouring of self-expression. In this view, much was made of Pollock's birth in Cody, Wyoming, and he was depicted as a sort of all-American, lonesome cowboy hero. The most sophisticated presentation of this line was by the critic Harold Rosenberg, who spoke of the transformation of painting into an existential drama in which 'what was to go on the canvas was not a picture but an event', and who wrote: 'The big moment came when it was decided to paint "just to paint". The gesture on the canvas was a gesture of liberation from value – political, aesthetic, moral.'

The third account, associated with Clement Greenberg, the most influential art critic of the 1950s and 1960s, was in sharp opposition to the second. It proclaimed abstract expressionism, and Pollock in particular, as the epitome of aesthetic value. It supported Pollock's work on formalistic grounds as simply the best painting of its day and the culmination of an art tradition going back via cubism and Cézanne to Manet, in which painting became ever 'purer' and more concentrated in what was 'essential' to it, the making of marks on a flat surface. It was this view which established Pollock's position in the modern art canon and became hegemonic in the art world until the late 1960s.

The 1960s radicalisation, however, gave rise to a fourth interpretation – a left critique – which located Pollock in his political context and attributed his success not to his formal merits but to his ideological usefulness to US imperialism. It was revealed that posthumous exhibitions of Pollock had been covertly sponsored by the CIA, and the argument was made that the US ruling class threw its weight behind this kind of art out of a nationalistic craving for a US avant-garde to supplant Paris, and a symbol of freedom to counterpose to Soviet insistence on social realism. Thus Pollock was promoted as, in the words of Eva Cockcroft, a 'weapon of the Cold War'.

Finally, there is a feminist revaluation of Pollock which looks askance at the machismo of the 'hero in the studio' and tends to see the whole drip-and-flick performance as the acting out of the phallocentric male fantasy on the symbolically supine canvas.

These political critiques were a salutary corrective to the romantic and nationalist mythmaking of the US bourgeoisie and the formalism of Greenberg that underwrote it. They disclosed the forces of ideology and material interest that lay behind the supposedly 'disinterested' judgments of the art world. That the Museum of Modern Art, the principal United States tastemaker in this area, was owned and controlled by the Rockefeller family, and that no Chinese wall separated their policy in art from their policy in Latin America and Southeast Asia, are facts to be reckoned with. Moreover, they are precisely the kind of facts that the art establishment – the Tate as well as MoMA – is anxious to marginalise. In his lengthy presentation at the exhibition's press view, Jeremy Lewison, the Tate's director of collections, made no mention of this left critique (though the feminist case was fully acknowledged), and in his book *Interpreting Pollock* he dismisses it in one line as some kind of paranoid conspiracy theory.

However, the limitation of this critique is that while it may help to explain Pollock's rapid rise to art superstardom, it tells us little of substance about the meaning and merit of his paintings. For if it is a fact that Pollock was used for Cold War purposes, it is no less a fact that he did not paint with that intention.

So what of the paintings themselves? This exhibition confirms that it is the drip paintings of 1947 to 1950 that are the real achievement. Some of the earlier works are surprisingly good, better than reproductions had led one to expect, especially in their colour. But *The She-Wolf* is the only really outstanding painting of this period, and in general the work does not get 'beyond' Picasso, with whose influence he was struggling.

The drip paintings are qualitatively different. This is where Pollock makes the breakthrough to a new way of painting and a distinct aesthetic vision. Even here, there are failures, pictures, like *Galaxy* and *Reflection of the Big Dipper*, which don't work. But there are masterpieces like *Full Fathom Five*, *Number 32, 1950* and *Lavender Mist,* which are among the great paintings of the century. It is a criticism of this show that not enough of these great paintings (e.g., *Autumn Rhythm*) are on view compared with the show when it was in New York and relative to the lesser earlier work.

What makes these paintings 'great'? The major paintings possess two qualities which relate to both form and content. First, they create order out of chaos. Without obvious patterning they achieve a total symphonic composition, and this speaks of the struggle against alienation, fragmentation and disintegration. Second, these compositions 'signify' at many levels – they convey by suggestion a multiplicity of 'meanings', meanings that are social, historical and political in character.

Let us take *Lavender Mist* as an example. On first seeing a reproduction of this, my eight-year-old granddaughter said instantly, 'It's like *EastEnders*!' She is right. It is suggestive of an aerial photograph of a city, but it is a city that has somehow been blasted. Here we must remember that this painting was done from above. It is also suggestive of astronomical photographs of nebulae and galaxies (in *Comet*, *Galaxy* and other works this is explicit, and Pollock is known to have been an avid stargazer), while at the same time, close-up details of this and other paintings resemble microscopic photos of molecular structures.

Add to these visual associations that these works were painted in the aftermath of Hiroshima and at the onset of the Cold War, and note Pollock's own statement that 'modern art to me is nothing more than the expression of contemporary aims of the age that we're living in ... the modern painter cannot express this age, the airplane, the atom bomb in the old forms of the Renaissance or of any other past culture. Each age finds its own technique'. Also recall again that this technique was to drip, flick and throw the paint onto the canvas from above. Put all this together and I think the connection between the work and the historical advent of the threat of nuclear annihilation is clear.

Of course, the relation is not direct – neither *Lavender Mist* nor, in fact, any of Pollock's other works is a painting of a nuclear explosion, nor is it anti-war agitprop. Pollock was attempting to paint out of his subconscious, but there is surely reason to believe that the prospect of nuclear holocaust would have been on his mind at this time. Nor is this any more than a partial account of the factors at work – other associations are with the improvisation of bebop and free-form jazz and with the young male rebels (Brando, Dean, Kerouac) of the time. Nevertheless, it is impossible to understand Pollock's art without historically locating him in this way.

This raises the question as to how such art was readily appropriated by the US ruling class. Clearly there were elements in the work that lent themselves to this – the passionate individualism, the absence of overt politics – but there are elements in Blake's 'Jerusalem' which allow that battle cry of freedom to be sung at the Last Night of the Proms.[1] And we are forced to note how often it has been the fate of great radical art, from Milton to van Gogh, to be taken up by our rulers. The solution is not to renounce the art but to expropriate our rulers.

Andy Warhol

First published in Socialist Review *261 (March 2002)*

In 1963 the pop artist Roy Lichtenstein painted *Whaam!* It was a huge blow-up of a comic-book image depicting a US fighter jet destroying an enemy plane at the press of a button. Nearly thirty years later, in the run-up to the Gulf War, *Socialist Review* put this picture on the front cover with the caption 'Stop Bush's Mad War'. Similarly, in 1962 Andy Warhol produced his *Marilyn Diptych*, with its rows of yellow-haired Marilyns, and thirty-six years later the *International Socialism* referenced Warhol on its cover with rows of yellow-haired Karl Marxes. Thus significant art, so often greeted as outlandish or absurd in its day, seeps gradually into the culture until it becomes part of the taken-for-granted collective visual consciousness, like van Gogh's *Sunflowers* or a Constable landscape.

It is therefore worth beginning a consideration of Warhol, whose exhibition has been the subject of such massive media attention, by noting just what a radical move (in historical, not political, terms) pop art represented at its inception. The art world in the 1950s, especially the New York art world, was dominated by the painting of the abstract expressionists and the criticism of their champion, Clement Greenberg. Greenberg's key theoretical statement, 'Avant-Garde and Kitsch', had previously defined 'high art' in opposition to the products of popular mass culture, of kitsch and 'Tin Pan Alley', as he called it. To try to make art out of the despised imagery of Hollywood and the supermarket was a daring and risky provocation, in the same way that a century earlier it was risky for Manet to present a nude working-class prostitute rather than a classical Venus or an Eastern odalisque.

It is true that it was Jasper Johns, Robert Rauschenberg, Richard Hamilton and others who were the first to take this road, but it was Warhol who took it furthest and mostly uncompromisingly with his stark, almost unembellished images of serial soup cans, Brillo boxes, Elvises and Marilyns. The word 'almost' is important here, and so is this impressive retrospective exhibition at the Tate Modern.

The casual viewer of Warhol reproductions in books, magazines and newspapers could easily get the impression that these are 'simple' mechanical reproductions of already-iconic images. But standing in front of the very large originals immediately makes it clear that these pictures are carefully and artfully constructed. For example, *210 Coca-Cola Bottles* (seven rows, thirty bottles each) actually presents us with 210 different bottles, each distinguished by variations in the quantity of the liquid, the highlights on the glass, the lettering on the bottle and so on, so that the pictures constitute not only an invocation of Coke and mass production but also a complex 'abstract' composition in its own right. The same applies to *S&H Green Stamps* and to *192 One Dollar Bills*, in which the bills all vary in tone and some are upside down. It's even more important where the Marilyn pictures are concerned. All the Marilyns derive from a single source, a clipped black-and-white still from the 1953 film *Niagara*, but each is different, and not only in colour. *Blue Shot Marilyn*, for example, has a white circle right between Monroe's eyes, clearly suggestive of a bullet hole. The *Marilyn Diptych* divides into twenty-five coloured Monroes on the left and twenty-five black-and-whites on the right, with the image passing through near-total blackening and disfiguration in the seventh column to extreme faintness on the far right. The more you look at the coloured panels, the more the hair, eyeshadow and lips look like paper cutouts that have been stuck on the faces, emphasising the artificially constructed nature of the Monroe 'image'. Also, the misregistration of the colour (the failure of the colour to fit exactly with the underlying black and white photograph) changes the expression on some of the faces from a smile almost to a snarl, especially where the red lipstick overlaps onto the teeth like blood.

The dark side of US life

Thus, while it is obvious that these works from the 1960s are 'about' mass production and celebrity, the actual paintings clearly undermine the oft-repeated view that Warhol's art is a simple celebration of either of these phenomena – 'fascinated critique' would be a more accurate designation. The images of Elvis also make this point. In the black-and-white *Double Elvis*, the left-hand figure is so darkened as to be virtually a black Elvis, while the red-shirted Elvis against a blue background has red lipstick – a camp, gay Elvis!

In fact, none of the early 'celebrity' works gives us a romanticised, glamorous publicity-type picture. They are certainly 'beautiful' in the sense that Warhol has created highly charged, highly memorable images, but they all share the same flat, impersonal, distanced quality, reflecting the fragile, alienated nature of the fame they represent.

This exhibition also gives prominence to the social-political works – the suicides, car crashes, race riots, electric chairs and so on – in which Warhol documented the dark side of US life in the 1960s. Some of these Warhol has called 'Disasters', in reference to Goya's *Disasters of War*, and indeed his subjects and themes are to some extent similar to Goya's. All of these large silkscreen prints make a strong visual and emotional impact – Warhol has a brilliant eye for the telling image.

Three of them I found especially powerful: the huge black and red *Atomic Bomb* in which the awesome blackening mushroom cloud is given the horns of the devil; the chilling *Big Electric Chair*, made more so by its use of dilapidated ordinariness; and the whited-out *White Disaster I*, depicting a lynching with a black man hanging from a telegraph pole and a burning car. It is, I think, neither possible nor desirable to try to infer a coherent or developed political position from these pictures, but their basic sympathies seem unambiguous. If one wants to pin down Warhol's politics, his vicious portrait of Nixon above the slogan 'Vote McGovern' is a fairly straightforward clue (McGovern was an anti–Vietnam-War left Democrat presidential candidate).

The exhibition also brings out other aspects of Warhol's art – his humour in his 'Mona Lisa' series, cheekily entitled *Thirty Are Better Than One*, produced to coincide with the original's much-trumpeted trip to New York. His chaotic avant-gardist capacity to annoy the authorities is seen in his *Thirteen Most Wanted Men* series, offered as a mural to represent the United States on the facade of the New York State Pavilion at the 1964 World Fair. Particularly surprising to me was the extract from *Empire*, his eight-hour film of the Empire State Building. Previously I had assumed this to be of only symbolic or conceptual significance, but the actual film showed that in the absence of any other motion, one became sensitised to every slight atmospheric variation in the air. Warhol's Empire State became Monet's paintings of Rouen Cathedral in a different light.

However, this exhibition unintentionally tells another story as well. It is a deep-seated tendency in both bourgeois art appreciation and the mass media's coverage of art to focus more on the artist's personality than the artist's work – to treat the work as simply an effect of the artist's innate 'genius'. This produces a situation where once an artist is established as a 'master', everything from his/her hand is automatically valued highly, both aesthetically and financially. In reality there are both great and poor Picassos, wonderful and mediocre Rembrandts. And this exhibition shows that there are good and bad Warhols.

At the beginning there are early paintings, influenced, I guess, by Johns and Rauschenberg, which do not work visually. More importantly there is a marked decline in the second half of the show, featuring work from the 1970s and '80s. Here the silkscreen portraits of Liza Minelli, Mick Jagger, Peter Ludwig and others have lost their edge, becoming 'pop' versions of the familiar saccharine society portrait, and some of the attempts at new directions, such as *Oxidation Paintings* and *Camouflage*, are not very interesting failures. Of course, Warhol had not lost all his talent, so there are exceptions, such as the beautiful *Portrait of Joseph Beuys*, but the general trend is downwards. Significantly, in his collaborations with his protégé Basquiat, it is the younger artist's style and work that predominate. It may be that Warhol's shooting by Valerie Solanas, author of the *Scum* (Society for Cutting Up Men) *Manifesto*, in 1968, was the turning point. Or it may be that he was the victim of his own success, his own celebrity.

Never mind. The show as a whole remains very impressive, and the first half offers the opportunity, probably unique for a generation, of a face-to-face engagement with some of the most surprising and telling art of the last fifty years.

Francis Bacon

First published in Socialist Review *329 (October 2008)*

Reviewing an exhibition is an invitation to comment both on the exhibition as such and on the art presented. Since performing both tasks satisfactorily is impossible in the space available, I shall concentrate on questions raised by Francis Bacon's work and say only this about the exhibition. Bacon is now widely proclaimed the greatest British artist of the twentieth century, and this show offers a selection of his best paintings from each phase of his career – it contains all the really 'iconic' works such as the 'Screaming Popes', the *Three Studies for Figures at the Base of a Crucifixion*, the Dyer triptychs, the self-portraits. For anyone interested in modern art, this is definitely a show to see.

Regarding Bacon's overall standing, I would say that he is not one of those artists, like Pablo Picasso, Marcel Duchamp, Piet Mondrian or Andy Warhol, who drove modern art forward to new forms of visual representation, or changed it so fundamentally that it became possible to conceive of an athlete sprinting through the Tate Britain as a work of art. He is, however, one of those, like Chaim Soutine or Alberto Giacometti, who, while using relatively traditional methods, made images of exceptional emotional power.

The source and nature of this emotional power remain much debated. One can point to a number of influences – Michelangelo, Diego Velázquez, Francisco Goya, Picasso, Giacometti and the photographs by Eadweard Muybridge, among others – and to certain repeated techniques and devices. For example, the way he uses cage structures to suggest his subjects are prisoners or creatures on display; the way, often, they are placed on plinths, or beds, with a sense of space around them, so that they appear served up like meat or specimens on a dish; or the way he uses cubist forms, in his portraits, to knead the flesh round the bones of the skull. But if these are some of the means by which Bacon achieved his effects, they leave the driving force of those effects unidentified.

In other words, why is Bacon's pope screaming? Alternatively, what or who is he screaming at? I pose this question not just as a means of interrogating Bacon's best-known image but also as a way into discussing the general purport of his work.

We don't get a clear answer from Bacon himself. Like many artists he preferred to let his paintings speak for themselves, and his response to questions of this nature was to cite the visual sources of his imagery (Velázquez's *Pope Innocent X*, the nurse's scream in *Battleship Potemkin*), while saying nothing about its emotional sources.

Nevertheless, there is a range of plausible answers on offer: for instance, the pope is Bacon himself, screaming at the fear and loneliness of being a gay man at a time when homosexuality was still a crime; the pope is the pope and Bacon, screaming at the horrors of the world at the end of the war (Auschwitz, Hiroshima); the pope is the pope, screaming at the wreckage of his faith in a godless world; the pope is Papa, Bacon's brutal father, who attempted to beat his homosexuality out of him. This obvious Freudian interpretation was put to Bacon directly by the art critic David Sylvester in one of their famous interviews – Bacon simply deflected it.

The pope's scream, like the figures at the base of a crucifixion, is Bacon's visceral response to the human condition as a whole – a world of violence and despair, hopelessness and terror, essentially meaningless, in which we are all simply 'meat'. There is probably truth in all these answers; indeed, artists often choose images precisely because they carry multiple associations.

However, there is no doubt that the final reading is the one favoured by the art establishment and by Tate Britain. This is because it enables them to assimilate Bacon to Michelangelo, Rembrandt and others, as a producer of 'timeless' truths about life, and because it dovetails with the notion of an unchanging human nature. The bourgeoisie has a place for art that shows the horribleness of life, so long as they can also claim it shows that nothing can be done about it.

For this reason, many on the left, including John Berger, have long been suspicious of, even hostile to, Bacon. And it has to be said that much of Bacon's outlook was reactionary: he was a kind of Nietzschean, adhering to a sort of 'exhilarated despair', and a positive supporter of social inequality as part of 'the texture of life'.

Nevertheless, I do not believe that the Left should reject Bacon's work, as opposed to his views, and I'm pleased that Berger has recently revised his judgment. The horror he so powerfully expressed is in reality a product not of human nature but of alienation, in all its aspects, internal and external. And that can be changed. Moreover, those artists such as Franz Kafka, Samuel Beckett and Bacon, who look into the abyss, who take on the horror and stare it down, do, through their work, make a form of resistance, a defiance, from which we can benefit and draw hope, whether they did or not.

Peter Paul Rubens

First published in Socialist Worker, *August 2006*

Peter Paul Rubens (1577–1640) was a great painter. Anyone who enjoys painting or is interested in the history of art will gain pleasure, and perhaps inspiration, from the exhibition of his work, *Rubens: A Master in the Making*, at the National Gallery in London. Nevertheless, this exhibition is also a good example of how the art establishment, and its traditional approach to art, acts as a barrier to its understanding and real appreciation.

The exhibition focusses on the artistic influences that shaped Rubens's style. This is the 'art connoisseur' approach, which isolates art history from the rest of human history. It contains valuable information, but the problem is what it leaves out. In this show it means the absence of Rubens's best work, which dates from later in his life, and of any attempt to locate his art in its social and political context. Where Rubens is concerned, this is particularly damaging.

To understand his art, it is necessary both to be aware of the basic facts of European history at the time, and to have some understanding of the real social meaning of those facts. Rubens's life coincided with a momentous struggle waged right across Europe. In traditional history, and especially in art history, this is treated as simply a religious struggle between Catholicism and Protestantism, Reformation and Counter-Reformation. In essence, however, it was a struggle between the rising middle class or bourgeoisie and the old aristocracy – a battle between capitalism and feudalism, fought out under the banner of religion. It was a struggle that, in the long run, was to determine the destiny of Europe and the world.

One of the front lines of this conflict was in the Netherlands, where Rubens spent most of his life. The Netherlands were initially not a nation but merely provinces of the vehemently Catholic and feudal Habsburg Empire, based in Spain, and at that time the dominant military power in Europe. The Netherlands, however, were a centre of early capitalist economic development and of Calvinism, the most militant and revolutionary wing of Protestantism. In 1566, the Netherlands rose in revolt against Habsburg rule, and the Spanish king, Philip II, responded by sending an army to crush this revolution. In the southern Netherlands this counterrevolutionary repression was successful, and this area (later to become Belgium) remained under Spanish rule. But in the north the revolution held out. This area was to emerge as the Dutch Republic, the world's first capitalist state.

Rubens's father was a lawyer in Antwerp and a strong Calvinist. In 1568, to escape repression, he fled to Westphalia in Germany, where Rubens was born. In 1587, Rubens's father died, and in 1589 he and his mother returned to Antwerp, where Rubens converted to Catholicism. In the circumstances, that meant joining the counterrevolution.

This had a massive impact on Rubens's art, for it was a time when the Catholic Church was consciously mobilising art as a cultural weapon of the Counter-Reformation. It meant that Rubens went to Italy as a court painter to the Duke of Mantua and studied the art of ancient Rome and of the Renaissance masters (and of the rebel, Caravaggio). It meant that he received innumerable commissions to paint vast canvasses of dramatically swirling figures to adorn the walls of churches and palaces. It meant that while Dutch artists such as Rembrandt and Hals died in poverty, and Caravaggio died on the run, Rubens died the richest and most famous artist in Europe – honoured by the kings of France, Spain and England.

Does the fact that Rubens was the artist of counterrevolution make his art poor or of no interest?

No; he was immensely skilled and talented, and expressed with great vigour the values appropriate to his cause – the power and glory of his church and religion. At the same time his work celebrated (under the cover of classical mythology) the sensuous pleasures of the flesh. But his politics did damage and restrict his art. They made it tend to the overly grandiose and ensured that the life of the people and the insight, sympathy and solidarity, so evident in Hals and Rembrandt, were lacking. His greatest works, such as his landscape *Het Steen* and his nude portrait of Helena Fourment in fur, came at the end of his life, when he was painting for himself, not his patrons.

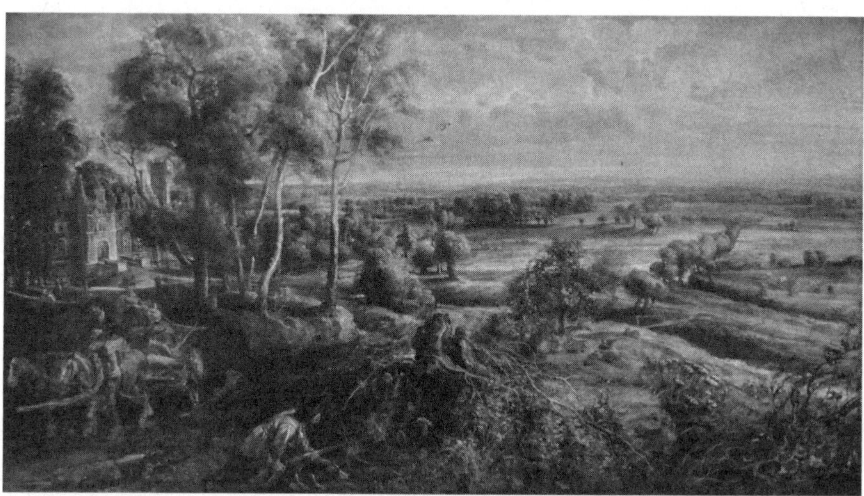

Peter Paul Rubens, *A View of Het Steen in the Early Morning* (1636)

CHAPTER 10

How Art Develops

A comprehensive analysis of the development of art self-evidently requires a study on the scale of Ernst Gombrich's *Story of Art* or Arnold Hauser's *Social History*. In a relatively short essay such as this, all that can be offered, and all that is offered, are a few general reflections on the subject, which hopefully will be of interest in stimulating debate.

For a historical materialist account of art's development, the starting point has to be Marx's famous distinction between base and superstructure:

> In the social production of their existence, men inevitably enter into definite relations, which are independent of their will, namely relations of production appropriate to a given stage in the development of their material forces of production. The totality of these relations of production constitutes the economic structure of society, the real foundation, on which arises a legal and political superstructure and to which correspond definite forms of social consciousness. The mode of production of material life conditions the general process of social, political and intellectual life. It is not the consciousness of men that determines their existence, but their social existence that determines their consciousness.[1]

Clearly 'art' is part of the superstructure, the 'general process of social, political and intellectual life' conditioned by the 'mode of production of material life', and Marx confirms this later in the same text when he writes:

> The changes in the economic foundation lead sooner or later to the transformation of the whole immense superstructure.

> In studying such transformations it is always necessary to distinguish between the material transformation of the economic conditions of production, which can be determined with the precision of natural science, and the legal, political, religious, *artistic* or philosophic – in short, ideological forms in which men become conscious of this conflict and fight it out.[2]

As does Engels when he states: 'The political, legal, philosophical, artistic, etc, development rest upon the economic. But they all react upon one another and upon the economic base.'[3]

I say 'starting point' here because the base/superstructure model is a point of departure, not of arrival, and it must be recognised at the outset, as Engels himself stressed in his late letters on historical materialism, that the relationship between the economic base and the various elements of the superstructure is not at all mechanically determined but rather always a complex mediated interaction. Nevertheless, it remains a *necessary* starting point for a materialist analysis. It is necessary on philosophical grounds in order to avoid falling into the notion that ideas in general, and artistic conceptions and images in particular, drop into the minds of artists 'from the sky' or arrive there by 'divine inspiration'. And it is necessary if we are going to avoid the idea, beloved of many cultural commentators, of a mysterious zeitgeist that floats through history, undergoing this or that transformation and development, independent of material conditions and production. The base/superstructure framework is also capable, I would suggest, of large-scale empirical confirmation by actually looking at concrete works of art.

Leaving aside the innumerable works tied to specific historic events, such as Uccello's *The Battle of San Romano*, Michelangelo's *David*, Goya's *The Third of May 1808* and David's *Death of Marat*, Delacroix's *Liberty Leading the People*, Picasso's *Guernica*, among others, it is nonetheless clear with virtually any work of significance that it could only have been painted within a definite and fairly limited time frame. Consider, for example, portraits. When an artist paints the portrait of an important or famous person, it is not just that the work is tied to a particular individual at a particular moment in time (as it is, of course). It depicts not only that individual's personal appearance, but also the role and institution they embody – the monarchy, empire, admiral, merchant, business tycoon and so on – and the social relationship that role and institution have with the artist, which is, in turn, one instance within a wider network of social relations at a specific stage of development. Thus when Holbein paints the portrait of Henry VIII, he is painting not just the man, Henry Tudor, but the institution of kingship at that moment in English history; likewise Bellini's *Doge Loredan*, Velázquez's *Pope Innocent X* and Hyacinthe Rigaud's *Portrait of Louis XIV* give us, respectively, depictions of what it is to be a doge, a pope, and an absolute monarch in Venice, Rome and Versailles in the sixteenth and seventeenth centuries. And that, in turn, is a product of the particular stage of development of the forces and relations of production. Thus absolutism was an expression, on the one hand, of the crisis of feudalism and the weakness of the old aristocracy, now unable to rule in the old way; and on the other, of the rise of a bourgeoisie not yet at the point where it was able to take over the rulership of society. In this crisis and in the contradiction between these forces, the absolute monarchs were able to raise themselves 'above' society and acquire unbridled power. All of which finds powerful expression in Rigaud's portrait.[4]

Nor do matters stand differently when the subject is much less elevated: Hals's portraits of the *Regents* and *Regentesses of the Old Men's Almshouse*, Courbet's *The Stone Breakers* and van Gogh's *Postman Roulin* are all testimony and responses to networks of social relations which are the products of very specific historical developments. The Hals paintings were discussed by John Berger in *Ways of Seeing*, so there is no need to repeat the discussion here. *The Stone Breakers*, painted in 1849, a simultaneously realist and heroic depiction of impoverished toilers at their labour, is inconceivable without the events of the 1848 Revolution, which itself was impossible without the emergence onto the stage of history of the modern proletariat. (The Chartists, the world's first mass workers' organisation, had developed in the previous decade, *The Communist* Manifesto was published at the beginning of 1848 and June 1848 in Paris saw the first distinctively working-class insurrection.)

It may seem that this argument applies less fully to landscape painting, until we recall that landscape painting as such[5] only really becomes a significant feature of European art with Dutch art of the seventeenth century – that is, in a society which, for the first time in history, is becoming urbanised. Moreover, the landscape which is depicted in, say, Jacob van Ruisdael's famous *Windmill at Wijk bij Duurstede*, or his pupil Hobbema's *The Avenue at Middelharnis,* is very evidently one that bears the mark of human labour to a huge degree. The same is obviously true of Gainsborough's *Mr and Mrs Andrews*, which shows us a countryside shaped by the rise in eighteenth-century England of capitalist agriculture, and with it of a rural capitalist gentry. And when we come, at the turn of the century, to Constable's rural idylls, such as *The Hay Wain* and *The Leaping Horse*, so long seen as representing the quintessence of 'Englishness', it is clear that the animating factor in both their production and their reception is the contrast between the scenes presented and the reality and prospect of the industrial revolution then sweeping England, while later phases in the development of that industrial revolution – the advent of the railway age – are the precondition and driving force of works such as Turner's *Rain, Steam and Speed* or Monet's *Gare Saint-Lazare* (*The Auteuil Line*).

Even where the most abstract art is concerned, the conditioning by the historical development of productive forces and social relations remains evident. Take Mondrian's abstract works from the mid- to late 1930s, characterised by grids of black lines on white with small boxes of primary colours, such as *Composition with Blue* (1937); it is clear that these works are intimately associated with modern design, architecture, construction materials (steel, glass, plastic, fibreglass, etc.) and with aspects of the experience of the twentieth-century city. It is significant that Rietveld's *Red and Blue Chair*, made in 1917–18, is actually in advance of Mondrian's trajectory in the development of his neo-plastic aesthetic. Mondrian's work constitutes an aestheticisation (to a very high degree) of a material reality created by twentieth-century production.[6] This connection with a specific time and place becomes explicit in his New York paintings such as *New York, New York* (1941–2), *New York City I* (1942) and *New York City II* (1942–4) and *Broadway Boogie Woogie* (1942–3).

I have tried here to give examples from different genres and different periods in which the link to the economic base is evident and can be easily described, but in reality this can be done for all significant works of art – indeed, as we have seen, it is one of the key factors that makes them significant. If it is otherwise with second- and third-rate works, this is frequently because of their derivative character. Thus it is possible to produce, or rather *try* to produce, landscapes à la Constable or Monet, or figures à la Picasso, long beyond the time and the place that gave the originals their artistic charge and vitality. The attribute of timelessness is often bandied around as a great compliment in sloppy art history and criticism, when in reality it should be regarded as a mark of inferiority.

If individual artworks are conditioned by the economic and social base and always stand in a definite relation to it, the same is true of broad developments in art history – 'movements' and 'periods'.

The Renaissance, 1300–1500 (i.e., from Giotto to Michelangelo), was a product of the early development of capitalism, within a feudal framework, in the Italian city-states, above all Florence and Venice. Its economic foundation lay in the prosperity generated by the textile industry and wool trade, and by banking, which allowed for increasing resources to be devoted to architecture and the arts. Its intellectual and ideological underpinning was the rise of humanism, which emphasised the study of human potential and found its visual expression in art, manifesting itself in increasing plasticity, naturalism, single-point perspective, individuation and thematic secularisation.

The early bourgeoisie established itself first in the independent city-communes, but its upper ranks, such as the Medicis, bought their way into the aristocracy and turned against the rising middle class. As a result, the bourgeoisie failed to make a decisive breakthrough on the Italian Peninsula – indeed, there would not be a national democratic revolution in Italy until the Risorgimento in the nineteenth century. With the emerging threat of the Protestant Reformation, the Sack of Rome in 1527 and the reestablishment of the Medicis as hereditary rulers of Florence, the tide turned decisively towards reaction. After a short 'mannerist' interlude, this absolutist counterrevolution – the Counter-Reformation – gave rise to a new art movement, the Baroque.

The dominant characteristics of Baroque art as seen in the work of leading representatives such as Bernini, Zurbarán, Rubens and van Dyke are the passionate emotive character of its religious works, its grandiloquence, its large size and the swirling cascades of figures in its secular works; all these features dovetailed with the propaganda needs of the Counter-Reformation, the absolute monarchs and the nobility who commissioned it.

In sharp contrast to this stands the art of the Dutch 'Golden Age': the likes of Hals, Rembrandt, de Hooch, van Ruisdael, Vermeer and many others. In chronological terms it is often included by conventional art history within 'the Baroque'. However, I would argue that this is misleading because both its social roots and its artistic characteristics are very different, indeed more or less diametrically opposed to those of the Baroque. The art of the Dutch Republic was the product of a successful national bourgeois revolution, precisely what did not occur in Italy or Germany, and every aspect of it is marked by this: its patrons were burghers, not emperors or popes; its venues were houses and municipal halls, not cathedrals and palaces (and therefore, its dimensions matched); its subject matter was domestic interiors, still lives, tavern life, middle-class portraits and group portraits; and its style was sombre and intimate, versus grandiose and extravagant. The contrast is most striking in the work of Rembrandt and Rubens, whose artistic careers overlapped and who were operating within a hundred miles of each other, but in fundamentally different societies.[7]

Moving forward to the nineteenth century, we see successive art movements – romanticism, realism, impressionism and so on – reflecting successive phases of the development of modern capitalist society. Romanticism in both painting and literature – Constable, Blake, Wordsworth, Delacroix, Keats, Shelley – sought to turn away from the 'dark satanic mills' of the Industrial Revolution to the 'purity' and 'beauty' of nature. Realism and impressionism, through Courbet, Manet and Monet, moved back towards the urban, beginning to embrace and express the lifestyle of the modern metropolis.

This raises the much-contested question of modernism. I will mention here two Marxist views of modernism, both of which have much to recommend them; that of Marshall Berman and that of Perry Anderson (which I also discussed in chapter 5). In his important work *All That Is Solid Melts into Air*, Berman treats modernism as a cultural expression of modern capitalism as whole. In this analysis, everything from Goethe, Baudelaire and Dostoyevsky to Joyce and Ginsberg, in literature, or Turner and Courbet through Manet, Picasso, Mondrian, Pollock and Warhol, in art, is a product of capitalism's restless and relentless drive to accumulate. It is a society which, in the words of the *Communist Manifesto*, 'cannot exist without constantly revolutionising the instruments of production, and thereby the relations of production, and with them the whole relations of society'. One in which

> constant revolutionising of production, uninterrupted disturbance of all social conditions, everlasting uncertainty and agitation distinguish the bourgeois epoch from all earlier ones. All fixed, fast-frozen relations, with their train of ancient and venerable prejudices and opinions, are swept away, all new-formed ones become antiquated before they can ossify. All that is solid melts into air, all that is holy is profaned.[8]

In 'Modernity and Revolution', his critical review of Berman, Perry Anderson proposes a much-narrower more historically specific, view of modernism:

> In my view, 'modernism' can best be understood as a cultural field triangulated by three decisive coordinates. The first . . . was the codification of a highly formalised academicism in the visual and other arts, which itself was institutionalised within official regimes of states and society still massively pervaded, often dominated, by aristocratic or landowning classes. . . . The second coordinate is . . . the still incipient, hence essentially novel, emergence within these societies of the key technologies or inventions of the second industrial revolution: telephone, radio, automobile, aircraft and so on. . . . The third coordinate . . . I would argue, was the imaginative proximity of social revolution.[9]

On this basis Anderson dates the birth of modernism to the first five to ten years of the twentieth century, while also seeing the Second World War as marking its, more or less, terminal decline. (This was, in

Anderson's view, due to the demise of the aristocratic ancien régime, the restabilisation of capitalism, and the eclipse of any hope of socialist revolution.) While his differences with Berman are important,[10] it is also possible to see merits both in the concept of a 'broad' modernism arising from capitalism in its totality and continuing to this day – encompassing (in visual art) everything from Courbet and Manet to Warhol and Hirst – and in the analysis of a specific 'modernist moment' in and around the period from 1905 to 1914. It is one which we might call the moment of Picasso, Stravinsky and Proust (or, with John Berger, the 'moment of cubism') which exhausted itself in the late thirties or forties.

But whatever view we take of this particular debate, what these accounts – along with the examples given above regarding the Renaissance, the Baroque, the Dutch Golden Age and so on – demonstrate is the possibility and legitimacy of relating broad movements in art to developments in the economic base of society, that is, in the forces and relations of production.

Mediations and Complications

Saying that the development of art can and should be related to developments in the economic foundations of society raises the question of the exact nature of this relationship, of how it should be understood and conceptualised. As I noted at the beginning of this chapter, it is certainly not a simple, straightforward or mechanical relationship, and no serious Marxist, no halfway-sophisticated practitioner of historical materialism, has ever claimed that it was.

One term that has often been used to characterise the relation between art and the base, or between art and society as a whole, is 'reflection', as in the propositions that the art of the Renaissance *reflects* the rise of capitalism in Italy, or that pop art *reflects* the emergence of mass consumerism in the postwar United States. If this term is taken to mean simply that there is a connection between Renaissance art and the rise of capitalism, or between pop art and mass consumerism, then it is relatively unproblematic. But if it is taken to imply any kind of one-to-one mechanical relationship, any literal reflection (as in a mirror), then it is clearly unsatisfactory. Take, for example, the claim that Constable's

The Hay Wain reflects the Industrial Revolution. If this means there is a definite relation between this painting and the Industrial Revolution taking place at this time, the claim is valid. If it means *The Hay Wain* is a mirror image of that revolution, it is plain silly. For these reasons I would generally avoid the term 'reflection' as too suggestive of mechanical determinism, but I do not reject it completely, nor always object to its use by others.

In the 1859 'Preface' quoted at the beginning of this chapter, Marx uses the terms 'correspond' and 'conditions': 'The totality of these relations of production constitutes the economic structure of society, the real foundation, on which arises a legal and political superstructure and to which *correspond* definite forms of social consciousness. The mode of production of material life *conditions* the general process of social, political and intellectual life.'[11] Both have their merits, but both also have drawbacks. 'Correspond' suggests a parallelism that is overstated and somewhat mechanical, whereas 'conditions' is certainly true, but perhaps a little weak. You could also say that art is conditioned by climate (think of the change in van Gogh's work as he moved to the sunbaked South of France), but the relationship between the economic base and art is, I believe, stronger and more foundational than that. Another possibility is to replace 'reflect' with 'refract', as in, 'The bourgeois development of English agriculture found its artistic *refraction* in the work of Gainsborough and Stubbs.' 'Refraction' is good in that it preserves the concept of a close relation and the primacy of the base without the idea of a simple mirror image.

However, the common defect of 'reflect', 'correspond', 'condition' and 'refract' is that they are all suggestive of one-way traffic – from the base to the art – whereas even as we insist on the foundational role of the economic base, we also have to recognise the specific agency of the artist. My preference, therefore, is to say that art *reflects and responds* to developments in the economic base and in society as a whole.

To respond to a development is, of course, to be conditioned by it, but it is possible to respond differently. Contemporaneous artists in the same or nearby locations may respond to the same external situation in divergent ways – they make different social, political and artistic choices.

The choices open to them are not 'free' in the sense of being unlimited, unconstrained or unconditioned, but they are nonetheless real. This combination of the terms 'reflect' and 'respond' is designed to express this duality of determination and agency.[12]

To advance this question further it is helpful to move beyond choice of terminology to spelling out concretely some of the mediations that exist between the economic foundations and their expression in art.

The economic base consists of the forces and the relations of production. The relations of production, since the passing of primitive communist foraging societies, have been exploitative relations which have divided society into opposing classes and generated class struggle.[13] This struggle, 'now hidden, now open' as Marx put it, is the most important mediating factor between the base and the artistic element of the superstructure.

In the first place we have to note that the ruling class in any given society – for instance, the slave owners in antiquity, the nobility and church hierarchy in the Middle Ages, the bourgeoisie in modern society – dominate the production and consumption of art. Marx says in *The German Ideology* that

> [t]he ideas of the ruling class are in every epoch the ruling ideas, i.e. the class which is the ruling material force of society, is at the same time its ruling intellectual force. The class which has the means of material production at its disposal, has control at the same time over the means of mental production, so that thereby, generally speaking, the ideas of those who lack the means of mental production are subject to it.[14]

This applies with particular force to art because visual art-objects (sculptures, murals, paintings, installations) require physical resources (blocks of marble, walls, gallery space) and are thus subject to private and state ownership to a greater degree than poems, novels, songs, music and the like. Consequently, from the Pharaohs of ancient Egypt to the Medicis and the popes to the Rockefellers' Museum of Modern Art and the Guggenheims and the Saatchis (not forgetting the CIA), the stamp of the ruling classes on the content and form of visual art has been palpable. They have used it for a variety of purposes, ranging from their private delectation to their public glorification, from the subtle articulation of their worldview to propaganda for the masses and the mockery of their enemies. Almost always, they have basked in the reflected cultural glory of owning and being associated with the greatest works, even when the values embedded in those works were sharply at odds with their own.[15]

But in a history where there is not only class but also class struggle, there appears, again and again, art which bears witness to the claims and resistance of oppressed and subordinate classes, whether that of the bourgeoisie under feudalism and absolutism (Bruegel, David, Repin under the tsars), the age-old plight of the peasantry (Millet, van Gogh) or, in modern times, the struggle of the proletariat and oppressed groups and nations (Kollwitz, Léger, constructivism, Grosz, Heartfield, Rivera, Kahlo, Jacob Lawrence, Romare Bearden, Basquiat, Mary Kelly, Martha Rosler, etc. – the list is very long). In addition to the art which can be seen to represent the influence of oppressed classes and groups more or less directly, there is also always a massive indirect or refracted influence of the class struggle on art. This is particularly evident in the whole history of modern art.

In capitalist society, the typical social position of the artist is petty bourgeois. I do not mean by this that most artists come from petty bourgeois class backgrounds (though statistically that is probably the case), but that objectively they operate as small, self-employed entrepreneurs who own and control their means of production (canvas, paints, studios, etc.) and, initially, the products of their labour, but then endeavour to sell these products on the market. Every now and again a massively successful artist – a Warhol, Koons or Hirst – makes it into the ranks of the bourgeoisie proper, but this is not typical. Far more common is that the artist is unable to survive purely by selling their work and is obliged also to sell their labour power (probably as a teacher of some kind) and is thus part petty bourgeois and part worker.

The effect of this is that modern artists and their art are continually pulled this way and that, continually buffeted by the struggle of the basic classes; torn between the fact that many of their sympathies lie with the poor and the oppressed and the even more powerful fact that the key to their economic survival and success lies with pleasing the rich and superrich.[16] The story of these conflicting influences and pressures is etched into the history of modern art, from Courbet and Manet, Pissarro, van Gogh and Cézanne to Bacon, Basquiat, Emin and Banksy.

Further, we should note that between the economic base, with its fundamental relations of production, and the ideological superstructure, of which visual art is one component, there lie a multitude of other social relations: between parents and children, husbands and wives and lovers, masters and servants and so on (as outlined in chapter 2). These innumerable relations, which are, of course, continually shaped and modified by changes in the economic base and the course of the class struggle, are the stuff of vast amounts of art. Think of van Eyck, Bruegel, Hals, Rembrandt, Hogarth, Goya, Courbet, just to give obvious examples.

The influence on art of the class struggle and of these changing intermediate social relations is in turn mediated by ideology and politics (by 'politics' here I mean specific political events). Ideologies are, in the final analysis, refractions of class interests, but this does not mean, as Engels noted, that they do not exercise a certain independent influence.[17] Religious ideology has manifestly exercised huge influence on the history of art, especially during certain periods – most obviously the middle ages and early modern era – and not only religion in general but also specific religious doctrines. Thus there is a manifest difference between the 'Catholic' and the Protestant images of Christ: compare, for example, della Francesca's serene and triumphant Christ with Grünewald's agonised Christ on the cross; and in Dalí's famous *Christ of St John of the Cross*, we see the visual representation of the (heretical) doctrine of Christ being permanently crucified for the sins of the world. In the nineteenth and twentieth centuries, the impact on art of varieties of socialist and Marxist ideology has been very considerable: Courbet, Kollwitz, Léger, the constructivists, the surrealists, Grosz, Heartfield, Rivera, Kahlo, Siqueiros, Orozco, Motherwell, Andre, Beuys, Guttoso, Tàpies, Kelly, Spero, Art and Language, Metzger and Wallinger all bear witness to this. Particular political events, above all wars and revolutions (which represent politics at their most intense), also repeatedly leave their mark on art, as in David's *Death of Marat*, Goya's *Third of May* and *Disasters of War*, Delacroix's *Liberty Leading the People*, Nash, Nevinson and other First World War artists, El Lissitzky's *Beat the Whites with the Red Wedge*, Picasso's *Guernica*, Golub's Vietnam paintings and so on.

Another mediation is the artistic tradition within which a particular work or body of work is being produced. This certainly looms large in the consciousness of many artists who closely observe and engage with the work of other artists past and present – look at the influence of Titian on Manet, of Velázquez on Bacon, of Schiele and Kahlo on Emin. There are reasons why this should not be overstated. First, because the tradition itself needs to be explained; second, because it is also necessary to explain which tradition or which artist/s was chosen to be an influence. Picasso *chose* to be influenced by Cézanne and Velázquez more than by Monet and Renoir. Third, because while artists are influenced by tradition and/or recent trends, they frequently react against it like Rembrandt against Rubens or Pollock against Picasso. Nevertheless it remains a factor which is real and has to be taken into account.

Finally, there is the role of the artist's personal biography. I deliberately place this last, whereas conventional art history places it first. We must recognise that the main features of an individual's biography, and this applies as much to artists (even artists of 'genius') as it does to anyone else, are particular intersections and condensations of social forces. The specific biography of Michelangelo, including his sponsorship by Lorenzo de' Medici and his rebellion against the Medicis, his commission for *David*, his work on the Sistine Chapel, his work on St Peter's, and his rise to artistic superstardom, would not have been possible either a century earlier or anywhere other than Renaissance Italy. Similarly there was no previous period in which a young woman with Tracey Emin's start in life and early experiences could have become the Emin we know. The very possibility of this occurring depended on changes in the social position of women and in public attitudes to sexuality, especially female sexuality. Her most famous work, *My Bed*, is, as I discussed earlier, an 'in your face' declaration of exactly this.[18]

But understanding this does not (or should not) imply that an individual artist's biography is a totally negligible factor in shaping their art. There are certainly occasions when particular and more or less unique features of an artist's biography play a major role in their art. Obvious examples are Henri de Toulouse-Lautrec's disability and subsequent retreat into bohemia, and the beatings inflicted on the young Francis Bacon at the behest of his father. There may even be the odd occasion when specific biographical factors play a major role in propelling an artist's work in a direction or way that significantly impacts the overall development of art. John Berger makes such a case in relation to Picasso in *The Success and Failure of Picasso*. But while this means that biography certainly has to be taken into account, I would submit this is only as the final link in a chain that is profoundly social.[19]

Finally, when considering all these mediations, we have to bear in mind that in their shaping the development of art, each of them acts not in isolation but always in complex dialectical interaction with the others.

Art and Progress

At this point it is necessary to address a major difficulty facing any attempt to relate the development of art to developments in the economic base of society (no matter how mediated that relationship may be). Marx points to this difficulty in the introduction to the *Grundrisse*, where he states that '[i]n the case of the arts, it is well known that certain periods of their flowering are out of all proportion to the general development of society, hence also to the material foundation, the skeletal structure as it were, of its organisation. For example, the Greeks compared to the moderns or also Shakespeare.' He then goes on to demonstrate the dependence of ancient Greek literature on Greek mythology, and of that mythology on the undeveloped state of Greek economy. But, he says, 'the difficulty lies not in understanding that the Greek arts and epic are bound up with certain forms of social development. The difficulty is that they still afford us artistic pleasure and that in a certain respect they count as a norm and as an unattainable model.'[20]

As regards why Homer and Aeschylus still 'afford us artistic pleasure', Trotsky supplied a more convincing answer than Marx himself. (Indeed, Marx's answer that the appeal of Greek art is bound up with Greek society representing the 'childhood' of society seems forced and implausible.) Trotsky, in the course of debating the relevance of Dante, asks:

> How is it thinkable that there should be not an historical but a directly aesthetic relationship between us and a mediaeval Italian book? This is explained by the fact that in class society, in spite of all its changeability, there are certain common features.... Let us take, for instance, such an elementary psychological feeling as fear of death. This feeling is characteristic not only of man but also of animals. In man it first found simple articulate expression, and later also artistic expression. In different ages, in different social milieux, this expression has changed, that is to say, men have feared death in different ways. And nevertheless what was said on this score not only by Shakespeare, Byron, Goethe, but also by the Psalmist, can move us.[21]

On this basis Trotsky argues that Shakespeare will still be needed when Marx's *Capital* has been reduced to the status of a mere historical document. But if this explains the transhistorical appeal of great art, it leaves unanswered the problem of why art, despite its dependence on the economic base, does not develop alongside that base; why, that is, there doesn't appear to be any progress in art. The development in the productive forces since the time of Aeschylus and Praxiteles or the days of Michelangelo and Titian is immense and continues decade by decade, year by year. But it can hardly be argued, either, that the leading artists of the twenty-first century, whoever they may be considered to be, are superior to the 'Old Masters' or that 'the average' level of art now is higher than 'the average' in ancient Greece or in the Renaissance.

The answer to this problem seems to me to be that the economic base whose development is reflected in the history of art consists of both forces and relations of production, and that it is the relations of production, not the forces, that exercise the principal influence on the development of art. And whereas there has been enormous advance in the productive forces, there has not been comparable advance in the relations of production, which, since the end of pre-class society, have remained antagonistic and exploitative. Certainly it is possible to argue that the abolition of slavery, serfdom and feudal land ownership constitute elements of progress, but capitalist wage labour still generates inequality, brutality, war, alienation, oppression, racism and environmental devastation on an increasing scale. Moreover, if slaves (ancient and modern) and serfs were excluded from the world of art and from being able to produce it, the same largely applies to wage slaves (and peasants) of today – that is, to the large majority of the population. In this context, we have to recall Marx's observation – discussed in chapter 1 – that 'capitalist production is hostile to certain branches of spiritual production, for example, art and poetry'.[22]

But if there is no *overall* progress in art, from the caves of Lascaux to Damien Hirst, as it were, there are nevertheless definite 'periods' or 'moments', limited in time and location, of great artistic flowering – ancient Greece in the fifth and fourth centuries BCE, Renaissance Europe from about 1300 to the mid-sixteenth century and the Dutch 'Golden Age' being obvious examples. Another candidate period is Western Europe, especially France, in the nineteenth and early twentieth centuries, say, from Courbet to Picasso.

In these periods it is possible to discern qualitative advance on what came immediately before so that, say, art in Italy from 1300 to 1550 (from Giotto to the deaths of Michelangelo and Titian), seems clearly richer, more complex, 'better', than art in Italy between 800 and 1300. Similarly, art in the Dutch Republic during the seventeenth century seems superior to art in the same geographical area in the fifteenth and sixteenth centuries. And also, within these periods we can see particular lines of development which appear cumulative and progressive; for example, towards three-dimensional plasticity, from Giotto, via Mantegna and Masaccio, to Leonardo and Raphael; or from Courbet's 'realism', via Manet, Seurat, Gauguin and Cézanne, to the cubism of Picasso and Braque.

If, however, there are such moments of flowering and advance but at the same time no overall progress, then the periods of advance must be succeeded and negated by periods of regression. This is indeed the case. Art in Italy during the seventeenth and eighteenth centuries (with the solitary exception of Caravaggio) does not stand comparison with the art of the Renaissance. After Rembrandt, Vermeer and Hobbema there is no comparable Dutch art until van Gogh. After the 1930s there is a decline in the quality of French art, and in the standing in art history of Paris and Paris-based artists.

Clearly there are numerous aesthetic value judgments involved in these assertions, and doubtless many of them could be contested. It must also be borne in mind that the picture for any one historical period is always very complex and contradictory, and that the more one tries to evaluate the situation internationally, rather than nationally, the more difficult it gets. Thus French art may have declined after the 1930s, but what about art in the United States? I would judge the emergence of abstract expressionism, followed by pop art, as an advance on prewar US art. And whatever about Renaissance Europe; what happens when we throw Chinese, Japanese, Indian, Central and South American and African art into the mix?

Nevertheless, despite all these difficulties, I think it is reasonable to say that the history of art consists of periods of progress and regression, and this raises the important question as to what determines these broad patterns or phases. Of course, in each case a concrete analysis is necessary, as with Perry Anderson's and John Berger's aforementioned analyses of the 'moment of cubism', but it is possible to advance a few general propositions.

First, because visual art is costly, a period of flowering is likely to be one of prosperity, in which the dominant classes have a relatively substantial surplus available for investment in cultural projects. This was the case for classical Athens. According to classical historian Josiah Ober, 'The Greek economy grew steeply and steadily from 1000 to 300 BCE', and by the fourth century BCE 'it was densely populated and remarkably urbanised, yet living standards remained high'.[23] Regarding Florence, Frederick Antal writes that its 'great economic power . . . grew up chiefly in the twelfth century, and expanded during the thirteenth and fourteenth centuries to dimensions unparalleled elsewhere in Italy or indeed in Europe.'[24] Likewise the Dutch Republic in the first half of the seventeenth century was, for that short time, the richest region in the world. According to economic historian Angus Maddison, Italy's per capita GDP of 1100 (1990 international Geary-Kharmis dollars) in 1500 was the highest in the world. By 1600 it had been overtaken by the Netherlands, which had reached 1381.[25] By the mid-nineteenth century, Western Europe had established its global economic and political dominance and enjoyed a standard of living much higher than any other part of the world except the United States. And while Britain occupied first place as the leading European economy, France was not very far behind. Of course, this should not be understood mechanically – Britain was economically ahead of France, but French art was more influential than British.

Second, these episodes of dramatic artistic advance seem usually to be highly concentrated geographically in certain cities – Athens, Florence, Venice, Amsterdam, Paris (plus Berlin) and later New York – which function both as centres of artistic production and as poles of attraction, drawing in artists from elsewhere. The development of art, despite the dominance of the concept of individual genius, is a collective social affair in which major artists cooperate, compete and learn from one another – da Vinci, Michelangelo and Raphael; Rubens, Rembrandt, Hals; the impressionists and post-impressionists; Matisse, Picasso and Braque.

Third, and this is connected to the first point, they are associated with the rise of a social class and the emergence of a new form of society that is experienced as opening up new horizons for people. This is clearest in the case of the Renaissance, in contrast to the feudal Middle Ages, but it was also the case in the mid-nineteenth and early twentieth centuries, with the rise of the bourgeoisie and the growth of a culture-consuming middle class, accompanied also by the rise (both alongside it and in opposition to it) of the proletariat. The imprint of both these classes, and their interaction as mediated by bohemia, on the art of the time is manifested repeatedly from Baudelaire's call to 'paint the heroism of modern life' via Courbet's *The Stone Breakers*, Manet's *Olympia*, Seurat's *Bathers* and *A Sunday Afternoon on the Isle de la Grande Jatte* to Toulouse-Lautrec's brothels and Picasso's 'blue period'.

When it comes to periods of artistic regression, these are likewise linked to economic decline or stagnation. This can range from extreme cases of general social collapse, such as the onset of the so-called Dark Ages in Europe in the fifth and sixth centuries (when the European population fell dramatically and urban life came close to disappearing), to the milder but telling example of what happened in post-Renaissance

Italy. As we noted above, Italy's per capita GDP in 1500 stood at 1100, the highest in Europe, but it then flatlined completely for over three centuries. This serious decline, relative to developments elsewhere in Europe, was not, of course, accidental. It was a product of the failure of the bourgeoisie in Italy to carry through a national democratic bourgeois revolution – not until the Risorgimento would the Italian economy experience serious growth – which simultaneously had the effect of closing down the cultural atmosphere of hope and liberation that characterised the Renaissance. As a result, the era of Giotto, Donatello, della Francesca and Michelangelo would give way to the era of Canaletto and Canova, while the centre of gravity in European art moved northward to the Netherlands.

The economic, social and political advances that underlay the emergence and rise of modernism in the nineteenth and early twentieth centuries culminated, due to the contradictions of imperialism and capitalism, in the catastrophe of the First World War and the revolutionary crisis of 1916 to 1923. But the revolutionary wave that followed the October Revolution was everywhere defeated, and by the time we reach the 1930s, we see economic depression and the triumph of extreme counterrevolution in both Russia and Germany (along with a number of other states – Italy, Poland, Austria, Rumania, Spain, etc.) and a general defeat of the Left. The result was the outright crushing and near extinction of the modernist artistic tradition in its heartlands. What survived continued largely in exile, and what emerged in Europe after the Second World War (although including very valuable work, such as that of Bacon) lacked the dynamic charge of the earlier period.

In making these broad generalisations (in order to illustrate the concept of progress and regression in art), it is immediately necessary to acknowledge that they constitute enormous simplifications of what are extremely complex processes, in which phases and moments of advance and of retreat continuously interact, and individual examples of great art stand out against the stream, even in very dark times.

CHAPTER 11

The Dialectics of Modernism

For a Marxist all change is dialectical, but I think it is possible to identify two particular dialectical processes at work within the overall trajectory of modernism.

The first I would call a 'dialectic of differentiation'. Trotsky wrote that 'a protest against reality, either conscious or unconscious, active or passive, optimistic or pessimistic, always forms part of a really creative piece of work', and consequently:

> Every new tendency in art has begun with rebellion. Bourgeois society showed its strength throughout long periods of history in the fact that, combining repression, and encouragement, boycott and flattery, it was able to control and assimilate every 'rebel' movement in art and raise it to the level of official 'recognition.' But each time this 'recognition' betokened, when all is said and done, the approach of trouble. It was then that from the left wing of the academic school or below it – i.e. from the ranks of new generation of bohemian artists – a fresh revolt would surge up to attain in its turn, after a decent interval, the steps of the academy. Through these stages passed classicism, romanticism, realism, naturalism, symbolism, impressionism, cubism, futurism.[1]

Each generation or, more accurately, each cohort – the revolts and movements arise at a faster pace than generations – tends to stress its differences with the cohort that precedes it. Thus impressionism, which emphasised light and colour at the expense of form, was followed immediately by Seurat and then Cézanne, who reintroduced form. At the beginning of the twentieth century, Matisse and the fauves concentrated on innovative juxtaposition of nonnaturalistic colours only to be challenged almost immediately by Picasso and Braque, whose analytic cubism engaged in intense deconstruction/reconstruction of form on the basis of a very limited palette. Filippo Tommaso Marinetti and the futurists declared war on the art of the 'museums, libraries and academies' and proclaimed, '[A] roaring car that seems to ride on grapeshot is more beautiful than the *Victory of Samothrace*.'[2] 'What was truth for the painters of yesterday is falsehood today' said his collaborator Umberto Boccioni.[3] To be followed by the suprematist Malevich, with his 'point zero' *Black Square on White* and the statement 'We have abandoned Futurism; and we, the most daring, have spat on the altar of its art.'[4] Meanwhile Dadaism was holed up in Zurich and denouncing the entire culture that had produced the catastrophe of the First World War, and Marcel Duchamp was producing his *Fountain.*

A later episode in this dialectic can be observed after the Second World War. Abstract expressionism in the United States defined itself as 'American' painting, in opposition to the hitherto-dominant European tradition, and its leading exponent, Jackson Pollock,[5] abandoned the brushstroke (in its traditional sense), all but eschewing the representation of three-dimensional space.[6] But the American art that followed abstract expressionism – Jasper Johns and Robert Rauschenberg, then pop art proper with Warhol, Lichtenstein and so on – is not only representational, but also based on imagery from popular culture that would have been anathema to the preceding generation and dismissed as kitsch. Pop art was then countered by the minimalism of Carl Andre, Donald Judd and others, and by the near disappearance of the object in highly theorised conceptual art. This in turn was succeeded by the 'vulgar' and apparently anti-theoretical populism of Hirst, Emin and the Young British Artists, and then by relational art and the social turn.

If we reflect on the causes of this dialectic of differentiation, they can be said to be (a) the rapid pace of social change unleashed by the dynamic of modern capitalism; (b) the privileging of 'originality' and 'the new' which accompanies this; and (c) the necessary self-assertion of emerging schools or trends in the competitive jungle of the art market and art world.

The second major dialectic at work in modernism is that of democratisation and elitism. The democratisation process in art is a reflection of and response to the rise of political democracy, initiated primarily by the American and French Revolutions, which, despite innumerable setbacks and reverses, has nevertheless spread round the world. Initially this rise in political democracy resulted, usually in very restricted form, from the struggle of the bourgeoisie; then it grew, in wider form, from the pressure exerted by the working class on the bourgeoisie.

In art, democratisation asserts itself first in the choice of subjects. From Géricault and Courbet onwards, there is a dramatic shift away from the depiction of royalty, aristocracy and mythology towards painting the people – the middle classes, the peasantry, the poor and, occasionally, the workers. This is manifest in a succession of paintings, such as Courbet's *The Stone Breakers* and *A Burial at Ornans*, Manet's *Olympia* and *Barmaid at the Folies-Bergère*, Seurat's *Bathers*, Millet's, Pissarro's and van Gogh's peasants, Cézanne's card players, Degas's laundresses, Toulouse-Lautrec's *Moulin Rouge* and brothel pictures, Picasso's 'blue' and 'rose' periods. After this shift, the portraits of monarchs and generals, of the rich and powerful, continue, of course, but as the work of mediocre and minor artists, not that of major figures as it was in the days of Holbein, Titian, Velázquez, Goya, David and Ingres.[7] The shift in subject matter is followed by a revision of the artistic hierarchy in terms of genres. Especially with Cézanne, and then with cubism, the hitherto-lowly genre of still life moves to the front, and the formerly dominant category of history painting fades.

The democratic impulse is also seen in the use of materials. Up to the twentieth century, oils in painting, and bronze and marble in sculpture remain mandatory for major art. This is challenged first by synthetic cubism, with its use of newsprint, pieces of linen and so on, and then by the European avant-garde as a whole, which rapidly embraces all sorts of materials – think of the sculpture of Picasso, with its metamorphoses of bicycle handlebars and saddles, or Duchamp's urinal, bottle rack and bicycle wheel. The expanded use of everyday 'nonartistic' materials is resumed in American modernism with Pollock's sticks and industrial paints, Rauschenberg's combines (with street detritus), Warhol's Brillo boxes, Andre's bricks, Kelly's diapers and so on. Outsider art and arte povera also embody these democratic aspirations, as does Joseph Beuys with his deployment of felt and lard, among other materials.

In general terms, it has been a major animating goal of modernist art to make art out of subjects and materials that would hitherto have been rejected as vulgar or unaesthetic. Time and again it is precisely this endeavour that has generated the most 'shock' and controversy (usually under the rubric that 'this is not art'), and this has continued all the way through to Tracey Emin's *My Bed*, Sarah Lucas's use of tabloid sub-journalism and Chris Ofili's of elephant dung.

Finally, the democratic aspiration is seen in recent trends towards street art, with the likes of Keith Haring and Banksy, and towards relational aesthetics and participatory art, socially engaged art, community art, and social practice (of which more later).

However, the tendency towards democratisation has always existed in dialectical tension with a strong pull towards elitism. This derives from structural features of capitalism. First, there is the continued control of the art world – its museums, galleries, dealerships and so on – by a combination of the superrich themselves (the Rockefellers, Guggenheims, Gettys, Saatchis, Thyssens, Gagosians, etc.) and their bourgeois or upper-middle-class representatives (Alfred H. Barr Jr, Kenneth Clark, Nicholas Serota, etc.). This is particularly important in relation to works of visual art, where both financial success and recognition are determined largely by the ability to appeal to a minority of wealthy and privileged 'patrons', rather than, as with music or literature, by mass popularity and mass sales.

Second, there is the objective division of the culture into high and popular culture, with avant-garde art firmly located within the former. As a result, there has been an alienation from and even hostility to modern art, fostered by the populist end of the media, on the part of large numbers of 'ordinary' people. These features, along with the hierarchical nature of class society in general, can push artists into an elitist view of themselves as an embattled, innately superior 'creative' minority. All this is reinforced by the tendency for young and impoverished artists to be located within 'outsider' and 'bohemian' strata of society – Montmartre, Montparnasse, Soho and SoHo, Hackney and Hoxton – and for the tiny minority who become very successful to live in isolated bubbles, surrounded by sycophants. The effect of this on Picasso was analysed by John Berger, but we can also see it at work with artists ranging from Dalí to Henry Moore, Andy Warhol, David Hockney and Damien Hirst. It often manifests itself in the 'drying up' of the artist's sources of creative imagination, from which their privileged social position can cut them off. This elitist tendency is most clearly evident in Italian futurism and its gravitation towards fascism.

However, given the powerful social pressures operating in its favour, I think it is fair to say that the damaging consequences of elitism for the work of the major artists have been relatively restricted, and less than might have been expected: artists such as Picasso, Matisse, Miró, Moore, even Emin, became very privileged but produced fine work. On the other hand, various forms of elitism have exercised a considerable appeal to a number of influential art critics, notably Roger Fry, Clive Bell, Clement Greenberg and Rosalind Krauss, and it is interesting to note that one of the most famous 'cultural debates' within Marxism, that between Theodor Adorno and Walter Benjamin in the 1930s, focussed on the question of elitist versus democratic tendencies in modernism. Mention of Adorno brings to the fore the fact that one driver that has propelled certain artists in an 'elitist' direction has been hostility to, or disdain for, the crudity, vulgarity and venality of capitalist mass culture.[8] This was a factor in the work of some of the abstract expressionists, such as Clyfford Still and, perhaps surprisingly, Carl Andre's minimalism.

Where Are We Now?

All of this brings us to the difficult questions: Where is art at present, and where might it be going?

It has always been much harder to write wisely and accurately about art of the present than art of the past,[9] and there are several reasons why this should be especially so right now. At the start of *Bad New Days*, Hal Foster writes, 'Contemporary art is so vast, so diverse, and, yes, so present as to frustrate any historical overview.'[10] And if that is sensible caution in relation to a whole book, how much more it applies to one section of one essay. I am therefore restricting myself to, as it were, 'flagging up' some issues which illustrate the current dialectics of modernism. These are: (a) internationalisation; (b) production values; (c) the social turn; and (d) climate change and the Anthropocene.

Obviously the implication of such an attempt is that I still consider the contemporary to be 'modernism', and that I reject the multitude of arguments advanced, from the late seventies onwards, to the effect that modernism is over and we have entered the era of postmodernism, complete with postmodern culture and art. This is a major topic – the subject of a vast literature – which cannot be properly discussed here; I will simply say that I have never been persuaded by the case for postmodernism – philosophically, economically, politically or in terms of art history. I do not accept Jean-François Lyotard's thesis of 'the end of all grand narratives', Jean Baudrillard's claims about the replacement of material production by the production of images and simulacra, or Fredric Jameson's argument that visual art since Andy Warhol has been characterised by depthlessness and 'the waning of affect'. I do not even accept this in relation to Jameson's paradigmatic example of Warhol's *Diamond Dust Shoes*, and there is plenty of 'depth' and 'affect' in the work of Jean-Michel Basquiat, Anselm Kiefer, Chris Ofili or Tracey Emin, for example. Postmodernism was at most a fad, not an era, and I prefer the broad view of modernism articulated (as referred to above) by Marshall Berman and which remains, in the phrase of Jürgen Habermas, 'an incomplete project'.[11]

Internationalisation

The internationalisation of the art world is one of the most evident and dramatic features of the last twenty years or so, and it is one the main factors that makes it so 'vast' as to 'frustrate an overview'. From its beginning, let us say, in the mid-nineteenth century until well into the twentieth, the story of modernist art was essentially a story of Europe,[12] and then, from about the thirties, of Europe and the Americas, with the US rise to dominance during World War II and after. But in the present century, we have seen a major expansion and opening up to the rest of the world, and especially to Asia.

Most striking is the spectacular rise of China as a centre of modern art. These trends are obviously difficult to quantify in any exact way, but the Chinese presence in the global art scene has clearly mushroomed. Looking at an online list of the thirty 'most popular' contemporary artists, based on prices recently fetched at auction, I notice that six out of the thirty are Chinese (and two are Japanese).[13] In 2013 Zeng Fanzhi's *Last Supper* sold for a $23.3 million at auction – a record price for Asian contemporary art. Chinese art writers are also featuring in the international discourse; for instance, the e-flux book *What Is Contemporary Art?* contains two contributions from China out of thirteen, alongside work from Mexico, Slovenia, India, Germany, the Netherlands and Switzerland, and three from the United States. But if China leads the way, there has also been a significant move to include contemporary art from eastern Europe and, to a certain extent, from Africa, while on the above-mentioned list of thirty top sellers, the first prize goes to Jean-Michel Basquiat.

Other things being equal, this is clearly a welcome and progressive development. However, it would be an illusion to see at as primarily a manifestation of left-wing internationalism. Doubtless the sustained and powerful critique of Eurocentrism (and advocacy of multiculturalism) which spread through many academic disciplines in the eighties and nineties, especially in the United States, has had an effect; but the main driver has been capitalist globalisation. What we are seeing is, first and foremost, a superstructural reflection of the economic rise of Southeast Asia, and above all the emergence of China as the world's second economic power. To return to the sale of Zeng's *Last Supper*. This is reported by *CNN Business* as follows:

> The 4-meter wide painting was sold to a private collector, who wanted to remain anonymous, after 15 minutes of tense telephone bidding at an evening auction held by auction giant Sotheby's on Saturday. Bidding started at $9 million.
>
> The 2001 work is a recreation of 'The Last Supper' by Italian master Leonardo Da Vinci, which depicts the last meal between Jesus and the 12 disciples when Jesus foretold his betrayal by Judas.

> In Zeng's work, the religious figures have been replaced by young communists with red neckties. The figure replacing Judas wears a western-style yellow tie – symbolizing China's move toward capitalism, said Evelyn Lin, Sotheby's head of contemporary Asian art.
>
> 'The painting represents a transformative period in Chinese society,' she said.[14]

Both the fact that this is reported by *CNN Business* and the content of the report testify to the real cultural meaning of this event. (This is compounded by the work's lack, in my eyes at least, of any great aesthetic merit.)

The domination of the internationalisation of modern art by big capital and the 1 per cent should not come as a surprise. The materiality of visual art – its embodiment in unique and expensive physical objects, and its attendant costs of production, display and storage[15] – has always been an important factor favouring its control by the rich and powerful, and this is compounded at an international level. Who but the richest individuals, corporations and institutions can afford to fly in and store a major sculpture or installation by Ai Weiwei or Yayoi Kusama?

In some ways, the figure of Ai Weiwei epitomises the whole process. In no previous period could such a contemporary artist from China have achieved such fame and success in the Western and global modern art scene. The merest glance at Ai Weiwei's biography reveals a set and type of experiences radically at variance with those of any recent Western artist. Born in 1957, Ai Weiwei is the son of a poet father who was persecuted during the Cultural Revolution, and sent into exile to perform hard labour in the Gobi Desert; Ai Weiwei went with him for sixteen years. Later, in 2011, Ai Weiwei himself was arrested and held for eighty-one days without charge. Officials hinted at 'economic crimes', but manifestly he was being punished for his criticism of the Chinese Communist Party regime and corruption. Ai Weiwei's rebelliousness, from a standpoint of strong liberal humanitarianism,[16] makes him a 'dangerous' artist in the eyes of the Chinese state, but he has also attacked the West's callous response to the refugee crisis, in particular in his moving and powerful documentary *Human Flow* (2017). At the same time, he was and is a multimillionaire who has engaged in many huge projects, including the design, with Swiss architects Herzog and de Meuron,[17] of the 'Bird's Nest' National Stadium for the 2008 Beijing Olympics and the installation of one hundred million sunflower seeds in the Turbine Hall at the Tate Modern in 2010.

Another of Ai Weiwei's more recent works, *The Law of the Journey* (2017) is a concentrate of this contradiction. Installed in the National Gallery in Prague, its centrepiece is a massive, 230-foot-long black inflatable boat carrying 258 faceless refugees. It is undoubtedly a powerful image, but it also raises the question of the extent to which its power depends on its sheer scale more than any other artistic quality. Moreover, it is impossible to work on such a scale without vast resources and the collaboration (i.e., permission) of powerful institutions. This, in turn, may set limits on the artistic and political radicalism allowed within such a framework. The role of production values in modern art is far from simple and merits attention in its own right.

Production values

Unsurprisingly, many artists relish the opportunity to work on a large scale, but the opportunity to do is only given to a few, essentially those supported by the very rich and, in one form or another, by the state. Sometimes the artists supported by the 1 per cent or the 0.1 per cent are great artists of the day, as was the case with Michelangelo, who was sponsored by the Medicis and the pope, or Jackson Pollock, who was put on a stipend by Peggy Guggenheim. But this is by no means always so. In the Dutch Republic, the defeat of the Habsburg Empire meant that the patronage and market for art shifted from the cathedrals of the Catholic Church and the palaces of the aristocracy to the emergent bourgeoisie, and that the scale of art adapted accordingly: compare Veronese and Rubens to Rembrandt and Vermeer. In the late nineteenth and early twentieth centuries, the finest art – the work of the impressionists, of van Gogh, Cézanne, of Picasso and Braque, among others – was oil painting on canvasses of relatively modest size.

Over the last couple of decades, it has become increasingly common to find large gallery spaces filled with huge works that have cost a large amount to construct and that cannot be stored in private homes (or even modest studios). And frequently these works have little to recommend them except the impressiveness that derives from their scale and high production values. Much of this is designated or designates itself 'conceptual art', but frequently it is very hard to identify any discernible concept – concept art without a concept. Obviously these are impressionistic judgments, as commentary on contemporary art often has to be, but I will cite two artists whose work seems to me to exemplify this trend: Anish Kapoor and Damien Hirst (both discussed earlier).

Kapoor is a sculptor whose speciality has always been visual tricks and effects. The 'meaning' of these tricks and effects, though it could be described in vague metaphysical terms – reaching for the infinite or connecting the individual to the cosmos or whatever – is very limited. As Kapoor has become more successful, he has executed these tricks on an ever-larger scale: *Cloud Gate* (2006), in the AT&T Plaza in Chicago's Millennium Park, is made up of 168 stainless-steel plates welded together, measures thirty-three by sixty-six by forty-two feet, and weighs 110 short tons; *Sky Mirror* (2001), costing £900,000 and weighing ten tons, was initially commissioned by Nottingham Playhouse, then installed in an even larger version at the Rockefeller Center in New York and later exhibited in Kensington Gardens, London; *Marsyas* (2003), designed with engineer Cecil Balmond for the Tate Modern's Turbine Hall, is a 492-foot-long, ten-story-high sculpture which may well be one of the largest works ever shown in a gallery; and the *ArcelorMittal Orbit* or 'Orbit Tower' (also designed with Cecil Balmond), commissioned for the London Olympics following a decision by London Mayor Boris Johnson and Olympics Minister Tessa Jowell, stands 376 feet high and cost approximately nineteen million pounds sterling (largely provided by Anglo-Indian steel billionaire Lakshmi Mittal). In 2013, Kapoor was knighted for his services to visual art, in 2016 he received the LennonOno Grant for Peace (along with Ai Weiwei) and in 2017, the one-million-dollar Genesis Prize, which 'recognises individuals who have attained excellence and international renown in their fields and whose actions and achievements express a commitment to Jewish values, the Jewish community and the State of Israel'.[18]

Commentary on Kapoor's work is littered with superlatives – biggest, largest, tallest, most expensive – but, leaving aside the question of the ethics and politics of this work, what aesthetic qualities does it possess? By the criteria outlined in chapter 2, very little; it is not particularly beautiful or emotionally powerful, nor is it original (except in size) or artistically critical; and above all, it neither expresses nor responds to human social relations.[19]

Damien Hirst began, in my opinion, as a much more interesting artist than Anish Kapoor. His work in the late eighties and nineties, when he was playing a pioneering role with the YBA generation, was often innovative, intelligent and sometimes genuinely challenging. I'm thinking of pieces like *A Thousand Years* (1990), *The Acquired Inability to Escape* (1991), *The Physical Impossibility of Death in the Mind of Someone Living* (1991) and, his best work, *Mother and Child Divided* (1993). All of these embody, in arresting forms, and in a way that had not been done before, astute reflections on contemporary social relations and relations with nature. But alongside these works there was always another side to Hirst, as manifested in his numerous spot and spin paintings. These were industrially manufactured works, lending themselves to mass reproduction on an unlimited scale and, while some of the spot paintings were arguably attractive as design, generally devoid of aesthetic quality or social meaning. As Hirst got older and richer, the entrepreneur increasingly displaced the artist. His series of vast butterfly paintings seemed little more than a cynical attempt to trade, on a mega scale, on his fame. Of course, butterflies are beautiful, but Hirst's use of them was visually crude and even ugly. *Hymn* (2000), a hugely blown-up anatomical toy, possibly bought by Charles Saatchi for one million pounds,[20] also depended entirely on size for its impact and had nothing of interest to say about the human condition. The whole process culminated, as everyone knows, in *For the Love of God*, the diamond encrusted skull, produced in 2007. Allegedly costing fourteen million pounds to make and allegedly sold for fifty million, this was a work in which the astronomical production values became the whole point, completely displacing artistic goals or criteria, and this has become characteristic of Hirst's shows as a whole.[21] His vast 2017 show in Venice, *Treasures from the Wreck of the Unbelievable*, was memorably, if almost certainly unfairly, described by Andrew Russeth as 'undoubtedly one of the worst exhibitions of contemporary art staged in the past decade'.[22] Its centrepiece was the sixty-foot-high *Demon with a Bowl*, among numerous other giant and tasteless statues.

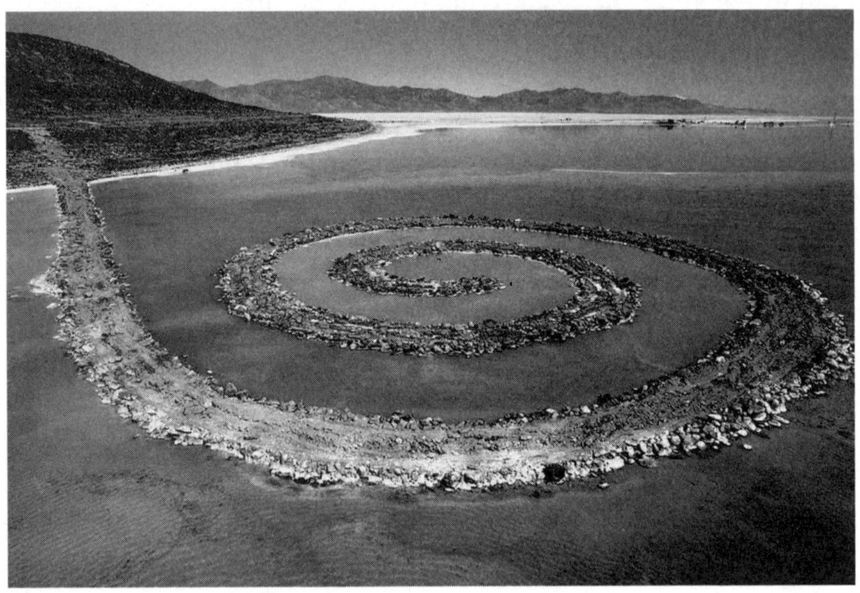

Robert Smithson, *Spiral Jetty* (1970)

I am not arguing here that big is bad, per se. The whole history of art, from the Sistine Chapel to Diego Rivera's 1935 *History of Mexico*, is there to refute such a proposition, and among more recent artists, strong cases could be made for the likes of Antony Gormley's *Angel of the North* (1998), Louise Bourgeois's *Spider* (1994) Robert Smithson's *Spiral Jetty* (1970), several Richard Serras and others. But when inflated production values become the norm and, in themselves, the key indicator of artistic merit, then not only do we have a powerful elitist pull, as is always there, but also a sinister corruption of the artistic endeavour. The corruption of art and artists is not the same as bribing a judge, policeman or politician; it is not a matter of providing a bung for services rendered. It is enough to create pressures and circumstances that separate the artist from the sources of their artistic inspiration, thus causing them to 'dry up' artistically. As noted earlier, John Berger showed how fabulous fame and wealth did that to Picasso, who was the greatest artistic talent of the age. Where lesser artists are concerned, it happens all the time.

The social turn

In terms of the dialectics of modernism, it was entirely to be expected that in the face of this transformation of art into the plaything of the superrich and the complicity of some of the foremost artists in this process, a 'fresh revolt', to use Trotsky's words, 'would surge up'. I'm calling this revolt 'the social turn'; however, many of those involved would prefer 'socially engaged art', 'dialogical art', 'community art', 'participatory art' 'social practice' or some other term to indicate that we are not dealing some specific group of artists with a specific style or practice (as in cubism, futurism or minimalism), but with a much broader and more diverse movement that has developed with different practices in different locations over a long period, perhaps two decades. Yates McKee, citing Claire Bishop, describes this development as follows:

> [T]he basic concern... was to move away from the idea of the art work as a finite object to be perceived in aesthetic terms by an individual understood as 'passive spectator'. Instead, the work of art was understood to variously incite, prompt or provoke the audience in such a manner as to transform it from distanced spectator to full and active collective participant in an open-ended socio-political process, performance, encounter, or experience.[23]

This 'turn' has, as Bishop has shown, many antecedents, stretching back to Italian futurism, Dadaism and the Russian Proletkult, as well as to the so-called 'happenings' of the sixties and, as McKee demonstrates, to much US activist art from the late eighties onwards. But since the turn of the century, it is an approach that has dominated what might be called the radical avant-garde, and it is now clear that this has been a major shift, not just a passing fad. One key moment in its development was Nicolas Bourriaud's theorisation of 'relational aesthetics' in his book of the same name.[24] Another was the 'Battle of Seattle' in 1999, a dramatic confrontation which stopped the World Trade Organization meeting in that city, and which announced the birth of a new alter-globalisation or anti-capitalist movement in the United States and then internationally.

It thus signified the reconstitution and reemergence of an international radical Left after the defeats of the seventies and eighties and the 'collapse of Communism', a process since continued by Occupy, Black Lives Matter, #MeToo and the Women's Marches, Bernie Sanders and many others.

Bourriaud offers these definitions:

> *Relational (aesthetics)*: Aesthetic theory consisting in judging artworks on the basis of the inter-human relations which they represent, produce or prompt.
>
> *Relational (art)*: A set of practices which take as their theoretical and practical point of departure the whole of human relations and their social context, rather than an independent and private space.[25]

On the face of it, there is a strong similarity here with what I specified in chapter 2 as the distinctive characteristic of Marxist aesthetics – the focus on human social relations. But by 'relational art' Bourriaud doesn't mean an art that was about social relations, in the sense that Rembrandt's, Goya's and Manet's were. He means art like that of Rirkrit Tiravanija, Félix Gonzalez-Torres and Carsten Höller, which induces viewer participation in the work as a necessary component of its completion and thereby stages a collaboration in the creation of an interhuman relationship. Thus Tiravanija made a work in which he presented the viewers/participants with the ingredients for a Thai curry and asked them to make the curry, with the whole process constituting the work. Gonzalez-Torres exhibited a large pile of sweets in a gallery, measured to maintain a weight equal to the weight of his partner, who died of AIDS, with instructions to visitors to take one or many sweets, so that their decision as to how to engage – refuse the sweets, take handfuls and so on – became 'the work'. Carsten Höller created *Test Site*, in which he installed several huge metal slides in the Tate Modern's Turbine Hall for visitors to ride down.

The practice and theory of relational aesthetics was, in my view, genuinely transformative. It opened art to new possibilities, including very radical possibilities. At the same time, the actual art instanced by Bourriaud as embodying the relational suffered a serious limitation: it was bland. The human relations it celebrated were overwhelmingly those of 'conviviality', and getting on well together, and being kind or loving towards each other. In his great poem 'To Posterity', Brecht wrote:

> The times I live in are bleak
> When an unwrinkled brow denotes insensitivity . . .
> And a conversation about trees is almost a crime
> for what it leaves unsaid.[26]

There is nothing wrong with conviviality and kindness, joy and fellowship. But after Auschwitz and Hiroshima in life, and Kafka and Beckett in literature and *Guernica* and the 'Screaming Pope' and Warhol's *Electric Chairs* in painting, an art which does not go beyond conviviality or 'bringing people together', to deal with the alienation and horror and the contradictions and conflicts of modern life, is simply not rising to the challenge of our times. However, the logic of the social turn and of the pervasive sense of emergency in the twenty-first century rapidly moved relational art beyond these limitations.

First, avant-garde art started to move out of the gallery to become 'socially engaged' with laypeople, not part of the 'art world', and to draw them into the process of its production.[27] This move was not, of course, original, but it was more sustained and involved more artists than previous forays, and it even became the orthodoxy in many art educational institutions, especially in the United States (though it was also an attempt to justify art education as socially useful in the face of right-wing and populist attack).[28] The move out of the gallery was a deliberate and conscious implementation of the democratic imperative, or pull, that I have identified as a major driver in modernist art, and it was accompanied by a quite heavily political/moral (some would say moralistic) focus on process over outcome. The goal became a highly egalitarian and democratic collaboration which rejected the notion of 'individual' authorship of art and the 'privileging' of the art professional over the lay participant.

Of course, such a strategy, operating within the profoundly unequal world of capitalist society, runs into numerous difficulties and contradictions, many of which have been diagnosed by Claire Bishop.[29]

Where does the funding for such community projects come from? Does the source, for example, local government in some form, set limits on the radicalism of the work, in either political or artistic terms? Is the collaboration with laypeople genuinely egalitarian, or mere window dressing masking the 'artist's' real control? And if it is the former, how does this impact on the radicalism of the work? Again, the danger of worthy blandness raises it head. That this was not universally the case is shown, for instance, by Jeremy Deller's 2001 reenactment of the Battle of Orgreave, from the British Miners' Strike of 1984–5.

Second, there has been a very considerable political radicalisation of artists and at least some of 'the art world'. There have, of course, been many radical moments in the history of modern art – 1848, Courbet and the Paris Commune, the Russian Revolution and its aftermath with suprematism, constructivism, surrealism, George Grosz and John Heartfield, the Mexican muralists, some of the sixties and so on. It is in the nature of art that this should be so. However, compared to the 1980s and '90s, the shift has been dramatic, and the politicisation has been not just in the artists but also in their work.[30] And this has occurred both within the established art world (the galleries, etc.) and outside it.

In his book *Strike Art*, which is by turns fascinating, challenging and irritating, Yates McKee tracks, at least for the United States and, especially New York, 'a dual process wherein artists have at once withdrawn from art as defined by the contemporary art system, and reinvented art as a force of radical imagination and direct action'.[31] In short, artists have become activists and taken their art with them to visually aestheticise protests, sit-ins, rallies, strikes and so on. Again, one can say this is not new: think of Heartfield's anti-fascist photomontages, of Peter Kennard's with the British peace movement, or the students' silk screen posters in May '68. But the sheer scale of the process in the United States makes it significant. The centrepiece of McKee's account and, in his view, the high point of this art activism is the mass occupation in autumn 2011 of Zuccotti Park, in the Financial District of Manhattan. Noting the very large number of artists actually involved in the organisation of Occupy, and the fact that it was 'summoned up' by an art image (the iconic ballerina surfing Wall Street's *Charging Bull*), McKee goes further to suggest that Occupy might itself be considered an artistic project in its own right' and quotes, among others, Martha Rosler as describing it as 'a grand public work of process art with a cast of thousands'.[32]

Not having actually been there, it is hard to know whether McKee is over-egging his pudding here and taking metaphors too literally. However, I'm not in principle averse to the notion of Occupy as constituting in its totality a work of art. In terms of the criteria for the definition of art set out in chapter 1 – as the product of unalienated labour, striving for a unity of form and content – it is the second term of this definition that causes a problem. Can an event or process which contains so many diverse actions and elements, many of them uncoordinated by any collective will, really achieve anything approaching a unity of form and content? Perhaps some elements of it can. Certainly that is what many of the organisers were striving for, insofar as they wanted the operation of the camp to prefigure the cooperative, creative and democratic future they envisaged. This question does not require a definitive answer here, but McKee's proposition identifies a process of the aestheticisation of political action that can take many forms.[33]

Another feature of McKee's narrative is the artistic character of many of the artefacts and paraphernalia of left movements: banners, posters, placards, flyers, and the like. Again, this is not, in principle, anything new. Many of the early banners of the British trade union movement had an indisputably artistic character,[34] and one recalls the role played by creative design skills in the Anti-Nazi League in the seventies and the Stop the War Coalition in 2003. But is this tendency on the increase? McKee would suggest it is. One reason for his emphasis on this is the strategy that the Occupy camp embodied, one which McKee, along with many anarchists, advocates: prefigurative organising. There is a name for this strategy in the Marxist lexicon, namely 'utopian socialism', and it stretches back to Saint Simon, Fourier, and Robert Owen. It is the idea, also prevalent in the communes of the sixties, that it is possible either to escape from capitalist social relations (to the countryside, usually) or to carve out 'autonomous' spaces in the interstices of the system where prefigurative egalitarian politics and/or living can be practiced.

Politically, Marxists, while not denying it any progressive character, have always pointed to the limitations of this strategy. On the one hand, it is a minority strategy, not open to the mass of the working class, and as such it contains no mechanism for actually defeating the ruling class and its state. On the other hand, as with the communes, cooperatives and phalansteries of the past, the longer the prefigurative 'autonomous space' is maintained, the more it becomes subject to and corrupted by the economic and social pressures of capitalism. It is significant here that the occupation of Tahrir Square in the Egyptian Revolution earlier in 2011, which served as an inspiration for Occupy, was primarily engaged not in prefiguration but in a literal life-and-death struggle with the Mubarak regime, and its police and its thugs; and that movement was able, by virtue of its mass character, to win that struggle at least temporarily. But the role of art in Tahrir and in the Egyptian Revolution, while not nonexistent, was much more subordinate to the role of fighting.

But the weakness of utopianism as a political strategy does not necessarily correspond to its weakness in art. Utopian impulses, from William Morris to Fernand Léger and beyond, can undoubtedly generate important art. Nevertheless, there are problems here too. McKee himself describes how, following the eviction of Occupy, many of the artistic energies involved in Zuccotti Park returned to a focus on and within the art world. Illuminator projected the figure of the 1 per cent on the walls of the Guggenheim Museum and Global Ultra Luxury Faction (GULF) staged carefully, and beautifully, choreographed interventions within the gallery space.[35] There may be nothing wrong with this in itself, but it marks a partial retreat from the 'withdrawal from art as defined by the contemporary art system' and 'the reinvention of art as a force radical imagination and direct action' proclaimed by McKee. A different but parallel phenomenon is the way in which Banksy's once-illegal street art is now selling for huge sums. It shows that in the dialectic of democracy and elitism, the pulling power of elitism within contemporary art (even among those ostensibly most committed to the opposite) has not disappeared, and will not disappear, while capitalism survives.

There remains to discuss one overarching problem with the art of the social turn as a whole: namely its overall failure to produce visually powerful art objects. This failure is not absolute, but compared to other art movements, it is real. Compared, for example, to the YBAs, the artists of the social turn are more ethical and politically aware. But where are the memorable images to stand with Hirst's *Mother and Child Divided*, Emin's *My Bed* or Whiteread's *House*?[36] This absence was very evident in the Turner Prize show at the Tate Britain in 2018. The exhibition featured four nominees: Forensic Architecture, Naeem Mohaiemen, Charlotte Prodger, and Luke Willis Thompson. All of their work tackles, as the Tate says, 'pressing social issues' – Palestine, anti-colonialism and Islamism, queer identity and black victims of police violence – from a human rights point of view, by means of video, documentary, archivism, film and so on. It reflects the rather extraordinary politicisation of contemporary art. But the whole show contains virtually nothing in the way of an aesthetically powerful object.

I want to be precise in my argument here. I am not claiming that because of this absence current art is all worthless or heading downhill, or that 'the social turn' was a wrong turn. Rather, I'm suggesting merely that this tendency (not absolute of course) to the loss of objecthood is a *real loss*, in the same sense that the loss of form, in favour of light effects, was a real loss in impressionism or the loss of colour in Picasso's and Braque's synthetic cubism was a real loss. And given that human beings have been making 'beautiful' and expressively powerful pictures and objects for over thirty thousand years, it is most unlikely that this will cease now. After impressionism, form made its return with Seurat and Cézanne; after synthetic cubism, colour was developed by Matisse and Miró. The question arises, therefore, as to whether the dialectic of modernism will result in avant-garde art, in its next phase, finding a way back to the object without losing all the gains – also real – of the social turn and its accompanying politicisation. In the next section, I will try to suggest a possible answer.

Climate Change and the Anthropocene

It is obviously impossible to know the precise effect climate change will have on art, but what is certain is that the effect will be enormous. The Industrial Revolution, the French Revolution, modern urbanism, the

First World War – all of these historical developments had a profound impact on the history of art. Climate change is a historic development of the same or greater magnitude. If it is allowed to proceed unchecked, and there are strong signs that this is what is going to happen, the consequences (unless the scientists are completely wrong) will be global catastrophe of almost unimaginable proportions. It will affect the daily life of everyone on the planet, and this will necessarily be reflected in art. But in order to halt or even seriously mitigate climate change (it is already too late to 'stop' it completely), there will also need to be a profound change, probably a revolutionary change, in the character of our global society and its relations with nature.[37] This, too, cannot fail to transform art.

As I pointed out in chapter 2, human relations with nature are always a function of human social relations, and vice versa. There is always a dialectical interaction, and we see this reflected throughout the history of art. The walls of the caves at Chauvet and Lascaux speak eloquently of a classless society and its symbiotic relationship with the natural world; Rembrandt's magnificent *Slaughtered Ox* and Stubbs's paintings of prize bulls and thoroughbred stallions depict, in their different ways, the commodification of animals, as does Damien Hirst's *Mother and Child Divided* today; Gainsborough in *Mr and Mrs Andrews* does the same for land. Constable and Turner represent different responses to nature in the face of industrialisation and so on.

When it comes to climate change, the historic moment is very different from the Industrial Revolution or the birth of capitalism, in that we have scientific knowledge in advance of the change that is heading our way, and that change is clearly not progressive. The question arises, therefore, as to the role that art can play in influencing our individual and societal responses to the challenge. This raises a major political divergence. The dominant discourse regarding the prevention or curbing of climate change is that what is needed is for 'all of us' to change our behaviour (eat less beef, drive cars less, fly less in planes, etc.), and in this scenario it is likely that attempts will be made by the rich and powerful to enlist artists, along with the media and public relations 'experts', in the cause of altering popular attitudes and habits. It is also likely that this role will appeal to some artists. The Marxist view – my view – of climate change is that its cause and its solution lie not in the behaviour of ordinary people but in the behaviour of giant corporations and states, governed by the central drive of capitalism to accumulate capital.[38] No amount of art, no matter how powerful or exquisite, will be able to negate that drive or significantly modify the behaviour of ExxonMobil and BP, or the US and Chinese state machines. Insofar as art has a part to play in this, it will be rousing and expressing the anger of 'ordinary' people against those who are presiding recklessly over the trashing of the planet on which we depend.

I do not mean by this that art which responds to climate change and the many other challenges of the Anthropocene, such as plastification and acidification of the oceans, mounting air pollution in our cities and the mass extinction of species, will primarily be focussed on agitation and propaganda – though there will doubtless be a place for that. There will also, I would expect, be a place for art that expresses the full range of human emotions generated by this 'metabolic rift'[39] opened up between humanity and nature: rage, grief, loss, despair, hope and the rest.

In terms of precedents from the art of the past, there are a number of individual works that might serve as points of reference because they attempt to depict human and environmental catastrophes. For example Turner's *Snow Storm*, Henri Rousseau's *War*, Hokusai's *Wave*, Munch's *The Scream*, Paul Nash's *We Are Making a New World*, Ernst's *Europe after the Rain*, Picasso's *Guernica*, Pollock's *Lavender Mist*, *One (Number 31)* and others, Anselm Kiefer's Sao Paulo dystopia *Lilith*, and the auto-destructive art of Gustav Metzger and Jean Tinguely. However, it is obvious that the scale of the catastrophes represented in these works is tiny compared to the disaster that will befall humanity and the planet in the event of runaway climate change.

When it comes to dealing with climate change and the wider matter of the Anthropocene, the art of the past that most immediately springs to mind as relevant is the land (or earth) art of the sixties and seventies. Land art, associated with artists such as Richard Long, Robert Smithson and Andy Goldsworthy, arose in response to the new ecological movement of that time, sparked and epitomised by Rachel Carson's 1962

Silent Spring. It sought to respond to impending ecological crisis not by exposing, depicting or protesting environmental damage, but by encouraging and celebrating a new, positive and reverential attitude to nature. In art historical terms it emerged 'out of' sculpture, in opposition to the abstract hard metal sculptures of David Smith and Anthony Caro,[40] and as an extension of the minimalism of Judd and Andre.

Like all art 'movements', land art produced diverse work of varying quality. At one end of its spectrum was Goldsworthy, whose sculptures using natural materials 'in nature' were certainly pretty, arguably beautiful, but always slightly saccharine and sentimental. Long's work, which ranged from records of marks made by walking in remote places to flat circles and lines of natural stone in galleries, was a more radical departure from previous art – more austere and more ambitious and, to my eye, often authentically beautiful. But the outstanding work of this category and time was by Smithson. It was he who made the single-most memorable image/object, namely the 1970 *Spiral Jetty*, and whose art raised the toughest questions about the effects of human actions on nature. But the period of its production meant that land art did not have to deal with anything on the scale of the destruction and calamity threatened in the Anthropocene, and which, therefore, would seem to demand a much 'angrier', more urgent or, possibly, more tragic response.

What seems worth mooting is the possibility – and I don't think predicting the future of art can be more definite than this[41] – that what will emerge in the coming period will be a kind of synthesis, a dialectical overcoming, of what is strongest in 'the social turn' with the aesthetic materiality of land art. This would imply large collective art projects, out there in the environmentally threatened world (rather than in the gallery), engaging with threatened communities – all our communities, globally, will be threatened – which would also involve physical transformations of sites into visually powerful works of art. Can it be done? Maybe. If it happens, it will likely be the first truly global art movement.

At the start of this book, I argued that art is a product of creative (i.e., unalienated) labour. In contrast, climate change is, along with nuclear war, one of supreme products of alienated labour. Not alienated labour as understood by the sociologists – feeling unhappy at work – but as analysed by Marx: as an objective social relation in which human beings come to be dominated by the products of their own labour, which stand over them as an alien and hostile power. Climate change is this in the most literal sense, and in endangering the future of humanity, it obviously also endangers the future of art. It is, therefore, fitting that the forces of art should be mobilised against this deadly force of destruction.

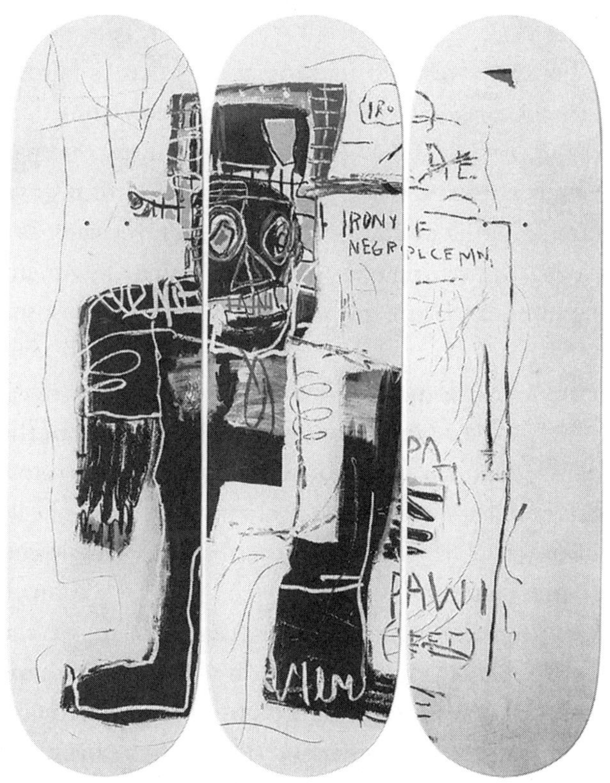

Jean-Michel Basquiat, *Irony of a Negro Policeman* (1981)

Conclusion

We know that human beings have been making things that today we would call 'art' for a very long time: the oldest carved sculptures date from approximately 38,000 BCE, and the oldest cave paintings from perhaps 60,000 BCE. Works as complex (and beautiful) as the paintings in Chauvet and Lascaux are 33,000 and 22,000 years old, respectively. We are therefore dealing with something very fundamental to being human, and indeed, every human culture we know of has produced some form of visual 'art'.

This is to be expected because makers is what we humans are. As Marx put it back in 1844, 'The *entire so-called history of the world* is nothing but the creation of man through human labour'.[1] The development of agriculture about ten thousand years ago, and, hard on its heels, living in towns and the dawn of 'civilisation', brought a huge explosion in the powers and range of cultural labour. It gave us the pyramids and the Sphinx; Homer, the Parthenon and Praxiteles; Khajahuro, the Bhagavad Gita and the Terracotta Army. But with this huge advance came terrible loss – the commencement of exploitation and alienation, the division of society into classes, the oppression of women, slavery and many other forms of oppression. It meant that from this time onwards, the finest products of human cultural labour were owned and controlled by a tiny proportion of the population.

Even in the days of classical Greece and Rome, there was still not yet a concept of art or the arts as a distinct and separate activity, counterposed to ordinary nonartistic labour. Poets, sculptors, painters, playwrights and musicians were not yet 'artists' as opposed to artisans and skilled labourers. This came only with capitalism. 'Art', in the modern sense and the sense discussed in this book, emerged with and, simultaneously, in opposition to capitalism, which took its first steps in the city-states of medieval Italy and then spread across Europe in the fifteenth and sixteenth centuries.

This development also brought enormous cultural enrichment: the Renaissance, Shakespeare, the Dutch 'Golden Age' and the rest, including the Scientific Revolution. In art, religion and philosophy, it meant, above all, the exploration of the consciousness and personality of the individual: Luther and Calvin, Descartes's 'Cogito, ergo sum', Michelangelo's *David*; *Hamlet* and *Macbeth*, the portraits and self-portraits of Rembrandt, Milton's Satan. But, again, there was also loss. The emergence of 'art' as a separate realm and 'artists' as 'specially gifted' and 'divinely inspired' individuals – geniuses even – set in motion a tendency which reached fruition in the twentieth century, namely the division of the culture into high and low (or 'popular'). With this came the alienation of the mass of the population from high culture, and especially from modern art, along with the development of the culture industry and its production of low-grade, soporific and sensationalist entertainment for the masses.

Serious artists have responded to this damaging schism in a variety of ways. Many have accepted it as 'natural' and inevitable, a product of the innate incapacity of the masses to make or even appreciate the finer things in life. Others, more or less reluctantly, have accepted it not as natural but as unavoidable, due to the downtrodden condition of the masses under capitalism. But it has also long been an aspiration of sections of the avant-garde to produce 'art for all', to proclaim that 'everyone is an artist' (Joseph Beuys) and to attempt to heal the rift between 'art and life' by their own efforts. This noble and democratic endeavour has produced much challenging and innovative art, from constructivism to pop art to the social turn, yet ultimately, it remains utopian in a class-divided society which rests on exploitation and alienation. Only in a society not based on the alienated labour of the majority will free artistic production become the property and practice of all.

Until that is achieved, art will take its place in the quest and fight for human freedom, if not on the front line – which will be occupied by the masses in struggle in the workplaces, the streets and on the barricades – then as an important ally and essential supplier of spiritual nourishment, as necessary, in its way, as boots and medicine.

Notes

Introduction

1 David Brooks, 'When Beauty Strikes', *New York Times*, 15 January 2016, https://www.nytimes.com/2016/01/15/opinion/when-beauty-strikes.html.
2 Leon Trotsky, *Literature and Revolution* (London: Redwords, 1991), 253.
3 Clearly I have not included in this list any of the many Marxists who were specifically art historians or art critics: Max Raphael, Frederick Antal, Arnold Hauser, John Berger, T. J. Clark and Carol Duncan, among others.

Chapter 1: What Is Art?

1 'The prize (if there were one) for the most vexing, the most widely and constantly worried question in aesthetics over the past three decades – at least in English-speaking countries – would surely go to the question "What is art?"' Monroe C. Beardsley, 'Redefining Art', in *Theories of Art and Beauty*, Robert Wilkinson, ed. (Milton Keynes: Open University, 1996), 43.
2 E. H. Gombrich, *The Story of Art* (Oxford: Phaidon, 1978), 4.
3 Angus Stevenson, ed., *The Concise Oxford Dictionary* (Oxford: Clarendon Press, 1980), 269.
4 The so-called 'Bricks in the Tate' – a rectangular arrangement of 120 bricks in two layers of sixty each, regarded in the art world as a classic example of 'minimalism'.
5 For example, I do not much like the work of Bernini or Canova or Chicago. I dislike Bouguereau and disapprove of some of the work of the Chapman brothers (see chapter 6), but all these works would meet my criteria for being art.
6 Leon Trotsky, *Trotsky's Notebooks 1933–35: Writings on Lenin, Dialectics and Evolutionism* (New York: Columbia University Press, 1986), 78.
7 Władysław Tatarkiewicz, 'Art: History of the Concept', in Wilkinson, *Art and Beauty*, 14–15.
8 Tatarkiewicz, 'Art: History of the Concept', 14–15.
9 Arnold Hauser, *The Social History of Art*, vol. 2 (London: Routledge & Kegan Paul, 1961), 61.
10 Tatarkiewicz, 'Art: History of the Concept', 25.
11 Karl Marx, *Feuerbach: Opposition of the Materialist and Idealist Outlooks* (Moscow: Progress Publishers, 1976), 96.

12 Nigel Warburton, *The Art Question* (London: Routledge, 2004), 70.
13 Morris Weitz, 'The Role of Theory in Aesthetics', cited in Warburton, *The Art Question*, 76.
14 Stephen Davies, 'Definitions of Art', in *The Routledge Companion to Aesthetics*, Berys Laut and Dominic McIver Lopes, eds. (London: Routledge, 2003), 171.
15 Karl Marx, *Economic and Philosophic Manuscripts of 1844* (Moscow: Progress Publishers, 1967), 106. Emphasis in original, unless otherwise noted.
16 Karl Marx and Frederick Engels, *The German Ideology*, in *Karl Marx: Selected Writings*, D. McClellan, ed. (London: Oxford, 1977), 160.
17 Karl Marx, *Capital*, vol. 1 (1867, repr., London: Lawrence & Wishart, 1970), 173.
18 There is currently an unpleasant vogue among some artists and 'arty' people to describe themselves as 'creatives', as if they were a different breed from the rest of humanity. The origin of this usage of the word seems to be from the corporate world.
19 Marx, *Economic and Philosophic Manuscripts*, 66.
20 Marx, *Economic and Philosophic Manuscripts*, 68.
21 Marx, *Economic and Philosophic Manuscripts*, 69.
22 Of course, I mean this in a way that was not true when Marx wrote it.
23 André Breton famously pointed out that Salvador Dalí was an anagram of 'Avida Dollars'.
24 See T. S. Eliot, *Selected Prose* (Harmondsworth: Penguin, 1965), 102–3.
25 Except by myself in John Molyneux, 'The Legitimacy of Modern Art', *International Socialism* 80 (autumn, 1998).
26 Karl Marx, 'On the Freedom of the Press', cited in *Marx and Engels on Literature and Art*, L. Baxandall and S. Morawski, eds. (New York: Telos Press, 1977), 60–61.
27 Karl Marx, *Theories of Surplus Value* (Moscow: Progress Publishers, 1963), 401. All emphasis original, except where noted otherwise.
28 Karl Marx, *Grundrisse* (London: Penguin, 1972), 610.
29 Marx, *Theories of Surplus Value*, 285.
30 I yield to no one in my respect and admiration for Marx, but I also think we have to guard against the tendency among some Marxists to assume that the fact that Marx said something means it must be true. Marx himself would have been the first to denounce such idolatry.
31 According to Engels, who had reason to know, 'There never were greater boors than our modern bourgeois.' Frederick Engels, *The Housing Question* (London: Lawrence & Wishart, 1942), 26.
32 William Morris, 'The Beauty of Life', in *Hopes and Fears for Art*, available at https://www.marxists.org/archive/morris/works/1882/hopes/chapters/chapter3.htm. Of course, it can be argued that Morris's view of the Middle Ages was idealised and romantic – and perhaps it was – but it is worth noting that Marx wrote (in another of those undeveloped asides) just after describing composing as 'really free working' of 'the semi-artistic worker of the Middle Ages'. Marx, *Grundrisse*, 610.
33 William Morris, 'Art or No Art? Who Shall Settle It?' (1884), available at https://www.marxists.org/archive/morris/works/1884/justice/06artno.htm.

34 As cited in Leon Trotksy, *Leon Trotsky on Literature and Art* (New York: Pathfinder, 1977), 96–97.
35 Trotsky, *Literature and Art*, 106 and 114.
36 Trotsky, *Literature and Art*, 119–20.
37 John Berger, 'The Work of Art', in *Selected Essays* (London: Bloomsbury, 2001), 434, my emphasis.
38 Berger, *Selected Essays*, 432–3.
39 As Renoir said, 'Without tubes of paint [which could be transported outside] there would have been no Impressionism.' I owe this point to Ben Davis.
40 In the case of Godot, there are only lead actors, but in many plays and most films there are bit parts and 'extras' whose labour has very little artistic (i.e., self-directed) element.
41 This differentiation is especially clear in art schools where there is a need to designate and distinguish academic disciplines and degree courses.
42 John Berger, *Ways of Seeing* (London: BBC and Penguin, 1972), 129.
43 The nature of those barriers, which are both very considerable, is worth an essay in its own right.
44 John Molyneux, *The Future Socialist Society* (London: Bookmarks, 1987), 34, available at https://www.marxists.org/history/etol/writers/molyneux/1987/future/index.html.

Chapter 2: How We Judge Art

1 This was the original position, later revised, of John Berger, who compared Bacon not to Goya but to Walt Disney. See John Berger, 'Francis Bacon and Walt Disney', in *John Berger: Selected Essays*, Geoff Dyer, ed. (London: Bloomsbury, 2001), 315.
2 Hockney's *Portrait of an Artist (Pool with Two Figures)* is, at the time of writing, expected to sell at auction for $80 million, the highest price for a living artist.
3 I am here essentially speaking about the Western art world (i.e., North America and Europe). In a sense, this is not just limited but also wrong in that the art world in the twenty-first century has gone global in a way that was never the case before, particularly with the inclusion of China. I return to his point in chapter 11.
4 See Eva Cockcroft, 'Abstract Expressionism: Weapon of the Cold War', *Artforum*, Summer 1974, https://www.artforum.com/print/197406/abstract-expressionism-weapon-of-the-cold-war-38017.
5 See Clive Bell, 'The Aesthetic Hypothesis', in *Art in Theory (1900–1990)*, Charles Harrison and Paul Wood, eds. (Oxford: Blackwell, 1993), 113.
6 'Aesthetic judgments are immediate, intuitive, undeliberate and involuntary ... they leave no room for the conscious application of standards, criteria, rules or precepts.' Clement Greenberg, 'Complaints of an Art Critic', cited in Charles Harrison, Francis Fascina and Gill Perry, *Primitivism, Cubism, Abstraction: The Early Twentieth Century* (London: Open University, 1993), 221.
7 Lenin, the greatest political leader of modern times, wrote that it is 'one of the functions of a party organisation and of party leaders worthy of the name ... to evolve the knowledge, the experience and – in addition to knowledge and

experience – the political *instinct* necessary for the speedy and correct solution of intricate political problems'. Vladimir Lenin, *Left Wing Communism: An Infantile Disorder* (Peking: Foreign Language Press, 1970), 65, my emphasis.

8 For example, I consider the element of mimesis to be a significant quality in the ink drawings of Tracey Emin.

9 Herbert Read, *The Meaning of Art* (Suffolk: Pelican, 1950), 16.

10 Aristotle, *Poetics*, chapter 7, cited in Robert Wilkinson, ed., *Theories of Art and Beauty* (Milton Keynes: Open University, 1996), 472.

11 Read, *The Meaning of Art*, 16.

12 It is conventionally attributed to Longinus, or 'Pseudo-Longinus'.

13 Barnett Newman, in his 'manifesto' of 1948, 'The Sublime Is Now', sees the sublime not as a complement to the idea of beauty, but as its antagonist and replacement: 'The impulse of modern art was this desire to destroy beauty . . . here in America, some of us, free from the weight of European culture, are finding the answer, by completely denying that art has any concern with the problem of beauty.' Cited in Alex Danchev, *100 Artists' Manifestos* (Harmondsworth: Penguin, 2012), 324–25.

14 Thus the Tate Britain devoted an exhibition to this theme in 2009.

15 'I must admit that, either from temperament or taste, or from both, I am quite incapable of understanding how any work of art can be criticised from a moral standpoint. The sphere of art and the sphere of ethics are absolutely distinct and separate.' Oscar Wilde, cited in Stuart Mason, ed., *Art and Morality* (London: J. Jacobs, 1908), available at http://www.gutenberg.org/files/33689/33689-h/33689-h.htm.

16 This also resulted in the painting over of genitals in the Sistine Chapel.

17 Marcel Duchamp, 'The Richard Mutt Case', cited in Harrison and Wood, *Art in Theory (1900–1990)*, 248.

18 'Efforts to brand some work as "communist" no longer worked by the 1980s. . . . Instead, US censorship campaigns have mostly taken the form of moral panics meant to mobilize authoritarian minded religious fundamentalists." Martha Rosler, 'Take the Money and Run? Can Political and Socio-critical Art Survive?', in *What Is Contemporary Art?*, Julieta Aranda, Brian Kuan Wood and Anton Vidokle, eds. (Berlin: Sternberg Press, 2010), 121.

19 See my review in chapter 6.

20 George Orwell would be an example of this.

21 This was pioneered by John Berger in *Ways of Seeing*.

22 My own view would tend to the third option, with the understanding (a) that the critique does not apply automatically and on principle to all representations of the female nude (a point acknowledged by Berger); (b) that the aesthetic criticism of sexist representation of the nude has to be concretely demonstrated, as it can be, for example, with Velázquez's *Rokeby Venus*; and (c) that where the case is convincingly demonstrated it should not be seen as annulling all artistic merit in the work – the *Rokeby Venus* again being an example.

23 Jean-Baptiste Du Bos, *Critical Reflections upon Poetry and Painting*, cited in Lionello Venturi, *History of Art Criticism* (New York: E.P. Dutton & Co., 1964), 113.

24 'The activity of art is based on the fact that a man receiving through his sense of hearing or sight another man's expression of feeling, is capable of experiencing the emotion which moved the man who expressed it.' Leo Tolstoy, *What Is Art?*, in Wilkinson, *Art and Beauty*, 325. It is worth noting that Tolstoy took this theory to its extreme and thereby condemned all the impressionists and their like as 'not art' because of their failure (at that time) to communicate with the mass of people.

25 Henry Matisse, 'Notes of a Painter' (1908), in Harrison and Wood, *Art in Theory (1900–1990)*, 72.

26 'To record the manners, ideas and aspect of the age as I myself saw them ... that is my aim'. Gustave Courbet, 'Statement on Realism', in *Art in Theory (1815–1900)*, Charles Harrison, Paul Wood and Jason Gaiger, eds. (Milton Keynes: Open University Press, 1998), 372.

27 Frederick Engels, 'Letter to Margaret Harkness', in Harrison, Wood and Gaiger, *Art in Theory (1815–1900*), 762. Engels was a brilliant mind who seldom wrote anything foolish, but the elevation of this passing comment in a private letter to canonical status smacks of a semi-religious attitude to the founders of historical materialism.

28 Hence the work of photographers such as Lewis B. Hine, Paul Strand, August Sander and Henri Cartier-Bresson, and film directors such as Jean Renoir, Roberto Rossellini, Luchino Visconti and latterly, Ken Loach.

29 Georgio Vasari, *Lives of the Artists* (Oxford: Oxford University Press, 1991), 58.

30 Vasari, *Lives of the Artists*, 124.

31 This is four to five years earlier than Kandinsky's first claimed abstract work in 1911.

32 This makes it possible for the gift shop in the Fundació Joan Miró museum in Barcelona to do a roaring trade in Miró-styled artefacts.

33 Rosler, 'Take the Money and Run?', 106. She may be thinking of Goya or Géricault here, but, as noted above, I date its origins a little later.

34 Blake, Goya and Géricault could all be cited as forerunners, but I think Courbet is the starting point for a major shift in the direction of art.

35 It could be said that Manet's main subject was the depiction of middle-class leisure, but (a) such depiction in 'high art' was itself radical at the time; and (b) *the way* he did it in, for example, *Déjeuner sur l'Herbe* and *A Bar at the Folies-Bergère* was decidedly 'critical' and 'edgy'.

36 'A superior consciousness of history-more precisely, the appearance of a new kind of criticism of society, an historical criticism-made this possible [Greenberg means Marxism here].... Thus our present bourgeois social order was shown to be, not an eternal, "natural" condition of life, but simply the latest term in a succession of social orders. New perspectives of this kind, becoming a part of the advanced intellectual conscience of the fifth and sixth decades of the nineteenth century, soon were absorbed by artists and poets, even if unconsciously for the most part. It was no accident, therefore, that the birth of the avant-garde coincided chronologically-and geographically, too-with the first bold development of scientific revolutionary thought in Europe.... True, the first settlers of bohemia-which was then identical with the avant-garde-turned out soon to be demonstratively uninterested in

politics. Nevertheless, without the circulation of revolutionary ideas in the air about them, they would never have been able to isolate their concept of the "bourgeois" in order to define what they were not. Nor, without the moral aid of revolutionary political attitudes would they have had the courage to assert themselves as aggressively as they did against the prevailing standards of society.' Clement Greenberg, 'Avant-garde and Kitsch', in Harrison and Wood, *Art in Theory (1900–90)*, 531.

37 See the description in Yates McKee, *Strike Art* (London and New York: Verso, 2017), 1–5.

38 These statements do not just designate general stages in the development of Marx's thought, but also specific texts: *The Critique of Hegel's Philosophy of Right, Economic and Philosophic Manuscripts of 1844, The Theses on Feuerbach, The German Ideology, A Contribution to the Critique of Political Economy* and *Capital: A Critical Analysis of Capitalist Production.*

39 Theodor Adorno, 'Commitment', in Harrison and Wood, *Art in Theory (1900–1990)*, 763.

40 Theodor Adorno, *Aesthetic Theory* (1970; repr., London: Bloomsbury, 2009), 296.

41 Leon Trotsky, 'Art and Politics in our Epoch', in *Leon Trotsky on Literature and Art* (New York: Pathfinder, 1977), 104.

42 Clement Greenberg, 'Modernist Painting', cited in Harrison and Wood, *Art and Theory (1900–1990)*, 754.

43 See Michael Fried, 'Three American Painters', in Harrison and Wood, *Art and Theory (1900–1990)*, 769–74.

44 The number of such adjectives deployed is vast. Art writers, especially the writers of catalogue notes and puff pieces, must make extensive use of their thesauruses. 'Mesmerising,' 'captivating', 'thrilling', 'celebrated', 'rigorous' – all of these are taken from a few paragraphs about one small show at the Tate Modern.

45 However, Frida Kahlo was herself a communist and would probably not have called herself a 'feminist'.

46 This is not to say this is the only quality to be found in Kahlo's work. For example, her *Self-Portrait along the Borderline between Mexico and the United States* makes a strong social statement, but the difference in emphasis with Rivera remains.

47 The same could, of course, be said, of a work of pop art, of minimalism, of conceptual art, of relational aesthetics and 'the social turn', but I think the broad principles of application would remain the same.

48 The works of both, especially Pollock's, often contain traces of figuration.

49 'The development of modern art from impressionism to abstract form… embodies the ever more frantic flight from content, i.e., from social reality, from all reality whatever, of the retrogressive capitalist class.… Far from achieving the emancipation of art, the destruction of content necessarily leads to the destruction also of form – a climax epically symbolized in the white square painted on a white canvas of white shape by the Suprematist Malevich. In its final decay the capitalist class destroys its art, as it destroys its science.' Francis Klingender, 'Content and Form in Art' (1935), in Harrison

and Wood, *Art in Theory (1900–1990)*, 421–22. Klingender was the British Communist Party's main theorist on visual art in the 1930s.

50 There is a general point here. Many works of modern and contemporary art which are attacked for lacking skill actually involve lots of skills, but they are different skills from those of a traditional painter or sculptor. For example, the work of Christo (who wrapped the Reichstag and much else besides) and of Rachel Whiteread (who cast the interior of a house) requires major organisational and engineering skills.

51 Barnett Newman, 'The Sublime is Now', in Harrison and Wood, *Art and Theory (1900–1990)*, 572–73.

52 Barnett Newman, 'Interview with Dorothy Gees Seckler', in Harrison and Wood, *Art and Theory (1900–1990)*, 766. It is relevant that at the time Newman made this comment, heated debates were taking place among the American Far Left as to the nature of Stalinist Russia, debates which included the theories that Russia was 'state capitalist', and that it was a new form of class society called 'bureaucratic collectivism'. Moreover, there was a certain crossover between avant-garde art circles and the Far Left, particularly via the *Partisan Review*, for which both Clement Greenberg and Harold Rosenberg had written important essays.

53 This was, among other things, the moment of Orwell's *1984* and Norman Mailer's *Barbary Shore*, which also referenced state capitalism and totalitarianism and, of course, McCarthyism.

54 Charles Harrison, 'Abstract Expressionism', in *Concepts of Modern Art*, Nikos Stangos, ed. (London: Thames & Hudson, 1983), 193.

55 For example: Plekhanov, Raphael, Antal, Hauser, Trotsky, Lukács, Benjamin, Brecht, Adorno, Caudwell, Klingender, Zhdanov, Sartre, Althusser, Macherey, Berger, Jameson, Hadjinicolaou, Lindsay, Clarke, Rifkin, Eagleton, Harrison, Wood, Edwards, Roberts, Duncan, Hemingway and many others.

56 Stuart Sim, 'Marxism and Aesthetics', in *Philosophical Aesthetics: An Introduction*, Oswald Hanfling, ed. (Oxford: Blackwell, 1995), 441–43.

57 I have made such an argument in relation to Rubens, where I suggest that, in comparison to Rembrandt, much of his work – though superb in many respects – is diminished in its depth and sensitivity by the sociopolitical nature of his clientele.

58 The high, or low, point was reached with Stalin's cultural supremo, A. A. Zhdanov, though a similar approach was adopted by Maoism, especially during the Cultural Revolution.

59 Karl Marx, 'Preface' to *A Contribution to the Critique of Political Economy*, in *Karl Marx and Frederick Engels: Selected Works*, vol. 1 (Moscow: Foreign Languages Press, 1962), 361.

60 Frederick Engels, 'Speech at the Grave of Karl Marx, 17 March 1883, Highgate Cemetery, London, available at https://www.marxists.org/archive/marx/works/1883/death/burial.htm.

61 Frederick Engels, Letter to H. Starkenburg (1884), in *Karl Marx and Frederick Engels: Selected Works*, vol. 2 (Moscow: Foreign Languages Press, 1962), 504.

62 See Mike Davis, *Old Gods, New Enigmas* (London and New York: Verso, 2018), 42–43.

63 There is an interesting comparison to be made between Mondrian's late work and the work of Robert Rauschenberg as representations of 'the city'.
64 They were subjects of a joint exhibition, *All Too Human*, at the Tate Britain in 2018. Exhibition guide available at https://www.tate.org.uk/whats-on/tate-britain/exhibition/all-too-human.
65 Nicolas Bourriaud, *Relational Aesthetics* (Dijon: Les Presses du réel, 2002), 113.
66 Carsten Höller, interview by Vincent Honoré (2006), Tate Modern official website, https://www.tate.org.uk/whats-on/tate-modern/exhibition/unilever-series/unilever-series-carsten-holler-test-site/carsten.
67 I regard this as a significant plus and one that has been built on and extended by work such as Superflex's *One, Two, Swing* installation of a brightly coloured child friendly surface on the entry ramp leading to numerous swings, also in the Turbine Hall, in 2017–18.
68 For clarity I should say that I am not maintaining that Marxism applies only to Western art. Historical materialism is a theory of world history, and the idea that 'great' art captures social relations should apply to the art of many cultures, but I have only demonstrated this in relation to the Western art due to my greater familiarity with that tradition.

Chapter 3: Michelangelo and Human Emancipation

1 Clearly this list could be made less Eurocentric by including figures such as Confucious, Rabindranath Tagore and Ibn Khaldun but, regardless of their objective stature, none of these non-European 'greats' has achieved the level of renown of their European counterparts, due to the global hegemony of European culture.
2 For what Newman actually *wrote* on the subject, see 'The Sublime is Now', in *Art in Theory (1900–1990)*, Charles Harrison and Paul Wood, eds. (Oxford: Blackwell, 1993), 573.
3 Georgio Vasari, *The Lives of the Artists* (Oxford: Oxford University Press, 1991), 414.
4 John A. Symonds, *The Life of Michelangelo Buonarroti*, vol. 2 (London: Macmillan, 1911), 174.
5 E. H. Gombrich, *The Story of Art* (Oxford: Phaidon, 1978), 217–18.
6 Vasari, *Lives of the Artists*, 277–78 and 280.
7 Rolf Schott, *Michelangelo* (London: Thames & Hudson, 1975), 7.
8 Charles de Tolnay, cited in C. Sala, *Michelangelo: Sculptor, Painter, Architect* (Paris: Terrail, 1995), 170.
9 There is now a 'gay' Vatican tour available: https://untoldhistorytour.com/tour/rome-vatican-museums-in-a-gay-light/. Thanks to Ben Davis for this point.
10 Frederick Engels, 'Introduction', *Dialectics of Nature* (London: Lawrence & Wishart, 1941), 1–2, available at http://www.marxists.org/archive/marx/works/1883/don/ch01.htm.
11 Frederick Antal, *Florentine Painting and Its Social Background* (London: Routledge & Keegan Paul, 1948), 11–13.
12 Arnold Hauser, *The Social History of Art*, vol. 2 (London: Routledge & Keegan Paul), 9–10.

13 Hauser, *Social History of Art*, 7.
14 Antonio Gramsci, *Selections from the Prison Notebooks* (London: Lawrence & Wishart, 1971), 351.
15 Hauser, *Social History of Art*, 105.
16 See Arnold Hauser, *Mannerism: The Crisis of the Renaissance and the Origin Of Modern Art* (London: Routledge & Keegan Paul, 1965), esp. 4–16.

Chapter 4: Rembrandt and Revolution

1 The other artist of the time most renowned for his use of chiaroscuro is the Italian Caravaggio (1573–1610). However, Caravaggio used the technique not for psychological depth but in order to freeze and capture the dramatic moment. See, for example, *The Supper at Emmaus* (ca. 1596–1602) in the National Gallery, where the 'moment' captured is the instant of the disciples' recognition of Christ.
2 The tendency to reduce the female nude to an armless and/or headless torso is a feature of the erotic representation of women from the *Venus de Milo* to the photographs of Bill Brandt, the woman thus being rendered 'armless' (pun intended) and mindless.
3 Impressionistic evidence suggests that in the capitalist epoch, most artists came from a middle- to lower-middle-class background (though in the twentieth century, there was also a significant working-class minority coming through the art colleges), but it is important to understand that the objective class position of the large majority of artists, whatever their background, is petty bourgeois in that they are predominantly self-employed or small employers, selling not their labour power, but the products of their labour, where possible, to the rich.
4 These figures are very rough because many of Rembrandt's works blur the categories (for example his 'portraits' of Christ or his 1651 'portrait' of King David) and because of arguments about attribution, but I am only interested in the general trend, which is clear.
5 Simon Schama, *Rembrandt's Eyes* (London: Allen Lane, 1999), 334–35. This is a huge and, in my opinion, very ill-judged book on Rembrandt (which I have reviewed very critically), but Schama's detailed knowledge enables him to make useful observations about particular paintings.
6 Schama, *Rembrandt's Eyes*, 337.
7 Ernst van de Wetering, 'The Multiple Functions of Rembrandt's Self-Portraits', in *Rembrandt by Himself*, Christopher White and Quentin Buvelot, eds. (London: Thames & Hudson, 1999), 10.
8 de Wetering, *Rembrandt by Himself*, flyleaf.
9 See the discussion of these themes in Arnold Hauser, *The Social History of Art*, vol. 2 (London: Routledge & Keegan Paul), 57–61.
10 Bertrand Russell, *History of Western Philosophy* (London: George Allen & Unwin, 1971), 579.
11 William Carlos Williams, introduction to Allen Ginsberg, *Howl and Other Poems* (San Francisco: City Lights, 1965), 1.
12 Hauser, *Social History of Art*, xxi.
13 John Berger, *Ways of Seeing* (London: Penguin, 1972), 112.

14 Berger, *Ways of Seeing*, 109.

15 Again, remember Marx in *The Communist Manifesto*: 'The weapons with which the bourgeoisie felled feudalism to the ground are now turned against the bourgeoisie itself.'

16 'Prints of beggars by the French artist, Callot, were popular in Holland at this time.... But what a difference! Callot's beggars are picturesque: at best sentimental, at worst designed to please those who derive pleasure from looking at those less fortunate than themselves.' Charles Fowkes, *The Life of Rembrandt* (London: Hamlyn, 1978), 39. See also John Berger's comments on Dutch genre painting in *Ways of Seeing* (103–4), and my discussion of Richard Billingham's photographs of his family in chapter 6 of this volume.

17 Kenneth Clark, *An Introduction to Rembrandt* (London: HarperCollins, 1978), 43.

18 Cited in Clark, *Introduction to Rembrandt*, 44.

19 See Jonathan Israel, *The Dutch Republic: Its Rise, Greatness and Fall* (Oxford: Oxford University Press, 1995) 376–77.

20 Fowkes, *Life of Rembrandt*, 9.

21 K. G. Boon, *Rembrandt: The Complete Etchings* (London: Thames & Hudson, 1963), i.

22 Kenneth Clark, *Rembrandt and the Italian Renaissance* (New York: New York University Press, 1966), 10.

23 Clark, *Rembrandt and the Italian Renaissance*, 12–13. A significant participant in this debate, and in the general debate on Rembrandt, is Nicos Hadjinicolaou, *Art History and Class Struggle* (London: Pluto Press, 1988), who mocks Clark's reaction and cites *The Rape of Ganymede* as an example of 'critical baroque visual ideology' (163–68). Hadjinicolaou attempts a rather mechanical application of Althusserian structuralist 'Marxism' to the discipline of art history. It is tempting to discuss the strengths and weaknesses of his approach and judgments at some length (it would require quite a long discussion), but time and space do not permit this. However, I will say that I disagree strongly with his tendency to reduce art to ideology.

24 There are two versions of *Slaughtered Ox*, one from 1635 and one from 1655. The experts say that the earlier work is probably not by Rembrandt himself. Both are fine paintings, but the later work, which I refer to here, is much more powerful.

25 Hélène Cixous, 'Bathsheba or the Interior Bible', in *Stigmata: Escaping Texts* (London: Routledge, 1998), 15–16.

26 See Marx's analysis of alienated labour in his *Economic and Philosophic Manuscripts*, in Karl Marx, *Early Writings* (London: Watts, 1963), 120–34.

27 Simon Schama makes a detailed analysis of this dynamic composition in *Rembrandt's Eyes*, 496–500.

28 Cited in Schama, *Rembrandt's Eyes*, 488.

29 Kenneth Clark, who refers repeatedly to Rembrandt as 'the rebel' in both his books on the artist, is unable to answer this question seriously and reduces Rembrandt's artistic radicalism to (a) a personal character trait; and (b) a rebellion against Italian classicism.

30 That is, artistically speaking. Politically, William Morris was a revolutionary socialist and identified with the working class.

31 In Pound's case, his critique of capitalism and idealisation of medieval Provence, the troubadours, Dante, and so on led him straight into the arms of Mussolini.
32 Cixous, 'Bathsheba', 7. This project has been five years in the making, and the overall argument and conclusion has been present almost since the beginning, but it was only right at the end that I came across this Cixous neologism that so well expresses my meaning.
33 This ended with Rembrandt scheming to have Geertje condemned to a house of correction, where she remained for five years – an act of cruelty for which it is hard to imagine any justification, although, or course, we do not know anything like the full story.
34 See Hauser, *Social History of Art*, xxxiii, xix and 106–7.
35 The title is from the nineteenth century, and it is not known who the couple were or whether they were really Jewish, but this is of little significance.
36 Karl Marx and Frederick Engels, *The Communist Manifesto* (1848, repr., New York: Penguin Books, 2011).

Chapter 5: A Revolution in Paint

1 See, for example, Jackie Wullschlager, 'The Day Modern Art Was Invented: Picasso's Demoiselles', *Financial Times,* 4 January 2007; or Jonathan Jones, 'Pablo's Punks', *Guardian*, 9 January 2007.
2 I am using 'realistic' here in the way it is used in everyday language, the media and mainstream art history, which basically accepts the method of representing the world developed in the Renaissance as true realism, and not in the specific Marxist sense developed by Frederick Engels, Georg Lukács and others. Lukács distinguished between 'naturalism', the more or less accurate depiction of surface appearances, and 'realism', which penetrated surface appearances to reveal the real driving forces in society. Lukács developed this distinction in relation to literature, so that for him Honoré de Balzac was a great realist, whereas Émile Zola was merely a naturalist, and 'the central aesthetic problem of realism is the adequate presentation of the complete human personality'. Georg Lukács, 'Preface', *Studies in European Realism* (London: Merlin Press, 2014), available at http://web.archive.org/web/20071228193901/http:/courses.essex.ac.uk/LT/LT204/lukacs_preface.htm). It can perhaps be applied to some 'traditional' (i.e., European 1300–1900) visual art, so that Rembrandt's 'realism' could be contrasted to the 'naturalism' of van Dyke or numerous hack portraitists. But it is very difficult to see how it can cope with post-1900 art, with its divergent phenomena such as geometric and expressionist abstraction, Dadaism, Marcel Duchamp and the 'readymade' tradition, pop art, conceptual art, installation art, performance art, and so on. And it cannot be used to understand the difference between 'traditional' art and 'modern' art, which is what I am concerned with here.
3 John Berger supplied the historical materialist explanation for this, linking it to the rise of capitalism and its fixation on property and commodities. See Berger, *Ways of Seeing*, 4.
4 Robert Hughes, *The Shock of the New* (London: Thames & Hudson, 1991), 24.

5 Carsten-Peter Warncke, *Picasso* (London: Taschen, 1997), 165. There is a significant difference between this and the outrage that greeted Manet and the impressionists in that the latter came from the public and the press, whereas this came from the artists in Picasso's immediate circle and resulted in the public not seeing the painting for nearly ten years.
6 Clement Greenberg, 'Modernist Painting', in *Art in Theory (1900–1990)*, Charles Harrison and Paul Wood, eds. (Oxford: Blackwell, 1993), 754.
7 Greenberg, 'Modernist Painting', 755.
8 Greenberg, 'Modernist Painting', 755–56. Neil Davidson has suggested that the position of the younger Greenberg in his essay 'Avant-Garde and Kitsch' is in some ways superior to the position cited here. I think that this is true, but space does not permit an account of the development of his views. Justice for Greenberg will have to wait.
9 According to John Berger, this was 'not so much a window on the world as a safe in the wall'.
10 Greenberg, 'Modernist Painting', 756.
11 See John Berger, 'The Moment of Cubism', in *Selected Essays and Articles: The Look of Things* (Harmondsworth: Penguin, 1972).
12 John Berger, *The Success and Failure of Picasso* (Harmondsworth: Penguin, 1965), 75.
13 Perry Anderson, 'Modernity and Revolution', *New Left Review* 144 March–April 1984.
14 Obviously such a periodisation requires a sustained argument of a depth and length that cannot be presented here.
15 Jones, 'Pablo's Punks'.
16 The story relates better to some of the numerous preliminary studies for *Les Demoiselles*, which feature two male figures – a sailor, and a student carrying a skull, a possible 'wages of sin' memento mori.
17 Berger, *Picasso*, 72.
18 On the first point, see John Molyneux, 'Picasso, Modernism and the Non-European', *Socialist Worker*, 22 April 2006.
19 Carol Duncan, *The Aesthetics of Power* (Cambridge, UK: Cambridge University Press, 1993), 112–13.
20 Duncan, *Aesthetics of Power*, 96–97.
21 Karl Marx, *Economic and Philosophic Manuscripts of 1844* (Moscow: Progress Publishers, 1967), 93.

Chapter 6: State of the Art

1 Louisa Buck, *Moving Targets: A User's Guide to British Art Now* (London: Tate Gallery Publishing, 1997), 7.
2 See E. Cockcroft, '*Abstract Expressionism, Weapon of the Cold War*', in *Pollock and After*, Francis Frascina, *ed.* (London: Harper & Row, 1985).
3 In 1988 Damien Hirst, in his second year at Goldsmith's College, curated the *Freeze* exhibition which marks the origin of Young British Art.
4 Leon Trotsky, *Leon Trotsky on Literature and Art* (London: Pathfinder, 1977), 105.

5 People get into the most absurd confusions about subject matter and 'art'. Can you make great art out of a man being slowly tortured to death? Yes! In fact it is probably the most common theme in the history of European art – the Crucifixion. Titian painted someone being hung upside down and flayed alive (*The Flaying of Marsyas*). Can you make art out of a pair of old boots? Both van Gogh and Chaplin managed it. The question is not what the subject matter is, but how it is painted, represented or used.
6 Royal Academy of Arts, *Sensation: Young British Artists from the Saatchi Collection* (London: Thames & Hudson, 1997), 198.
7 I am reminded of Vivienne Westwood and others associated with punk in 1976–77 attempting to 'play' with the swastika for shock value, attempts which socialists had to firmly oppose.
8 Royal Academy of Arts, *Sensation*, 194.
9 For example, such a defence might be offered in relation to the anti-Semitism in T. S. Eliot's poem 'Gerontion.'
10 All three of these arguments might be used to defend Nabokov's *Lolita*.
11 T. S. Eliot, *Selected Prose* (Harmondsworth: Penguin, 1965), 102.
12 It is worth noting that those works of art which became exceptionally well known – like the *Mona Lisa*, *The Hay Wain*, Monet's *Water Lilies*, Munch's *The Scream* – are often despised for this reason but usually are powerful and important works in their own right.
13 For this point, see David Batchelor, *Minimalism* (London: Tate Gallery Publishing, 1997), 95.
14 In fact, it *was* eventually constructed, after this essay was published. Originally scheduled to be finished on 9 November 1996, the fifty-eighth anniversary of Kristallnacht, it was finally unveiled on 25 October 2000.
15 Bitter controversy surrounded the decision by the local authority to destroy *House,* which had been erected on a temporary basis. Doubtless the decision was motivated by philistinism, and it can easily be seen as an artistic tragedy (as well as a financial blunder). However, it seems to me that there is also a sense in which, just as Duchamp decided to regard the cracks received in transit by *The Large Glass* as part of the work, so the demolition of *House* is its fitting dialectical completion.
16 As noted above, it was ultimately constructed.
17 It is worth noting that, of the forty-two artists represented, eleven are women – still a small minority but probably a higher proportion than would have been found in a supposedly representative survey of British art at any time in the past.
18 I have revised upwards my opinion of Lucas's work as a result of a number of discussions with students, colleagues and comrades, especially Sarah Dryden, Paul Clarke, Jenny Walden and Alison Jones.
19 Far more powerful are *Light Sentence* and *Corps Étranger,* by which Hatoum was represented in the Turner Prize show of 1995.
20 As depicted by Hogarth in the last of the *Rake's Progress* series (but Hogarth shows and implicitly condemns the voyeurs).
21 It is possible, thanks to the shift to the right in academia in the 1980s, that many of these artists do not know either the name or the analysis of the condition in which they are immersed.

22 Karl Marx and Frederick Engels, *The German Ideology* (London: Lawrence & Wishart, 1985), 55.
23 Traces of this are to be seen in some of the work, such as that by Chris Ofili, Glen Brown and Jason Martin.
24 'But love has pitched his mansion in / The place of excrement / For nothing can be sole or whole / That has not been rent.' W. B. Yeats, 'Crazy Jane Talks with the Bishop', *Collected Poems* (Ware: Wordsworth, 1982), 221.
25 After this article was written, the *Sensation* show was taken to the Brooklyn Museum in New York. There in 1999, the controversy was not about Harvey's Myra Hindley or the Chapman brothers, but Chris Ofili's *The Virgin Mary*. This was singled out for attack by New York Mayor Rudy Guliani (later legal advisor to President Donald Trump), who was no doubt trying to appeal to his Catholic base, as obscene and blasphemous because of its employment, alongside its Black Madonna, of small pornographic images and Ofili's trademark elephant dung. In this dispute I think we should stand clearly with Ofili.

Chapter 7: The Emin Phenomenon or the Phenomenal Emin

1 Amy Lane 'Bare-Faced Realities', *Socialist Review*, December 2004, 34.
2 Jennifer Doyle, 'The Effect of Intimacy', in *The Art of Tracey Emin*, Mandy Merck and Chris Townshend, eds. (London: Thames & Hudson, 2002), 102.

Chapter 8: The Liberty of Appearing

1 John Berger, *Ways of Seeing* (Harmondsworth: Penguin, 1988), 103.
2 Karl Marx and Frederick Engels, *The German Ideology* (1846; repr., London: Lawrence & Wishart, 1991), 10.
3 Karl Marx, *Economic and Philosophic Manuscripts of 1844* (Moscow: Progress Publishers, 1967), 98.
4 Karl Marx and Frederick Engels, *The Communist Manifesto* (1848, repr., New York: Penguin Books, 2011).

Chapter 9: Shorter Reviews

1 For non-British readers, this is a famous 'patriotic' concert.

Chapter 10: How Art Develops

1 Karl Marx, 'Preface', *A Contribution to the Critique of Political Economy*', in *Karl Marx and Frederick Engels: Selected Works*, vol. 1 (Moscow: Foreign Languages Press, 1962), 361. The validity and usefulness of the 'base and superstructure' model has, of course, often been contested, most influentially, perhaps, by Raymond Williams in his book *Marxism and Literature* (Oxford: Oxford University Press, 1977). My view is that what is usually rejected is a

mechanical and deterministic conception of the relationship between base and superstructure. Thus Williams writes: 'Any modern approach to a Marxist theory of culture must begin by considering the proposition of a determining base and a determined superstructure.' (75) But this deterministic model is not what I am proposing here. An interesting debate on this question took place in *International Socialism* in 1986–87, with contributions by Chris Harman ('Base and Superstructure'), *International Socialism* 32, Summer 1986, and three critical comments by Colin Barker, Alex Callinicos and Duncan Hallas, respectively, in *International Socialism* 34, Winter 1987. For my own take on this, see John Molyneux, 'Is Marxism Deterministic?', *International Socialism* 68, Autumn 1995.

2 Marx, 'Preface', my emphasis.

3 Engels to Borgius, 25 January 1894, *New International* 1:3 (September–October 1934), 81–85, available at https://www.marxists.org/archive/marx/works/1894/letters/94_01_25a.htm.

4 Arnold Hauser tells us that at forty thousand francs, this was the highest paid picture of its time. Arnold Hauser, *The Social History of Art*, vol. 3 (London: Routledge, 1962), xxix.

5 As opposed to paintings where the landscape (however beautifully painted) is merely the background to the figures, as in Piero Della Francesca's *Baptism of Christ* or da Vinci's *Virgin of the Rocks*.

6 However, he himself had a very complex Theosophist/spiritual reasoning for what he did.

7 For a fuller exploration of the relationship between Dutch art, especially that of Rembrandt, and the Dutch bourgeois revolution, see John Molyneux, *Rembrandt and Revolution* (London: Redwords, 2001).

8 Karl Marx and Frederick Engels, *The Communist Manifesto* (1848, repr., New York: Penguin Books, 2011).

9 Perry Anderson, 'Modernity and Revolution', *New Left Review* 1:144, January–February 1984.

10 The most important difference concerns not the dating of the origin of modernism, but the contrast between Anderson's pessimistic, almost miserabilist, view of modernism and culture in decline (which also leaves the door wide open to postmodernism) and Berman's more open and optimistic view of modernism as an ongoing project. See Marshall Berman, 'The Signs in the Street: A Response to Perry Anderson', *New Left Review* 1:144, January–February 1984. I am very much inclined to agree with Berman on this. See my critique of Anderson in John Molyneux, 'The Legitimacy of Modern Art', *International Socialism* 80, Autumn 1998.

11 Marx, 'Preface'.

12 This discussion of conditions, conditioning and agency in relation to art is clearly a subset of the wider debate about circumstances and agency which always gone on within and around the Marxist tradition. See Alex Callinicos, *Making History* (Oxford: Polity, 1989); and John Molyneux, 'Is Marxism Deterministic?', *International Socialism* 68 (1995). With some justification one could paraphrase Marx to say, 'People make art but they do not make it as they please, in circumstances of their own choosing.'

13 For elaboration of this view of class struggle as rooted in exploitative relations of production, rather than unequal consumption and life chances, see John Molyneux, *The Point Is to Change It! An Introduction to Marxist Philosophy* (London: Bookmarks, 2012), chapter 3; and G. E. M de Ste Croix, *The Class Struggle in the Ancient Greek World* (London: Duckworth,1983), 43–44.
14 Karl Marx, *The German Ideology* (1846; repr., London: Lawrence & Wishart, 1991).
15 Think of the tsars with their collection of Rembrandts, or Japanese corporations buying up van Goghs.
16 We should note the difference here between visual art and music, literature, film and so on. In the latter categories, an artist can a build a career by achieving either a mass or significant niche audience. In visual art almost the only way for artists to earn reasonable amounts of money directly from their art is by appealing to the rich and powerful.
17 See Engels to Bloch (1890), in Marx and Engels, *Selected Works*, vol. 2 (Moscow: Progress Publishers, 1962), 489.
18 The same is true of her video work *Why I Never Became a Dancer* and of the photo series *Life Model Goes Mad*. See chapter 7 in this volume.
19 There is a parallel here with the argument made by Trotsky in his *History of the Russian Revolution* that without Lenin the October Revolution would not have succeeded, but that Lenin was only the final link in a chain that stretched back to the fundamental facts of Russia's historical development.
20 Karl Marx, *Grundrisse* (Harmondsworth: Penguin, 1972), 110–11.
21 Leon Trotsky, *Class and Art* (London: New Park, 1968), 9–10.
22 Karl Marx, *Theories of Surplus Value*, vol.1 (1863; repr., London: Lawrence & Wishart, 1951), 285.
23 Josiah Ober, *The Rise and Fall of Classical Greece* (Princeton, NJ: Princeton University Press, 2015), cited in Peter Rose, 'The Secret of the Ancients?', *New Left Review* 2:103 (January–February 2017), 141.
24 Frederick Antal, *Florentine Painting and Its Social Background* (Cambridge, MA: Harvard University Press, 1986), 11.
25 Angus Maddison, *The World Economy: Historical Statistics* (Paris: OECD, 2003), 262.

Chapter 11: The Dialectics of Modernism

1 Leon Trotsky, 'Art and Politics in Our Epoch', in *Leon Trotsky on Literature and Art* (New York: Pathfinder, 1970), 104–5.
2 Filippo Marinetti, 'The Foundation and Manifesto of Futurism', in *Art in Theory (1900–1990)*, Charles Harrison and Paul Wood, eds. (Oxford: Blackwell, 1993), 147.
3 Umberto Boccione et al., 'Futurist Painting: Technical Manifesto', in Harrison and Wood, *Art in Theory (1900–1990)*, 150.
4 Kasimir Malevich, 'From Cubism to Futurism to Suprematism: The New Realism in Painting', in Harrison and Wood, *Art in Theory (1900–1990)*, 170.
5 Pollock had not been to Europe, and when asked 'Would you like to go abroad?' he replied, 'No. I don't see why the problems of modern painting

can't be solved here as well as elsewhere.' Jackson Pollock, 'Answers to a Questionnaire', in Harrison and Wood, *Art in Theory (1900–1990)*, 560.

6 'It is not in principle that Modernist painting in its latest phase has abandoned the representation of recognisable objects. What is has abandoned in principle is the representation of the kind of space that recognisable, three dimensional objects can inhabit'. Clement Greenberg, 'Modernist Painting' (1961), in Harrison and Wood, *Art in Theory (1900–1990)*, 756.

7 I may be mistaken, but, offhand, I cannot think of a single artistically important painting or sculpture of a royal in the Western tradition after David's and Ingres's paintings of Napoleon.

8 The question of capitalist mass or popular culture and the Marxist analysis thereof is complex and interesting, but it will have to wait for another day.

9 One of the distinguishing marks of the 'great' critic is that they are able to champion from the outset the art which history also decides was the leading work of the time. Baudelaire (and Manet), Roger Fry (and Cézanne), Clement Greenberg (and Jackson Pollock) are examples. But it also often happens that the same critic stumbles when art moves on to its next phase.

10 Hal Foster, *Bad New Days: Art, Criticism, Emergency* (London and New York: Verso, 2017), 1.

11 For some of the key texts in this debate, see *Jean-François Lyotard, The Postmodern Condition* (1979; repr. Manchester: Manchester University Press, 1984); Jean Baudrillard, *The Mirror of Production*, trans. Mark Poster (New York: Telos Press, 1975); Fredric Jameson, *Postmodernism, or the Cultural Logic of Late Capitalism* (Durham, NC: Duke University Press, 1991); Alex Callinicos, *Against Postmodernism: A Marxist Critique* (London: St Martin's Press, 1990); Terry Eagleton, *The Illusions of Postmodernis*m (Oxford: Blackwell, 1997); and Jürgen Habermas, 'Modernity: An Unfinished Project' (1980), in *Contemporary Sociological Theory*, Craig J. Calhoun, ed. (Oxford: Blackwell 2007).

12 Of course, there were very important non-European influences – from Japan, Africa, Polynesia, and others – but 'modern art' itself was made almost entirely in Europe and by Europeans.

13 Shira Y. Wolfe, 'The 30 most popular artists of our time', *Artland*, n.d., https://artlandapp.com/30-popular-contemporary-artists/?nabe=4797008188276736:0&utm_referrer=https%3A%2F%2Fwww.google.com%2F. I am not claiming any scientific value for this or similar lists, but it illustrates a real trend. As recently as, say, 1990, such a list would have not included any Chinese or Asians working in Asia.

14 Katie Hunt, 'Chinese Artist's "Last Supper" Sets Record for Asian Contemporary Art', *CNN Business*, 6 October 2013, https://edition.cnn.com/2013/10/06/business/record-asian-art/index.html.

15 Storage is a seldom-mentioned but ever-present problem for artists, with the exception of a tiny elite.

16 The interview with him on this video gives a good idea of his liberal outlook: 'Ai Weiwei Detained. Here Is His TED Film', YouTube, TED, https://www.youtube.com/watch?v=MVnH8ou3Kd4.

17 Jacques Herzog and Pierre de Meuron were responsible for converting the Bankside Power Station into the Tate Modern.

18 Genesis Prize official website, https://www.genesisprize.org/about.
19 Except in the alienated sense of being, by virtue of its scale and cost, an expression of the power of money.
20 It was strongly rumoured that the one million pound price tag was connived by Hirst and the supposed buyer, Saatchi, to boost the value of Hirst's work as whole.
21 Regarding these prices, the same caveat applies as with *Hymn*, and, of course, it is possible to claim that because it is a skull, *For the Love of God* is 'about death' and is somehow profound but, given that the use of a skull to signify death or serve as a memento mori goes back many centuries and that this work does not actually even attempt to say anything new or different about death, these claims lack any credibility.
22 This is palpably an exaggeration, and in fairness to Hirst, I quote Ben Davis here. 'I disagree with Andrew: I thought this show was very innovative for the way it wove together its individual works and a larger story, reflecting the present condition of art in relation to the media around it in an innovative way. It wasn't everyone's cup of tea, but it was impressive and extremely ambitious – definitely not the worst show of modern times!' Davis to JM, personal communication.
23 Yates McKee, *Strike Art: Contemporary Art and the Post-Occupy Condition* (London and New York: Verso, 2017), 77.
24 Nicolas Bourriaud, *Relational Aesthetics* (Dijon: Les Presses du réel, 2002).
25 Bourriaud, *Relational Aesthetics*, 112–13.
26 Bertolt Brecht, 'To Posterity' (1938), H. R. Hays, trans., available at https://allpoetry.com/To-Posterity.
27 Like Hal Foster, I 'keep faith with the old idea of an avant-garde' and have a good deal of sympathy with his description of it as 'immanent in a caustic way. Far from heroic, it does not pretend that it can break absolutely with the old order or found a new one; instead it seeks to trace fractures that already exist within the given order, to pressure them further, even to activate them somehow. Far from defunct, this avant garde is alive and well today.' Foster, *Bad New Days*, 4.
28 See Pablo Helguera, *Education for Socially Engaged Art: A Materials and Techniques Handbook* (New York: Jorge Pinto Books, 2011). Helguera is director of adult and academic programmes in the Department of Education at MoMA, no less.
29 In Claire Bishop, *Artificial Hells: Participatory Art and the Politics of Spectatorship* (London and New York: Verso, 2012), chapter 2.
30 It is quite possible for an artist to be 'of the left', and even of the far left, and for their work not to exhibit overt political content. Consider, for instance, Carl Andre, Antoni Tàpies, and 99 per cent of Picasso.
31 McKee, *Strike Art*, 237.
32 McKee, *Strike Art*, 101. McKee also quotes organiser Gan Golan saying it was an 'artistic spectacle' and Nathan Schneider calling it 'a living artwork' (100).
33 We should remember here that Walter Benjamin identified the aestheticisation of politics (and war) with fascism and said 'Communism responds by politicising art'. Walter Benjamin, *Illuminations* (London: Shocken, 1992), 235.

34 See John Gorman, *Banner Bright: An Illustrated History of the Banners of the British Trade Union Movement* (London: Scorpion Publishing, 1986).
35 See the account in McKee, *Strike Art*, 1–6 and 135–80.
36 I'm deliberately not setting the bar as high as I could here, by not making the comparison with, say, cubism or surrealism.
37 Two of a number of books that give very clear and persuasive accounts of this point of view are Ian Angus, *Facing the Anthropocene* (New York: Monthly Review Press, 2016); and Martin Empson, ed., *System Change not Climate Change* (London: Bookmarks, 2019).
38 'Accumulation for accumulation's sake', as Marx called it.
39 The concept of a 'metabolic rift' between society and nature caused by capitalism has been developed by Marxist ecologist John Bellamy Foster, on the basis of comments by Marx in *Capital* and the *Grundrisse*. See especially *Capital*, vol. 1 (1867; repr., London: Lawrence & Wishart, 1970), 637–38; and John Bellamy Foster, *Marx's Ecology* (New York: Monthly Review Press, 2000), chapter 5.
40 This was an instance of the dialectic of differentiation referred to earlier. Interestingly, Richard Long was taught by Anthony Caro at St Martin's School of Art (1966–68), where he rebelled against the prescriptions of his tutor. (They both ended up knighted.)
41 A quote from Gramsci (in a very different context) is apposite here. 'In reality one can "scientifically" foresee only the struggle, but not the concrete moments of the struggle, which cannot but be the result of opposing forces in continuous motion. . . . In reality one can "foresee" to the extent that one acts, to the extent that one applies a voluntary effort and therefore contributes concretely to creating the result "foreseen".' Antonio Gramsci, *Selections from the Prison Notebooks* (London: Lawrence & Wishart, 1971), 438. In this context I think this would signify that the only people really able to foresee what future art will look like are the artists who are making it.

Conclusion

1 Karl Marx, *Economic and Philosophic Manuscripts of 1844* (Moscow: Progress Publishers, 1967), 106.

Index

Page numbers in *italic* refer to illustrations. 'Passim' (literally 'scattered') indicates intermittent discussion of a topic over a cluster of pages.

abstract art, 24, 59, 64–66, 73, 124, 197. *See also* abstract expressionism
abstract expressionism, 53, 60, 217; American chauvinism and, 137, 214; CIA and, 45, 137, 182; Greenberg and, 126, 182, 185; Newman, 64–66. *See also* Pollock, Jackson
Adorno, Theodor, 61, 217
advertising, 38, 47
Aeschylus, 68, 207
aesthetic judgment. *See* judgment of artwork
The Agony and the Ecstasy (Stone), 77
Ai Weiwei, 69, 220–21, 222
alienated and unalienated labour, 4, 18–21 passim, 25–35 passim, 39, 42, 234–35, 237. *See also* artistic/creative labour
Alwan, Yasser, 171–80
Anatomy Lesson of Dr Nicolas Tulp (Rembrandt), 104–5, 118
ancient Greece arts, 207, 210, 211, 236
Anderson, Perry, 128–29, 200–201, 210
Andre, Carl, 7, 60, 205, 214, 217, 234, 256n30; *Equivalent VIII*, 8, *9*, 39, 50, 151–52, 216
Animal Farm (Orwell), 174
Antal, Frederick: *Florentine Painting and Its Social Background*, 87, 210
appliquéd blankets, 159–60, *160*
Arbus, Diane, 54, 175
architecture, 73, 231, 255n17
Aristotle, 49, 51, 77
Aristotle Contemplating the Bust of Homer (Rembrandt), 120
'ars' (Latin word), 10–11, 50
Art and Language, 41, 205
art canon. *See* canon
art collectors, 45, 46, 108, 137, 138, 219, 223
art critics, 45, 46, 48, 217, 255n9. *See also* Greenberg, Clement
Art History and Class Struggle (Hadjinicolaou), 31, 84, 248n13
art intervention, 60, 230
artistic/creative labour, 3, 4, 19–20, 24–25, 28, 32–40 passim, 117
artistic freedom, Trotsky views on, x–xi, 29–30
artistic progress and regression, 207–12 passim
artists' manifestos, 30–31, 59, 63, 242n13
art patrons, superrich. *See* superrich
art sales and purchases, 43, 117, 219, 223; *Portrait of Louis XIV* (Rigaud), 253n4
'Avant Garde and Kitsch' (Greenberg), 152, 185, 243–44n36

Bacon, Francis, x, 45, 56, 74, 128, 154, 189–91, 207; Freud and, 46, 74; influence on Hirst, 146;

'Screaming Pope', 67, 107, 189, 190, 227; Velázquez influence on, 189, 190, 206
Balthus, 39, 54
Balzac, Honoré de, 57, 68, 249n2
Banksy, 60, 216, 230
Baptism of Christ (Piero della Francesca), 2, 67, 107
Baroque movement, 198–99
Barr, Alfred H., Jr, 46, 63, 216
base and superstructure (Marxism), 68, 168, 194–95, 201, 205, 208, 252–53n1
Basquiat, Jean-Michel, 159, 166, 188, 204, 218, *235*
Bathers at Asnières (Seurat), 72, 151, 211, 215
Bathsheba (Rembrandt), 100–102, *101*, 120
'Battle of Seattle'. *See* World Trade Organization protests, Seattle, 1999
Baudelaire, Charles, 163, 200, 211, 255n9
Baudrillard, Jean, 81, 218
Beardsley, Monroe C., 239n1 (ch. 1)
Beatrizet, Nicolas, 115–16
beauty, 50–52, 74, 75, 80, 91, 125, 126, 242n13
Beckett, Samuel, 32, 35, 191, 227
Bell, Clive, 14–15, 47, 48, 217
Bellini, Giovanni, 109; *Portrait of Doge Leonardo Loredan*, 71, 98, 99, 121, 196
Benjamin, Walter, 217, 256n33
Berger, John, x, 4, 39, 58, 84, 115; on Dutch genre painting, 173; 'Moment of Cubism', 72, 210; on 'publicity' (advertising), 38; on Rembrandt self-portrait, 111–12; review of Hadjinicolaou's *Art History and Class Struggle*, 31; *Success and Failure of Picasso*, x, 72, 84, 207; view of Bacon, 191; views of cubism, 72, 128; views of Picasso, 132, 207, 217, 225; *Ways of Seeing*, x, 38, 49, 140, 196
Berman, Marshall, 59, 200–201, 218; *All That Is Solid Melts into Air*, 130, 200
Bernini, Gian Lorenzo, 199, 239n5
Berry, Chuck, 19, 36
Beuys, Joseph, 146, 205, 216, 237; Warhol portrait, 188
Billingham, Richard, 151
Birth of a Nation (Griffith), 39
Birth of Venus (Botticelli), 73, 99–100
Bishop, Claire, 225, 228
black artists, 159, 166, 168, 188, 204
Blake, William, 199; 'Jerusalem', 185, 199
Boccioni, Umberto, 214
Boon, K. G., 114
Borriaud, Nicolas, 74, 75
Bosch, Hieronymus, 124, 125
Botticelli, Sandro, 124, 125, 162; *Birth of Venus*, 73, 99–100; *Primavera*, viii, 52, 65
Boucher, François, 134, 162
Bouguereau, William-Adolphe, 47, 73, 239n5
Bourgeois, Louise: *Spider*, 224
Bourriaud, Nicolas, 225–26
Brâncuși, Constantin, 7, 39, 75, 152
Braque, Georges, 59, 124, 126, 131, 209, 231
Brassaï, 174, 175
Braverman, Harry: *Labour and Monopoly Capital*, 4
Brecht, Bertolt, 174, 227
Breton, André, 30, 63, 240n23
Breughel, Pieter, 57, 168, 172, 204, 205
'Bricks in the Tate' (Andre). See *Equivalent VIII* (Andre)
Brillo Boxes (Warhol), 21, 39, 186, 215–16
Broadway Boogie Woogie (Mondrian), 73, 197
Brooks, David, 1
Buck, Luisa: *Moving Targets*, 136–37
Burke, Edmund, 51; *Philosophical Enquiry into the Origin of Our Ideas of the Sublime and Beautiful*, 52
Burns, Robert: 'Red, Red Rose', 22–23
'But is it art?' *See* 'Is it art?'

Cabanel, Alexandre, 73
Callot, Jacques, 248n16
Canaletto, 92, 212
canon, 43, 47, 66, 128, 168, 182
Canova, Antonio, 92, 239n5
Capital (Marx), xi, xii, 17–18, 33, 208
Caravaggio, 192, 193, 209, 247n1
Caro, Anthony, 234, 257n40
Cartier-Bresson, Henri, 174, 175
Catholicism and Catholic Church, 2, 53, 192, 205, 221, 252n25; censorship, 93; popes in art, 58, 67, 71, 98, 99, 107, 189, 190, 227; Rubens and, 67, 192
cave paintings, 10, 116, 236
celebrity, 77, 154, 187, 189
censorship and repression of art, 40, 93, 161, 242n18
Central Intelligence Agency. *See* CIA
Cézanne, Paul, 20, 47, 60, 129, 138, 215, 231; *Bathers* series, 126; card players, 215; cubism and, 128; Fry and, 255n9; in lines of development, 55, 128, 209, 213; *Mont Sainte-Victoire* paintings, 16; as precursor to abstract expressionism, 182; still life and, 215
Chapman brothers, 54, 140–43, 158
Charging Bull (Di Modica), 229
China and Chinese artists, 219–21
Christ in art, 22, 107, 205; Caravaggio, 247n1; Dalí, 107, 205; Grünewald, 2, 22, 55, 71, 72, 107, 205; Michelangelo's *Pietà* statues, 1, 22, 55, 81, 91, 120; Piero della Francesca, 2, 67, 107; Rembrandt, 114, 120
Christian art, 53, 67, 107, 192–93, 205; Michelangelo and, 82, 90; Michelangelo's *Creation of Adam*, 81, 88, 89–90, *89, 94*; Michelangelo's *David*, 27, 34, 51, 80–83 passim, 88–90 passim, 94, 102, 195; Michelangelo's *Pietà* statues, 1, 22, 55, 81, 91, 120; Rembrandt, 100–102, *101*, 103, 119–20. *See also* Christ in art
Christian God. *See* God (Christianity)
Christo, 7, 148, 245n50
CIA, 45, 137, 182
Cixous, Hélène, 116, 119
Clark, Kenneth, 27, 46, 113, 115, 116, 138, 216
Clark, T. J., 153
Clark, Stephen Carlton, 46
class struggle, xi, 84, 203–5 passim. See also *Art History and Class Struggle* (Hadjinicolaou)
climate change, 231–35
Cockcroft, Eva, 182
Cold War, 45, 182, 183
collectors. *See* art collectors
Collishaw, Matt: *Bullet Hole*, 150
Colonna, Vittoria, 93
commodification, 20, 25, 135, 142, 167
commodity fetishism, xi–xii
Communist International, 57
The Communist Manifesto (Marx and Engels), 4, 111, 200, 248n15
conceptual art, 49, 214, 222
A Concise History of Modern Painting (Read), 55
Constable, John, 49, 70, 124, 185, 197, 199; *Hay Wain*, 197, 201–2, 251n12
content and form. *See* form and content
Contribution to the Critique of Political Economy (Marx), 68
Cornelis van Haarlem, 110
Corot, Jean-Baptiste-Camille, 57
Courbet, Gustave, 60, 124, 138, 199, 205, 215; cubism and, 128; as starting point, 57, 130, 209, 243n34; 'Statement on Realism', 243n26; *Stone Breakers*, 57, 196, 211, 215
Creation of Adam (Michelangelo), 81, 88, 89–90, *89, 94*
creative labour. *See* artistic/creative labour
critical art, 59–62, 74
critics. *See* art critics
Crucifixion (Grünewald), 2, 22, 55, 71, 72

cubism, 59, 64, 72, 84, 125, 182, 190, 214; line of development to, 209. *See also* synthetic cubism

Dadaism, 60, 125, 214, 225
Dalí, Salvador, 20, 22, 41, 45, 54, 73, 151, 217; Breton on, 240n23; *Christ of St John of the Cross*, 107, 205; patronization by bourgeoisie, 138
Dante, 207–8
Daumier, Honoré, 57
David (Michelangelo), 27, 34, 51, 80–83 passim, 88–90 passim, 94, 102, 195
David, Jacques-Louis, 97, 107, 130, 204; *Death of Marat*, 1, 195, 205; *Napoleon Crossing the Alps*, 107; patronization by bourgeoisie, 138
Davies, Stephen, 16
da Vinci, Leonardo. *See* Leonardo da Vinci
Dead Dad (Mueck), 143
Degas, Edgar, 215
de Hooch, Pieter, 115, 199
De Keyser, Thomas, 118
Delacroix, Ferdinand, 166, 199; *Liberty Leading the People*, 195, 205
della Francesca, Piero. *See* Piero della Francesca
Deller, Jeremy, 60, 228
de Meuron, Pierre, 221, 255n17
democratisation and elitism, 215, 216, 217, 230
Les Demoiselles d'Avignon (Picasso), 39, 115, 122–35, *123*
Derain, André, 126
Descartes, René, 109
design, graphic. *See* graphic design, product design, illustration, etc.
De Tolnay, Charles, 83
Dialectics of Nature (Engels), xi, 85
Di Modica, Arturo: *Charging Bull*, 229
Disasters of War series (Goya), 51, 140–41, 205
Donatello, 89
Doyle, Jennifer, 164
Du Bos, Jean-Baptiste, 55
Duchamp, Marcel, 21, 59, 60, 125, 144, 189, 215; *Fountain*, 39, 50, 53, 214; *Large Glass* (*Bride Stripped Bare*), 144, 146
Duncan, Carol, 132–33
Dürer, Albrecht, 86, 107
Dying Captive (*Dying Slave*) (Michelangelo), 83
Dylan, Bob, 19, 36

Educating Rita (Russell), 47–48
Egypt, 171–80 passim
Eliasson, Olafur, 53
Eliot, T. S., 24, 32, 77, 78; 'objective correlative', 144
elitism and democratisation. *See* democratisation and elitism
El Lissitzky. *See* Lissitzky, El
Emin, Tracy, 7, 20, 46, 69, 153–70, 206, 214–18 passim; blankets, 159–60, *160*, 166, 167; drawings, 157, 242n8; *Everyone I Have Ever Slept With, 1963–95*, 150, 156, 163; *Exorcism of the Last Painting I Ever Made*, 166; films, 160–61, 163–64, 165; *Homage to Edvard Munch and All My Dead Children*, 166; *Life Model Goes Mad*, 166–67; *Masculinity*, 163, 164; *My Bed*, 6, 7, 39, 70, 156–57, 165, 166, 206, 215; performance art, 166; *Pysco Slut*, 159–60, *160*; *Top Spot*, 161; *Why I Never Became a Dancer*, 160–61, 163–64, 165
emotional power and expression, 55–56, 71, 74, 75; Bacon, 189–90; Emin, 156, 157, 164–65; Hirst, 145, 146; Kahlo, 64; Michelangelo, 90–91; Newman, 65; Rembrandt, 121; Warhol, 187
Engels, Frederick, 4, 17, 57, 68–70 passim, 195, 240n31; *Communist Manifesto*, 4, 111, 200, 248n15; *Dialectics of Nature*, xi, 85–86
Equivalent VIII (Andre), 8, *9*, 39, 50, 151–52, 216
Ernst, Max, 58, 124; *Europe after the Rain*, 233

ethics and morality, 53–55, 242n15
Eurocentrism, 173, 219
evaluation of artwork. *See* judgment of artwork
Everyone I Have Ever Slept With, 1963–95 (Emin), 150, 156, 163

The Fall of an Avalanche in the Grissons (Turner), 52
fauvism, 213–14
Fell, Sheila, vii–viii
films, 36, 39, 40; Ai Weiwei's *Human Flow*, 220; Eisenstein's *Battleship Potemkin*, 190; Emin's *Why I Never Became a Dancer*, 160–61, 163–64, 165; Warhol's *Empire*, 188
flatness of paintings, 127–28
The Flaying of Marsyas (Titian), 251n5
Florentine Painting and Its Social Background (Antal), 87
Fontana, Lucio, 59
Forensic Architecture, 231
form and content, 21–24
Foster, Hal, 217, 256n27
Fowkes, Charles, 248n16
French Revolution, 1, 12, 87, 97, 107, 215
French Revolution of 1848 (February Revolution), 196
Freud, Lucian, 46, 58, 74
Fried, Michael, 61
Fry, Roger, 217, 255n9
furniture, modern, 197
futurism, 214, 217, 225

Gainsborough, Thomas, 124; *Mr and Mrs Andrews*, 115, 197
Gauguin, Paul, 129, 132, 147, 209
'genius', 11, 58, 77–79 passim, 109, 173, 188, 211, 237
Gentileschi, Artemisia: *Judith Slaying Holofernes*, 55
Géricault, Théodore, 58, 130, 215
Giacometti, Alberto, 32, 73–74, 189
Giorgione, 126; *Sleeping Venus*, 100
Giotto, 22, 49, 58, 78–80 passim, 90, 109, 198, 209
Giuliani, Rudy, 252n25
Global Ultra Luxury Faction (GULF), 60, 230
global warming. *See* climate change
God (Christianity), 109; in art, 89–90, *89*; as provider of Rembrandt's genius, 78–79
Goethe, Johann Wolfgang van, 2, 77, 130
Goldsworthy, Andy, 233, 234
Golub, Leon, 41, 206
Gombrich, Ernst H., 79, 80; *Story of Art*, 6, 49
Gonzalez-Torres, Felix, 226
Gormley, Antony, 53, 224
Goya, Francisco, 55, 107, 108, 124, 130, 138, 146; *Disasters of War* series, 51, 140–41, 205; female nudes, 126; influence on Bacon, 189; *Third of May 1808*, 195, 205
Gramsci, Antonio, 4, 68, 257n41
graphic design, product design, illustration, etc., 37–38
Great Deeds against the Dead (Chapman brothers), 140–41
Greek literature, 207
Greenberg, Clement, 46, 47, 48, 60, 126–28, 182–83; on aesthetic views, 241n6; 'Avant-Garde and Kitsch', 152, 185, 243–44n36; elitism and, 217; 'Modernist Painting', 61, 255n6; view of Manet, 59; view of pop art, 163; views of modernism, 61, 127, 255n6; views of Pollock, 182, 255n9
Griffith, D. W.: *Birth of a Nation*, 39
Grosz, George, 57, 60, 68
Grundrisse (Marx), 26, 207
Grünewald, Matthias: *Crucifixion*, 2, 22, 55, 71, 72, 107, 205
Guernica (Picasso), 2, 24, 33, 84, 89, 152, 195, 206, 227, 233; commissioning of, 108
Guggenheim, Peggy, 138, 221
Guggenheim family, 27, 45, 203, 216
Guggenheim Museum, 60, 230
Guerrilla Girls, 167
Guttoso, Renato, 57, 205

Habermas, Jürgen, 218
Hadjinicolau, Nicos: *Art History and Class Struggle*, 31, 84, 248n23
Hals, Frans, x, 57, 60, 70, 193, 196, 199
Hamilton, Richard, 59, 186
Hamlet (Shakespeare), 24, 109
Harrison, Charles, 66
Harvey, Marcus: *Myra*, 54, *56*, 137, 139–40, 142
Hatoum, Mona, 150, 251n19
Hauser, Arnold, 11, 87–88, 90–91, 111, 119–20
Heartfield, John, 41, 57, 139, 158, 204, 205, 228
Hegel, G. W. F., 60, 90
Hepworth, Barbara, 153–54
Herzog, Jacques, 221, 255n17
'high art' and 'low art', 42, 134, 185, 216, 237, 243n35
Hilma af Klimt, 59
Hine, Lewis, 174, 175
Hirst, Damien, 7, 46, 143–47, 214, 217, 223–24; *Away from the Flock*, 145, 146; class mobility, 204; *Demon with a Bowl*, 224; Emin compared, 159; *For the Love of God*, 223, 256n21; *Freeze* exhibition curation, 250n3; *Hymn*, 223; *Isolated Elements Swimming*, 145, 146; *Mother and Child Divided* (cows), 13, 116, 145–46, 147, 223; *Physical Impossibility of Death in the Mind of Someone Living* (shark), 39, 50, 144, 146, 223; paintings, 143, 223; Saatchi and, 137, 223; sculptures, 223, 224; *Thousand Years* (cow's head), 145, 147; Venice show (2017), 223–24
historical materialism, xi, 17, 68–69, 71, 84, 194, 195, 201
historical reenactment, 60, 228
History of Art Criticism (Venturi), 55
Hockney, David, 45, 217, 241n2; *Garrowby Hill*, 62–63
Hogarth, William, 51, 57, 124, 138
Hokusai, 233
Holbein, Hans, the Younger, 49, 60, 65, 124; *Ambassadors*, 98, 121; *Portrait of Henry VIII*, 71, 98, 107, 139, 196
Holiday, Billie, 23
Höller, Carsten: *Test Site*, 74–75, 226
homoeroticism: Michelangelo, 83, 90
homosexuality, 154, 190
Hopper, Edward, 57
Hughes, Robert, 78

illustration. *See* graphic design, product design, illustration, etc.
imitation. *See* mimesis
impressionism, 52, 72, 125, 129, 138, 199, 213; loss of form in, 231; mimesis of light effects, 49; Monet, 59; Trotsky view, 243n24
individualism, 58, 60, 108–9, 111, 185
Ingres, Jean-Auguste-Dominique, 49, 162; female nudes, 126, 134, 140
innovation in art, 58–59, 66, 72, 73, 214
installation art, 221
internationalisation of the art world, 218–21
International Socialism, x, 185
intervention. *See* art intervention
intuition (in judgment of art), 47–48
'Is it art?', 7, 21, 39, 162–63, 181

Jameson, Fredric, 218
Jesus Christ in art. *See* Christ in art
Jewish Bride (Rembrandt), 3, *3*, 91, 119, 121
Johns, Jasper, 186, 188, 214
Jones, Jonathan, 131
Joyce, James, 20, 200; *Dubliners*, 129; *Ulysses*, 33
Judd, Donald, 214, 234
Judenplatz Holocaust Memorial (proposed) (Whiteread), 147, 149–50

Kafka, Franz, 32, 129, 152, 191, 205, 227
Kahlo, Frida, 63–64, 153–54, 206, 244n45
Kandinsky, Wassily, 59, 124
Kant, Immanuel, 51, 52, 61, 130

Kapoor, Anish, 53, 73, 222–23
Keats, John, 24, 199
Kelly, Mary, 41, 204, 205, 216
Kerouac, Jack, 32, 184
Kiefer, Anselm, 218; *Lilith*, 233
Kipling, Rudyard: 'White Man's Burden', 39
kitsch, 77, 141, 163, 185, 214. *See also* 'Avant Garde and Kitsch' (Greenberg)
Klee, Paul, 124, 145
Klingender, Francis, 244–45n49
Kollwitz, Käthe, 57, 60, 158, 204
Kosuth, Joseph, 59

labour, alienated and unalienated. *See* alienated and unalienated labour
labour, artistic/creative. *See* artistic/creative labour
labour, productive and unproductive. *See* productive and unproductive labour
Labour and Monopoly Capital (Braverman), 4
land art, 224, *224*, 233–34
landscape paintings, 62–63, 193, *193*, 196–97; Constable, 70, 185; Rubens, 62–63, 193, *193*; Sheila Fell, vii
Lane, Amy, 161
Last Judgment (Michelangelo), 52, 83, 90–91, 93, 126
Lavender Mist (Pollock), 50, 181, 183, 184, 233
Le Blanc, Paul, vii
Left in Vision exhibitions, ix
Léger, Fernand, 41, 70, 204, 205, 230
Lenin, Vladimir, vii, 4, 68, 130, 138, 241–42n7, 254n19; *State of Revolution*, 22
Leonardo da Vinci, 58, 69, 77, 88, 90, 126; *Last Supper* appropriation, 166, 219–20; line of development to, 209; Michelangelo rivalry, 46; *Mona Lisa*, 77, 188, 251n12; Vasari on, 51; *Virgin of the Rocks*, 52; Warhol appropriation from, 166, 188
Lessing, Gotthold, 26, 51, 52
Lewison, Jeremy: *Interpreting Pollock*, 183
Lewitt, Sol, 146
Liberty Leading the People (Delacroix), 195, 205
The Liberty of Appearing: Photographs of Egyptian Working People (Alwan), 171–80
Lichtenstein, Roy, 214; *Whaam!*, 39, 185
Lissitzky, El, 206
literature, 19, 24, 33, 40, 47–48, 191, 203; alienation in, 32; distinction from other writing, 13; Lukács views, 249n2; Marx and, 68; modernism, 129, 201; moral/political offence and, 54; in *On the Sublime*, 52; Orwell, 174; pulp/genre fiction, hackwork, etc., 25, 33, 35, 37; realism, 57; reproduction and selling of, 167; Romanticism, 199; 'transitional' cases, 37; Trotsky on, 2; women authors, 168; working people in, 172. *See also* Shakespeare, William; poetry
Literature and Revolution (Trotsky), x, 2, 41
Long, Richard, 21, 39, 233, 234, 257n40
Louvre, 12, 83, 122, 138
'low art' and 'high art'. *See* 'high art' and 'low art'
Lowry, L. S., vii
Lucas, Sarah, 46, 150, 216, 251n18
Lukács, Georg, 4, 57, 61, 64, 129, 145, 152, 249n2
Luther, Martin, 86, 92
Luxemburg, Rosa, 4, 68
Lyotard, Jean-François, 218

Machiavelli, Niccolò, 86, 91, 92
Malevich, Kazimir, 124, 214; *Black Square on White*, 8, 39, 214, 244n49
Manet, Édouard, 57–60 passim, 70, 72, 124, 129, 138, 199, 243n35;

Bar at the Folies-Bergère, 131, 215, 243n35; Baudelaire and, 255n9; *Le Déjeuner sur l'Herbe*, 73, 243n35; in line of development, 209; *Olympia*, 73, 115, 126, 153, 166, 186, 211, 215; Rembrandt presaging of, 107; Titian influence on, 206
Manifesto for an Independent Revolutionary Art, 30–31, 63
manifestos, artists. *See* artists' manifestos
Mann, Sally, 54
Mantegna, Andrea, 49, 209
Marinetti, Filippo Tommaso, 214
Marx, Karl, 4, 24–33 passim, 86, 90, 93, 176–77, 202, 207–9 passim; base and superstructure, 168, 194–95, 203; *Capital*, xi, xii, 17–18, 33, 208; *Communist Manifesto*, 4, 111, 200, 248n15; *Contribution to the Critique of Political Economy*, 68; Engels on, 69; *German Ideology*, 42, 203; *Grundrisse*, 26, 207; Marxism of, 60–61; on prostitution, 135; 'social being determines social consciousness', 169–70; as stylist, 22; *Theories of Surplus Value*, 25, 26–27; theory of alienation, xi, 18–20, 28, 29, 32; *Theses on Feuerbach*, 12–13; view of art creation, 253n12; view of Greek literature, 207; view of Rembrandt, 97; views of labour, 4, 16–19 passim, 25, 26, 32; in Warhol-inspired graphic design, 185
Marxism, ix, xi, 1–2, 16, 54, 60–62 passim, 66–75 passim, 90; Adorno-Benjamin debate, 217; Greenberg views, 61; of Marx, 60–61; 'utopian socialism', 229; views of modernism 199–201. *See also* base and superstructure (Marxism); historical materialism
Masaccio, 49, 58–59, 209
Matisse, Henri, 19, 55, 58, 132, 217; colour, 52, 213–14, 231; Picasso and, 46, 126
McKee, Yates, 225, 228–30 passim
Medici family, 91–92, 93, 198, 203, 206, 221
Meeropol, Abel: 'Strange Fruit', 23
Metzger, Gustav, 32, 205, 233
Michelangelo, xi, 19, 45, 69, 77–95 passim, 138, 206; *Atlas*, 94, *94*; *Battle of the Centaurs*, 83; celebrity, 154; *Creation of Adam*, 81, 88, 89–90, *89*; *David*, 27, 34, 51, 80–83 passim, 88–90 passim, 94, 102, 195; as 'divine' genius, 78–79, 109; *Dying Slave*, 83, 94; Hauser view, 11; *Holy Family*, 83; homoeroticism, 83, 90; influence on Bacon, 189; *Last Judgment*, 52, 83, 90–91, 93, 126; Leonardo rivalry, 46; Medicis and, 91–92, 93, 206, 221; *Moses*, 80, 95; *Pietà* statues, 1, 22, 55, 81, 91, 120; *Rape of Ganymede*, 115–16; Renaissance marker, 198; 'slave' ('captive') sculptures, 83, 94–95
Millet, Jean-François, 57, 204, 215
Milton, John, 185; *Paradise Lost*, 25, 32
mimesis, 49–50, 52, 65, 71, 73, 80, 124–25, 242n8
minimalism, 7, 60, 146, 214, 217, 234; *Equivalent VIII* (Andre), 8, *9*, 39, 50, 151–52, 216
Miró, Joan, 58, 59, 124, 147, 217, 231
misogyny, 55, 132, 133, 154
modernism, 127–30, 199–201, 218
Modotti, Tina, 177
Mohaiemen, Naeem, 231
MoMA. *See* Museum of Modern Art (MoMA)
Mona Lisa (Leonardo), 77, 188
Mondrian, Piet, 24, 48, 58, 64, 70, 73, 124, 189, 197; *Broadway Boogie Woogie*, 73, 197; Hirst compared, 145; in line of development, 55; reproductions, 147
Monet, Claude, 19, 59, 125, 188, 199, 206; *Gare Saint-Lazare (The Auteuil Line)*, 197; as precursor to abstract expressionism, 182; *Water Lilies*, 251n12
monumental art, 221–24 passim

Moore, Henry, 73–74, 217
morality and ethics. *See* ethics and morality
Morris, William, 28–29, 119, 230
Mother and Child Divided (Hirst), 13, 116, 145–46, 147, 223
Moving Targets: A User's Guide to British Art (Buck), 136–37
Mueck, Ron: *Dead Dad*, 143
Munch, Edvard, 56, 132, 166; *Scream*, 233, 251n12
murals, 63–64, 138, 188, 203
Museum of Modern Art (MoMA), 46, 63, 122, 183, 203
music, 19, 23, 33, 35–36, 185, 203; modernism, 129, 201; Pollock and, 184; reproduction and selling of, 167
My Bed (Emin), 6, 7, 39, 70, 156–57, 165, 166, 206, 215

Nash, Paul, 57, 205; *We Are Making a New World*, 233
National Galley (UK), viii; absence of black artists, 168; Rembrandt exhibition, 107–8, 110; Rubens exhibition, 191–93; works in collection, 98, 102, 109, 110, 155, 247n1
nature: Marx views, 16, 17
Nazi Germany, 53
Newman, Barnett, 53, 78, 242n13; *Vir Heroicus Sublimis*, 64–66
The Night Watch (Rembrandt), 104, 112, 117–18, 120
Nineteen Eighty-Four (Orwell), 174
Nolde, Emil, 54
'nonartistic' materials, use of, 143–44, 215–16
nudes, female, 55, 73, 115, 126, 133, 140, 150, 242n22; armless and headless, 247n2; Botticelli, 73, 99–100; Harvey, 139–40; Manet, 73, 115, 126, 153, 166, 186, 211, 215; in Metropolitan Museum of Art, 167; Picasso, 122–35 passim; Rembrandt, 99–103 passim, *101*, 120, 126; Rubens, 126, 193; Saville, 150; Velázquez, 52, 100, 120, 126, 140, 242n22
nudes, male: Michelangelo, 83, 93; Michelangelo's *Creation of Adam*, 81, 88, 89–90, *89*; Michelangelo's *David*, 27, 34, 51, 80–83 passim, 88–90 passim, 94, 102, 195; Michelangelo's *Dying Slave*, 83, 94

Ober, Josiah, 210
Occupy movement, 228–29, 230
Ofili, Chris, 59, 216, 218, 252n25
Olympia (Manet), 73, 115, 126, 153, 166, 211, 215
On the Sublime, 52
originality. *See* innovation in art
Orozco, José Clemente, 41, 64, 205
Orwell, George, 174

paedophilia, 141–43
Paradise Lost (Milton), 25, 32
performance art, 166–67
photography, 50, 174–75; Alwan, 171–80; Arbus, 54, 175; Billingham, 151; Emin, 157; Modotti, 177; Muybridge, 189
Picasso, Pablo, 48, 51, 55, 58, 163, 188, 189, 217; apolitical content, 256n30; Berger views, 132, 207, 217, 225; 'blue period', 211,215; celebrity, 154; Cézanne influence on, 206; cubism, 39, 59, 143, 231; *Les Demoiselles d'Avignon*, 39, 115, 122–35, *123*; *Guernica*, 2, 24, 33, 84, 89, 108, 152, 195, 206, 227, 233; influence on Bacon, 189; 'is it art?', 7, 39; lifelong work, 19; line of development to, 209; Matisse rivalry, 46; 'modernist moment', 201; 'nonartistic' materials use, 143–44, 215; *Nude Woman in a Red Armchair*, 102; patronization by bourgeoisie, 138; Pollock reaction against, 206; references to other artists, 166; 'rose period', 215; sculptures, 143–44, 215; sexism, 132; Stalin and, 107; Velázquez influence on, 206. See

also *The Success and Failure of Picasso* (Berger)
Piero della Francesca, 49, 58, 66, 124, 205; *Baptism of Christ*, 2, 67, 107; *Resurrection*, 107
Pietà statues (Michelangelo), 1, 22, 55, 81, 91, 120
Pissarro, Camille, 215
Plato, 49
poetry, 16, 22–25 passim, 36, 77, 164, 252n24
Pollock, Jackson, x, 48, 53, 58, 64, 124, 181–85, 214; Greenberg and, 255n9; Guggenheim sponsorship of, 221; as innovator, 59; 'is it art?', 7, 39; *Lavender Mist*, 50, 181, 183, 184, 233; 'nonartistic' materials use, 215; on not traveling abroad, 254–55n5; patronization by bourgeoisie, 138; reaction against Picasso, 206; reproductions, 147
pop art, 59, 163, 185, 201, 210, 214; *Whaam!* (Lichtenstein), 39, 185. *See also* Warhol, Andy
popular culture and high culture. *See* 'high art' and 'low art'
Portrait of a Man (Titian), 98, 99, 109
Portrait of Doge Leonardo Loredan (Belini), 71, 98, 99, 121, 196
Portrait of Henry VIII (Holbein), 71, 98, 107, 139, 196
Portrait of Jan Six (Rembrandt), 106–7
Portrait of Louis XIV (Rigaud), 84, 196
Portrait of Nicolaes Ruts (Rembrandt), 106
Portrait of Pope Innocent X (Velázquez), 58, 71, 98, 99, 107, 190
Portrait of Postman Joseph Roulin, 71, 196
postmodernism, 218
Pound, Ezra, 41, 119, 249n31
Prodger, Charlotte, 231
productive and unproductive labour, 25, 26
progress in art. *See* artistic progress and regression
propaganda, 39, 199, 204, 233
psychological insight in portraiture, 58, 74, 114–17
'psychological realism', 58, 64

Quinn, Marc: *Self*, 150

The Rape of Ganymede (Rembrandt), 115–16, 248n23
The Rape of Proserpine (Rembrandt), 115
The Rape of Proserpine (Rubens), 115
Raphael, 51, 65, 88, 109, 126, 209
Raphael, Max, 31
Rauschenberg, Robert, viii, 186, 188, 214, 215; *Bed*, 166
Read, Herbert, 27, 50, 51; *Concise History of Modern Painting*, 55
realism, 57–58, 64, 74, 209, 249n2; Engels prescription for, 175. *See also* 'psychological realism'; socialist realism; social realism
Regentesses of the Old Men's Almhouse (Hals), x, 70, 196
Regents of the Old Men's Almhouse (Hals), x, 70, 196
regression in art. *See* artistic progress and regression
'relational aesthetics' (Bourriaud), 225–26
relational art, 74–76 passim, 226, 227
Rembrandt, x, xi, 60, 66, 69, 96–121, 124, 188, 221; *Anatomy Lesson of Doctor Deyman*, 120; *Anatomy Lesson of Dr Nicolas Tulp*, 104–5, 118; *Angel Stopping Abraham from Sacrificing Isaac to God*, 120; *Apostle Peter Denying Christ*, 120; *Aristotle Contemplating the Bust of Homer*, 120; Asian people, 114; *Bathsheba*, 100–102, *101*, 120; commodification, 20; beggars, 110, 113, 172; black people, 114; *Conspiracy of the Batavians*, 118–19; *Danaë*, 102, 120; drawings, 110, 116–17; etchings, 102–3, 109, 113, 172; female nudes, 100–102, *101*, 120, 126; *French Bed*, 102–3; *Jewish Bride*, 3, *3*, 91, 119, 121; Jews, 113–14; Maerten Soolmans portrait, 104, 105; *Night*

Watch, 104, 112, 117–18, 120; patronization by bourgeoisie, 138; *Portrait of Jan Six*, 106–7; *Portrait of Nicolaes Ruts*, 106; portraits of Jacob Trip and Margaretha de Geer, 98, 99, 105; poverty of, 114, 117, 193; *Rape of Ganymede*, 115–16, 248n23; *Rape of Proserpine*, 115; Rubens and, 199, 206; 'realism', 249n2; *Return of the Prodigal Son*, 119–20; *Sampling Officials* (*De Stalmeesters*), 105–6; self-portraits, 20, 55, 58, 91, 107–11; *Slaughtered Ox*, 116, 146, 248n24; *Woman Bathing in a Stream*, 102
Rembrandt by Himself (White and Buvelot), 108
Renoir, Pierre-Auguste, 19, 55, 126, 162, 206, 241n39
Repin, Ilya, 41, 57, 204
The Revolution Betrayed (Trotsky), 29–30
Riefenstahl, Leni: *Triumph of the Will*, 39
Rietveld, Gerrit: Red and Blue Chair, 197
Rigaud, Hyacinthe: *Portrait of Louis XIV*, 84, 196
Rivera, Diego, 30, 57, 63–64, 128, 138, 158, 205; *History of Mexico*, 224
Rockefeller family, 46, 63, 138, 183, 203, 216
Rodin, Auguste, 132, 162
Rokeby Venus (Velázquez), 52, 100, 120, 242n22
Rosenberg, Harold, 46, 182
Rosler, Martha, 59, 204, 229, 242n18
Rothko, Mark, 39, 53, 56, 124
Rousseau, Henri: War, 233
Rubens, Peter Paul, 191–93, 221; as Baroque exemplar, 199; Catholic Church and, 67, 192; celebrity, 154; clientele, 245n57; female nudes, 102, 126, 193; *Rape of Proserpine*, 115; Rembrandt reaction against, 206; self-portraits, 107; *Three Graces*, 100; *View of Het Steen in the Early Morning*, 62–63, 193, *193*
Rushdie, Salman, 40
Russell, Bertrand, 109
Russell, Willy: *Educating Rita*, 47–48
Russeth, Andrew, 224
Russian Revolution (Bolshevik Revolution), 1, 30, 42, 130, 212, 254n19
Russian Revolution of 1905, 129

Saatchi, Charles, 46, 137, 138, 223
Sala, Charles, 83
Salgado, Sebastião, 174, 179–80
Salmon, André, 123
Sander, August, 174, 175
Sandrart, Joachim von, 113, 118
Saville, Jenny, 150
Savonarola, Girolamo, 93
Schiele, Egon, 166, 206
Schott, Rolf, 82
The Scream (Munch), 233, 251n12
'Screaming Pope' (Bacon), 67, 107, 189, 190, 227
Sensation (exhibition): Brooklyn Museum (1999), 252; Royal Academy of Arts (1997), 54, 136–52, 154, 156
Serge, Victor, 4, 93
Serota, Nicholas, 46, 216
Serra, Richard, 53, 224
Seurat, Georges, 129, 138, 209, 213, 231; *Bathers at Asnières*, 72, 151, 211, 215
sex: Bacon, 154; Emin, 153, 155, 162–65; Picasso, 122–35 passim; Rembrandt, 102–3. *See also* homoeroticism; paedophilia
sexism, 54–55, 73, 132–34 passim, 139–40, 156–57, 165, 168–69
Shakespeare, William, 2, 68, 77, 91, 119, 173, 208; *Hamlet*, 24, 109
Shelley, Percy Bysshe, 16, 199
Sim, Stuart, 66–67
Siqueiros, David Alfaro, 41, 64, 205
Sistine Chapel, viii, 83, 89–90, 147, 206, 224. See also *Creation*

of Adam (Michelangelo); *Last Judgment* (Michelangelo)
skill, 50, 65, 71, 74, 98, 125, 245n50; beauty and, 52; Emin, 157; Michelangelo, 80; Rembrandt, 121; Rubens, 67, 193
Sky Mirror (Kapoor), 222
Slaughtered Ox (Rembrandt), 116, 146, 248n24
Smith, Adam, 26
Smith, David, 234
Smithson, Robert, 233; *Spiral Jetty*, 224, *224*, 234
socialist realism, 54, 61
social realism, 57, 62–64 passim
'social turn' in art, 60, 74, 216, 225–31
Soutine, Chaim, 189
Soviet Union, 31, 54, 24n525. *See also* Stalinism
Spencer, Stanley: *Resurrection in Cookham*, 107
Spero, Nancy, 41, 205
Spiral Jetty (Smithson), 224, *224*, 234
Stalinism, 31, 54, 61, 68, 93, 177, 245n52
Still, Clyfford, 53, 217
Stoffels, Hendrickje, 96, 100–101, 102, 119, 120
Stone, Irving, 77
The Story of Art (Gombrich), 6, 49
'Strange Fruit' (Meeropol), 23
Stravinsky, Igor, 129, 201
street art, 216, 230
Strike Art (McKee), 228
strikes, 4, 33, 34, 177–80 passim; reenactment, 60, 228
sublime (concept), 52–53, 65, 75, 126, 242n1
The Success and Failure of Picasso (Berger), x, 72, 84, 207
Sunflowers (van Gogh), 24, 185
superrich, 27, 45, 216, 221
superstructure and base (Marxism). *See* base and superstructure (Marxism)
Supper at Emmaus (Caravaggio), 247n1
Sylvester, David, viii
synthetic cubism, 143, 215, 231

Tahrir Square occupation, Cairo, 2011, 230
Tàpies, Antoni, 41, 205, 256n30
Tatarkiewicz, Władysław, 11, 12
'Tate Bricks' (Andre). See *Equivalent VIII* (Andre)
Tate Britain: Bacon exhibition, 189–91; Turner Prize show (1995), 251n19; Turner Prize show (1999), 155; Turner Prize show (2018), 231
Tate Gallery: Jackson Pollock retrospective (1999), 183
Tate Modern, 44; conversion from Bankside Power Station, 255n17; Turbine Hall installations, 44, 75, 221, 222, 226; Warhol retrospective, 185–89
'techne' (Greek word), 10–11
technical skill. *See* skill
television, 36–37, 142
Test Site (Höller), 74–75, 226
Theories of Surplus Value (Marx), 25, 26–27
Theses on Feuerbach (Marx), 12–13
Third International. *See* Communist International
Thompson, Luke Willis, 231
Thompson, Milly, 162
A Thousand Years (Hirst), 145, 147
Tintoretto: *Origin of the Milky Way*, 100
Tiravanija, Rirkrit, 226
Titian, 19, 70, 109, 124, 162; celebrity, 154; female nudes, 100, 126, 131, 134, 140, 166; *Flaying of Marsyas*, 251n5; influence on Manet, 206; mimetic skill, 49, 65; *Portrait of a Man*, 98, 99, 109; self-portraits, 107; *Venus d'Urbino*, 100, 131, 134, 166
Tolstoy, Leo, 19, 55, 57
Toulouse-Lautrec, Henri de, 126, 207, 211, 215
Triumph of the Will (Riefenstahl), 39
Trotsky, Leon, x–xi, 4, 54, 61, 68, 161, 213–14, 225; 'Art and Politics in Our Epoch', 137; on Dante,

207–8; *History of the Russian Revolution*, 254n19; *Literature and Revolution*, x, 2, 41; *Manifesto for an Independent Revolutionary Art*, 30–31, 63; *Philosophical Notebooks*, 9; *Revolution Betrayed*, 29–30; as stylist, 22; view of Rivera, 63; *What Is Art?*, 243n24
Turner, J. M. W., 52, 70; *Fall of an Avalanche in the Grissons*, 52; *Rain, Steam and Speed*, 197; *Snow Storm*, 233

Uccello, Paolo, 49, 195
University of Portsmouth, School of Art and Design, ix, 155
unproductive labour. *See* productive and unproductive labour
USSR. *See* Soviet Union
utopianism, 229, 230

van der Helst, Bartholomeus, 118
van der Wetering, Ernst, 108
van Dyck, Anthony, 98, 199, 249n2
van Eyck, Jan, 70, 124, 205
van Gogh, Vincent, 44, 56, 124, 129, 138, 204, 209; expropriation of, 185; move to South of France, 202; *Pair of Boots*, 163, 251n5; peasants, 215; *Portrait of Postman Joseph Roulin*, 71, 196; Read view, 55; reproductions, 147; self-portraits, 107; in Stone fiction, 77; *Sunflowers*, 24, 185
van Hoogstraten, Samuel, 118
van Ruisdael, Jacob, 199; *Windmill at Wijk bij Duurstede*, 197
Vasari, Giorgio, 51, 58, 78–80 passim
Velázquez, Diego, 57, 65, 66, 124, 138, 166; female nudes, 52, 100, 120, 126, 140, 242n22; influence on Bacon, 189, 190, 206; influence on Picasso, 206; *Portrait of Pope Innocent X*, 58, 71, 98, 99, 107, 190, 196; portraits of Philip IV, 98; *Rokeby Venus*, 52, 100, 120, 242n22
Venturi, Lionello: *History of Art Criticism*, 55
Venus d'Urbino (Titian), 100, 131, 134, 166
Vermeer, Johannes, 44, 199, 221
Veronese, Paolo, 221
Verrocchio, Andrea del, 78, 89
Vettriano, Jack, 45
View of Het Steen in the Early Morning (Rubens), 62–63, 193, *193*
Vir Heroicus Sublimis (Newman), 64–66

Wallinger, Mark, 41, 205
Warburton, Nigel, 15
War Disasters series (Goya). See *Disasters of War* series (Goya)
Warhol, Andy, 7, 21, 32, 40, 57, 185–89, 214, 217; *Brillo Boxes*, 21, 39, 186, 215–16; *Campbell's Soup Cans*, 21, 51, 70, 186; class mobility, 204; *Electric Chairs*, 227; influence on Hirst, 146; Jameson view, 218; *Marilyn Diptych*, 185, 186; 'Mona Lisa' series, 188; *192 One Dollar Bills*, 187; paintings, 188; *Thirteen Most Wanted Men*, 188; *210 Coca-Cola Bottles*, 186
Ways of Seeing (Berger), x, 38, 49, 140, 196
Ways of Seeing (television series), x
Weitz, Morris, 15
Welles, Orson, 40
Westwood, Vivienne, 251n7
Whaam! (Lichtenstein), 39, 185
What Is Art? (Trotsky), 243n24
Whiteread, Rachel, 7, 147–50, 245n50; *Ghost*, 149, 150; *House*, 39, 147, 149, 251n15
Why I Never Became a Dancer (Emin), 160–61, 163–64, 165
Wilde, Oscar, 32, 242n15
Williams, Raymond, 252–53n1
Williams, William Carlos, 111
Wittgenstein, Ludwig: *Philosophical Investigations*, 15, 16
Wordsworth, William, 119, 199

Workers: An Archaeology of the Industrial Age (Salgado), 180
World Trade Organization protests, Seattle, 1999, 225–26

Yeats, Jack, x, 41, 44, 57
Yeats, W. B., 13, 19, 252n24
Young British Artists (YBAs), ix, 136–52, 154, 214, 231, 250n3

Zeng Fanzhi: *Last Supper*, 219–20
Zeuxis, 49
Zola, Émile, 299n2
Zygotic Acceleration, Biogenetic, De-Sublimated Libidinal Model (Enlarged x 1000) (Chapman brothers), 141–43

About Haymarket Books

Haymarket Books is a radical, independent, nonprofit book publisher based in Chicago. Our mission is to publish books that contribute to struggles for social and economic justice. We strive to make our books a vibrant and organic part of social movements and the education and development of a critical, engaged, international left.

We take inspiration and courage from our namesakes, the Haymarket martyrs, who gave their lives fighting for a better world. Their 1886 struggle for the eight-hour day—which gave us May Day, the international workers' holiday—reminds workers around the world that ordinary people can organize and struggle for their own liberation. These struggles continue today across the globe—struggles against oppression, exploitation, poverty, and war.

Since our founding in 2001, Haymarket Books has published more than five hundred titles. Radically independent, we seek to drive a wedge into the risk-averse world of corporate book publishing. Our authors include Noam Chomsky, Arundhati Roy, Rebecca Solnit, Angela Y. Davis, Howard Zinn, Amy Goodman, Wallace Shawn, Mike Davis, Winona LaDuke, Ilan Pappé, Richard Wolff, Dave Zirin, Keeanga-Yamahtta Taylor, Nick Turse, Dahr Jamail, David Barsamian, Elizabeth Laird, Amira Hass, Mark Steel, Avi Lewis, Naomi Klein, and Neil Davidson. We are also the trade publishers of the acclaimed Historical Materialism Book Series and of Dispatch Books.

Also Available from Haymarket Books

9.5 Theses on Art and Class
Ben Davis

Making Art in Terrible Times
Ben Davis

Marxism and the Party
John Molyneux

A Moment on the Clock of the World
A Foundry Theatre Production
Edited by David Bruin and Melanie Joseph

Revolution Today
Susan Buck-Morss

This Is Modern Art: A Play
Kevin Coval and Idris Goodwin

Too Much Midnight
Krista Franklin

About the Author

John Molyneux is a socialist, activist, and writer. Formerly a lecturer in art history at Portsmouth University, he now lives in Dublin where he is a member of People Before Profit. His many books include *What Is the Real Marxist Tradition?*, *Rembrandt and Revolution*, *Lenin for Today*, *Will the Revolution be Televised?*, and *Marxism and the Party*. He is also a founder of the Global Ecosocialist Network.